'Global legal indicators play an increasingly important role in today's world. Yet their relationship with traditional legal rules often remains unclear. This book offers a much-needed foundational analysis of these indicators through the lens of comparative law. I highly recommend it!'

Mathias Siems, *European University Institute, Florence, Italy*

'Comparative lawyers were traditionally suspicious about quantification. In this century the mood has changed, and numbers have started to appear in comparative law. Some speak of the quantitative turn. This highly original book is part of the turn as it focuses on indicators and the role they play in societies. The authors show how the traditional practice of ranking legal systems is still part of the endeavour of understanding law comparatively. By analysing global legal indicators they make an innovative contribution. The book will be an excellent read for anyone interested in comparative law or globalising law.'

Jaakko Husa, *University of Helsinki, Finland*

Global Legal Indicators and Comparative Law

In recent times, comparative law has moved towards a new type of visualisation of the law, which is mainly based on indexes and indicators. Through these, legal scholars and practitioners measure legal systems against specific benchmarks; they no longer search for commonalities among legal systems but are interested in assessing how the law performs in economic terms. This book critically analyses this 'quantitative turn' in comparative law.

The work focuses on the role played by social indicators in general, and legal indicators in particular, in contemporary societies. It presents the evaluation of indicators as a pattern of governance as well as a driver promoting a change in the law from 'outside'. The authors explore a range of issues, including how and why the quantitative turn in comparative law has taken place; how legal indicators are created and for which purposes; whether indicators really act as a new form of legitimisation and law-making and, if so, if it is possible to resist or challenge their power; whether it is fair and equitable to measure the performance of diversified national legal frameworks through such managerial tools of governance; and ultimately, how legal indicators change the way we conceive of the law. The book addresses these issues by focusing on legal indicators, whose global ambitions are often related to societal concerns. To this extent, it examines how both non-economic and economic global indicators might have some bearing on the law.

The volume will be of interest to advanced students, researchers, and academics in comparative law, global law, transnational law, constitutional law, and law and economics.

Daniele D'Alvia is Lecturer in Banking and Finance Law at CCLS, Queen Mary University of London, UK, and Associate Researcher at the European Banking Institute in Frankfurt, Germany.

Matteo Nicolini is Associate Professor of Comparative Public Law in the Department of Law at the University of Verona, Italy; Visiting Lecturer at the Newcastle University Law School, UK; and External Partner of the Centre for the Study of Law in Theory and Practice (LTAP) at Liverpool John Moores University, UK.

Globalization: Law and Policy

Globalization: Law and Policy builds an integrated body of scholarship that critically addresses key issues and theoretical debates in comparative and transnational law and the principles governance and policy on which they are developed. Volumes in the series focus on the consequential effects of globalization, including emerging frameworks and processes for the internationalization, legal harmonization, juridification, and democratization of law among increasingly connected political, economic, religious, cultural, ethnic, and other functionally differentiated governance communities. Legal systems, their harmonization and incorporation in other governance orders, and their relationship to globalization are taking on new importance within a coordinated network of domestic legal orders, the legal orders of groups of states, and the governance frameworks of non-state actors. These legal orders engage a number of important actors, sources, principles, and tribunals-including multinational corporations as governance entities, contract and surveillance as forms of governance that substitute for traditional law, sovereign wealth funds and other new forms of state activity, hybrid supra national entities like the World Bank and the International Monetary Fund, and international tribunals with autonomous jurisdiction, including the International Criminal Court, the World Trade Organization, and regional human rights courts. The effects have been profound, especially with respect to the role of states, and especially of developed states as their long time position in global affairs undergoes significant transformation. Comparative and transnational law serve as natural nexus points for vigorous and sometimes interdisciplinary approaches to the study of state and non-state law systems, along with their linkages and interactions. The series is intended as a resource for scholars, students, policy makers, and civil society actors, and includes a balance of theoretical and policy studies in single-authored volumes and collections of original essays.

Larry Catá Backer is the W. Richard and Mary Eshelman Faculty Scholar, Professor of Law and International Affairs at the Pennsylvania State University. Previously he served as Executive Director of the Comparative and International Law Center at the University of Tulsa. He has published widely on comparative and transnational law.

Also in the series:

Multinationals and the Constitutionalization of the World Power System
Edited by Jean-Philippe Robé, Antoine Lyon-Caen and Stéphane Vernac

Power, Procedure, Participation and Legitimacy in Global Sustainability Norms
A Theory of Collaborative Regulation
Karin Buhmann

Chinese Constitutionalism in a Global Context
Peng Chengyi

Hostile Business and the Sovereign State
Privatized Governance, State Security and International Law
Michael J. Strauss

Legal and Rhetorical Foundations of Economic Globalization
An Atlas of Ritual Sacrifice in Late-Capitalism
Keren Wang

Armed Conflict and Human Rights Law
Protecting Civilians and International Humanitarian Law
Daniel Ivo Odon

Business, Compliance and Human Rights Law
The Effectiveness of Transnational Private Regulations for Vulnerable Stakeholders
Gabriel Webber Ziero

The United Nations Convention on the Law of the Sea
A System of Regulation
Edited by Kristina Siig, Birgit Feldtmann and Fenella M.W. Billing

Judicial Review in Greater China
Activism and Deference of Four Apex Courts
Shiling Xiao

Global Legal Indicators and Comparative Law
The Factory of Indexes
Daniele D'Alvia and Matteo Nicolini

For more information about this series, please visit: www.routledge.com/Globalization-Law-and-Policy/book-series/GLOBLP

Global Legal Indicators and Comparative Law

The Factory of Indexes

Daniele D'Alvia and Matteo Nicolini

Routledge
Taylor & Francis Group
LONDON AND NEW YORK

First published 2025
by Routledge
4 Park Square, Milton Park, Abingdon, Oxon OX14 4RN

and by Routledge
605 Third Avenue, New York, NY 10158

Routledge is an imprint of the Taylor & Francis Group, an informa business

Library of Congress Cataloging-in-Publication Data
Names: D'Alvia, Daniele author | Nicolini, Matteo author
Title: Global legal indicators and comparative law : the factory of indexes / Daniele D'Alvia, Matteo Nicolini.
Description: Abingdon, Oxon [UK] ; New York, NY : Routledge, 2025. | Series: Globalization : Law and policy | Includes bibliographical references and index.
Identifiers: LCCN 2025008082 (print) | LCCN 2025008083 (ebook) | ISBN 9781032302843 hardback | ISBN 9781032302850 paperback | ISBN 9781003304333 ebook
Subjects: LCSH: Legal polycentricity—Methodology | Law—Methodology | Comparative law | Conflict of laws
Classification: LCC K236 .D38 2025 (print) | LCC K236 (ebook) | DDC 340/.1—dc23/eng/20250305
LC record available at https://lccn.loc.gov/2025008082
LC ebook record available at https://lccn.loc.gov/2025008083

ISBN: 978-1-032-30284-3 (hbk)
ISBN: 978-1-032-30285-0 (pbk)
ISBN: 978-1-003-30433-3 (ebk)

DOI: 10.4324/9781003304333

Typeset in Galliard
by Apex CoVantage, LLC

To Vassia.
– Daniele D'Alvia

To Lisa, Tobia, and Valeria.
– Matteo Nicolini

Contents

About the Authors

Daniele D'Alvia is Lecturer in Banking and Finance Law at CCLS, Queen Mary University of London, and Associate Researcher at the European Banking Institute in Frankfurt. He has significantly contributed to the understanding of special-purpose acquisition companies. His scholarship adopts an interdisciplinary and cross-jurisdictional approach, with a particular emphasis on the role of comparative law in shaping financial and regulatory frameworks.

Matteo Nicolini is Associate Professor of Comparative Public Law, Department of Law, University of Verona (Italy); Visiting Lecturer at the Newcastle University Law School (UK); and External Partner of the Centre for the Study of Law in Theory and Practice (LTAP), Liverpool John Moores University (UK). His fields of research include comparative methodology, federal studies, constitutional adjudication, law and literature, African law, and legal geography. He is the author of several monographs, essays, and articles in Italian, Spanish, and English.

The book is the fruit of the joint efforts of both authors.

Matteo Nicolini is the author of Chapters 1 (Sections 1–4 and 9–10), 2, 3. Daniele D'Alvia is the author of Chapters 1 (Sections 5–7), 4, and 5. The Introduction, Chapter 1, Section 8, and Conclusions were written by both authors.
Proofread by Francis Gordon.

Introduction

Framing and Ranking the Law From 'The Outside'

1 Law-Mapping: A Constant in Comparative Law

As a cultural competence, the comparison of different legal systems has ancient roots, particularly when it comes to improving domestic legislation, with the aim of enabling the development of the law handed down from the past. To this extent, legends and accounts abound.

In the sixth century BCE, the Athenian statesman and lawgiver Solon compiled the laws of Athens; he succeeded by gathering and drawing inspiration from the laws of several city-states.[1] Likewise, in the fifth century BCE, the Romans reportedly perused the legislation of the colonies the Greek had founded in Sicily to draft the *Lex XII Tabularum* (Laws of the Twelve Tables). In the fourth century BCE, the philosopher Aristotle examined and then collected the constitutions of 158 Greek city-states when formulating a constitutional blueprint. Several practices and institutions that informed Roman law often originated in the imperial provinces: Indeed, 'many commercial institutions in Babylonian, Egyptian, Phoenician, and Greek law' were subsequently incorporated into the Roman legal system, particularly 'through the practice of international jurisdiction exercised by the *Praetor*'.[2] As is evident, those wishing to set up a 'better' legal system drew inspiration and example from the 'outside'.

However, these processes of borrowings and loans cannot be considered a thorough application of comparative legal methodology. Indeed, Greeks and Romans took no recognition of comparative law. Nor did universities in mediaeval Europe undertake exercises in legal comparison. And comparative law played no part in legal education. The aforementioned examples only testify to a sporadic and intermittent use of comparative law, mainly because

1 Solon (638–558 BC) was numbered among the Seven Wise Men of Greece. He is also known because he ended aristocratic control of the Athenian government, replaced it with a system of control by the wealthy, and introduced a new and more humane law code. Besides this, he was also a renowned poet.

2 PG Monateri, *Advanced Introduction to Comparative Legal Methods* (Edward Elgar 2021) 61–62.

DOI: 10.4324/9781003304333-1

it became an autonomous legal discipline only at the end of the nineteenth century.[3]

Indeed, the nineteenth century represented a turning point. It experienced codification of the law in several continental European countries, thus putting an end to the dualism that existed between an ideal system, as taught in universities, and the practice of the law. Codification paved the way to legal nationalism even in legal education. When a country makes its own national law the object of legal study and law students begin contrasting it with foreign counterparts, we can say that the approach towards comparative law has improved remarkably. This change was already apparent in the early nineteenth century. Legal journals were founded in Germany (1829) and France (1834).[4] For these reasons, comparative law is a modern – if not a contemporary – legal phenomenon.

More specifically, its modernity is crystallised when the comparison of legal institutions deserves a systematic approach to increase understanding of foreign cultures and to further legal progress. It is at this moment in history that the 'outside' of foreign laws becomes the 'inside' of legal studies and disciplines. This was particularly apparent in France: In 1831, the *Collège de France* set up a chair of comparative legislation; in 1846, a chair of comparative criminal law was established at the University of Paris. The *Société de Législation Comparée* (1869) and the *Institut de Droit International* (1873) soon ensued. Likewise, England had its *Society of Comparative Legislation* in 1895, and London University established the *Quain Professorship of Comparative Law* in 1894. Chairs in comparative law subsequently spread all over the continent, with particular vigour in France.

The year 1900 marked the birth of comparative law as a discipline; indeed, the First International Congress of Comparative Law was held in Paris. Scholars gathered to discuss the functions and aims of comparative law. The convenors of the Congress, Raymond Saleilles and Édouard Lambert, paved the way for an ambitious project. A specific focus was laid on the role of comparative law, which would be entrusted with the discovery of universal principles when drafting a 'common law for the civilised world'.[5] The stress was on comparative legislation and codification: the Congress attracted jurists from several European countries (also from the UK) to 'promote the convergence of legal systems through the elimination of the accidental differences in the

3 For more on legal comparison in ancient and mediaeval times, see George Mousourakis, *Comparative Law and Legal Traditions. Historical and Contemporary Perspectives* (Springer 2019) 49–58; Charles Donahue, 'Comparative Law Before the *Code Napoléon*' in Mathias Reimann and Reinhard Zimmermann (eds), *The Oxford Handbook of Comparative Law* (2nd edn, OUP 2019).

4 Respectively: the *Kritische Zeitschrift für Rechtswissenschaft und Gesetzgebung des Auslandes* edited by KJA von Mittermaier and Karl Salomo Zachariae; the *Revue étrangère de législation et d'économie politique*, founded by Jean Gaspard Foelix.

5 See B Fekete, *Paradigms in Modern European Comparative Law. A History* (Hart 2021) 77 and 92.

laws of peoples at similar stages of development'.[6] This moment in time was therefore essential to highlight a possible hegemonic role of comparative law in Europe. Comparative lawyers and professors applied a variety of markers to rank legal systems, also through their cartographic representation. Displayed on the world map, legal systems were grouped (and often coloured) to reflect their being members of a given legal family. Legal cartography was not an exercise in neutrality and objectivity; rather, it was framed with a clear idea in mind: the fabrication of colonial spaces through legal practices.[7]

Within this geopolitical competition, legal systems were not put on equal footing. Legal cartography assumed that 'superior' legal practices did exist, and that these could be used as benchmarks, against which the degrees of legal civilisation around the world could be assessed. These benchmarks acted as a '*centre*, an *omphalos*', in relation to which all other legal systems became a 'diffuse *periphery*'.[8] The centre was evidently the Western legal tradition, and the 'outside' were foreign legal systems that needed to be transformed by making them coalesce towards the Eurocentric legal systems. With this approach, the nascent comparative law assumed that only civilised systems – as said, the 'European' systems – were generalisable and exportable, thus setting the benchmark against which all systems could be 'measured'.[9]

It was not just a matter of mapping legal systems. Europeans considered legal cartography a transformative device, a cultural-cum-political competence. Owing to the superior fabrication of the Western legal tradition, comparative law promoted its dissemination across non-European communities. The rest of the world could attain the same cultural and economic superiority provided that they evolved through various stages of legal development, reaching the same level envisaged by European legal traditions.[10] This Eurocentric approach changed direction from World War I onwards, when European scholarly interests began to extend well beyond European continental law, thus encompassing the legal systems of common law countries, the socialist ones, and in the wake of decolonisation, those of the newly independent states

6 Mousourakis (n 3) 96.

7 On law-mapping, see Matteo Nicolini, *Legal Geography. Comparative Law and the Production of Space* (Springer 2022) 106 *et seq*. In some maps, legal systems were grouped after colours. RW Lee, 'The Civil Law and the Common Law – A World Survey' (1915) 14 Mich L Rev 89, displayed common-law jurisdictions in black; civil law ones were dotted, whereas mixed jurisdictions were striped. See also JH Wigmore, *A Panorama of the World's Legal Systems*, vol 1 (Washington Law Book Co. 1928), and University of Ottawa – World Legal Systems Research Group, 'JuriGlobe' <www.juriglobe.ca/default.php> accessed 7 February 2024.

8 Andrew Gordon and Bernard Klein, 'Introduction' in Id. (eds), *Literature, Mapping, and the Politics of Space in Early Modern Britain* (CUP 2001) 3.

9 Werner Menski, *Comparative Law in a Global Context. The Legal Systems of Asia and Africa* (2nd edn, CUP 2006) 26 *et seq*.

10 On comparative law and colonialism, see Upendra Baxi, 'The Colonial Heritage' in Pierre Legrand and Roderick Munday (eds), *Comparative Legal Studies: Traditions and Transitions* (CUP 2003); Marian Pargendler, 'The Rise and Decline of Legal Families' (2012) 60 Am J Com L 1043.

of Asia, Oceania, and Africa. This also explains why, in the second half of the twentieth century, comparative law focused on the similarities between former colonies and Western legal systems. By emphasising legal-colonial links, scholars ranked (and still rank) French, Spanish, Portuguese, Dutch, and Italian former colonies among the civil law legal systems; former British colonies and protectorates are ascribed to the common-law legal tradition; and countries with a mixed colonial past join the mixed jurisdictions.[11]

Furthermore, legal mapping conveyed a deliberate plan of change. Staging benchmarks for legal development was apparent, for example, in constitutional law. In the aftermath of colonialism and the Cold War, with its related human rights discourse, Western law enjoyed 'universal respect' and 'observance' because it set 'a common standard of achievement for all peoples and all nations'.[12] Likewise, in the twentieth century, contract law 'celebrated dispute' between consideration and *iusta causa* located jurisdictions on either side of the civil law–common law divide, with lasting effects on Southern African mixed jurisdictions.[13]

2 Mapping the Law in the New World Economic Order

The practice of ranking legal systems also characterises our time of globalisation, which is 'powerfully driven . . . by the urge to unify or harmonize law' or to promote legal change.[14] Comparative law is appreciated as a 'harmonising handmaiden' actively constructing common legal frameworks that favour the smooth flows of goods, capital, and services across frontiers and legal systems.[15]

Yet something has changed. There are no longer formal empires, whose politico-economic dominance imposes uniform commercial laws to avoid hindrances to trade. Nor is ours a time of legal nationalism, where comparative law is perused to improve the legal system of a given political community. The global context has its own institutions, transnational legal communities, and financial actors. What mainly matters now is how legal systems attract investments.

11 Reinhard Zimmermann and Daniel Visser, 'Introduction. South African Law as a Mixed Legal System' in Id. (eds), *Southern Cross: Civil Law and Common Law in South Africa* (Clarendon Press 1996) 7–8. On mixed jurisdictions, see Jacques Du Plessis, 'Comparative Law and the Study of Mixed Legal Systems' in Mathias Reimann and Reinhard Zimmermann (eds), *The Oxford Handbook of Comparative Law* (2nd edn, OUP 2019) 478.

12 Tom Bingham, *Widening Horizons: The Influence of Comparative Law and International Law on Domestic Law* (CUP 2010). Indeed, 'the basic principles of constitutional law' were deemed to be 'the same around the world'. See David Beatty, *Comparative Law in Theory and Practice* (University of Toronto Press 1995) 10.

13 See Dale Hutchison and C-J Pretorius (eds), *The Law of Contract in South Africa* (OUP Southern Africa 2010) 12, referring to the seminal judgement *Conradie v Rossouw* 1919 AD 279.

14 Roger Cotterell, 'Seeking Similarity, Appreciating Difference: Comparative Law and Communities' in Andrew Harding and Esin Örücü (eds), *Comparative Law in the 21st Century* (Kluwer 2002) 44.

15 Menski (9) 46.

Empowering countries – especially developing countries – to facilitate access to their domestic markets is deemed essential to attract foreign investors. Nowadays, domestic markets are the most desirable source of financing before issuing sovereign debt in the form of bonds; it is still preferable, therefore, to rely on internal proceeds rather than on external sources of lending.

To facilitate, say, the evolution and implementation of efficient domestic capital markets, a new type of legal mapping has arisen. This possesses a new meaning that distances itself from the Eurocentric origins of nineteenth-century comparative law we outlined earlier. More specifically, this new trend in comparative law is based on the constantly evolving economic conditions and competitive requirements imposed by globalisation, which are directly measured in terms of indexes and indicators – that is, two tools that are frequently used today to promote legal change from the 'outside' (Chapter 1).[16] This is the area of comparative legal methodology that Mathias Siems has labelled 'numerical comparative law'.[17] As an intriguing field of research, it focuses on how legal indicators assess changes affecting several ambits of the legal spectrum. Through them, legal scholars and policymakers measure legal systems against specific benchmarks; they no longer search for commonalities among legal systems but are interested in assessing how the law performs in economic terms (Chapter 2). And the ranking of legal systems depends on how they ensure such elevated economic performances.[18] This book, *inter alia*, focuses on such changes, and it dedicates three chapters to the illustration and examination of the evolution of the new world economic order in terms of constitutional law (Chapter 3) and finance law (Chapter 4), adding a specific focus on international insolvency law (Chapter 5), which has become a major point to promote the unification of the law at the domestic level.

Assessing legal systems is part of a broader scheme advocating new regulatory systems, facilitating legal harmonisation, and stimulating socioeconomic development. The rankability of legal systems now depends on their 'better' economic performativity. The assessment is usually conducted through indexes and indicators; countries are evaluated as regards their (more or less) democratic (and economically viable) outlook, as well as their (more or less) elevated economic performances. The major institutions delivering indexes – the World Trade Organisation (WTO), the International Monetary Fund (IMF), and the World Bank Group (WBG) – use indicators to map legal systems and measure them in terms of good governance and financial predictability.

16 KE Davis, B Kingsbury, and SE Merry, 'Introduction: Global Governance by Indicators' in Id. (eds), *Governance by Indicators: Global Power Through Quantification and Rankings* (OUP 2012) 10–21.

17 See Mathias Siems, 'Numerical Comparative Law: Do We Need Statistical Evidence in Law in Order to Reduce Complexity' (2005) 13 Cardozo J Int'l Comp L 521.

18 Richard Rottenburg and SE Merry, 'A World of Indicators: The Making of Governmental Knowledge Through Quantification' in Richard Rottenburg et al. (eds), *The World of Indicators. The Making of Governmental Knowledge Through Quantification* (CUP 2015) 3.

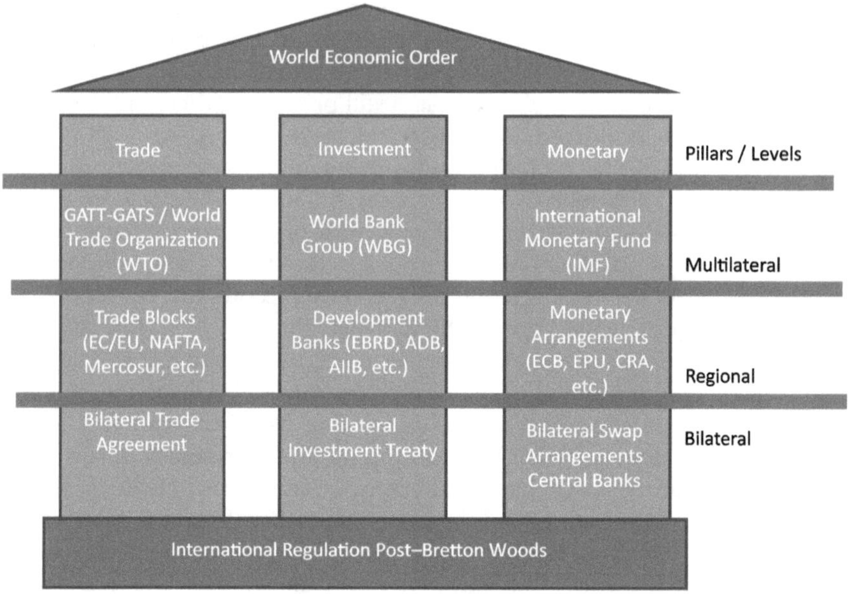

Figure 0.1 New economic order.

Note: This graphic has been taken from the slides concerning a series of lectures about international economic law at CCLS, Queen Mary University of London, and delivered by Prof. Rosa M. Lastra, who has been the mentor and intellectual 'mother' of Dr Daniele D'Alvia, one of the authors of this book.

The WTO, IMF, and WBG are also the three main multilateral international organisations that manage the three main pillars of the new world economic order, summarised in the following figure.

Rankability reflects the main concern of the transnational economic community. Specifically, business communities and states need uniform and efficient legal systems to facilitate business relationships among countries.[19] For instance, in 2004, the WBG released its *Doing Business Reports* in the effort to promote uniformity and help developing countries hone their business cultures and improve their domestic markets. In these *Reports* – discontinued in 2019 – the WBG encouraged legal generalisations based on one of the main functions of comparative law, that is, harmonisation. 'One Size Can Fit All – In the Manner of Business Regulation' is the title of a section of the *Doing Business Reports* (2004) that directly related to such an idea.[20] This is not so far removed from the early times of comparative law in the nineteenth century. Improving national legislation was the prime consideration of comparative

19 See RI Rotberg, 'Strengthening Governance: Ranking Countries Would Help' (2004–2005) 28 Washington Quarterly 71.

20 The World Bank, *Doing Business in 2004: Understanding Regulation* (OUP 2003). On the *Doing Business Reports* and their discontinuity, see Ch 2.3.

law in relation to countries that were codifying (or re-codifying) their legal systems, as well as enacting new legislation to boost their economies. For example, when the Code Napoleon was enacted in 1804, several provisions contained therein were not of Roman origin; legal solutions were indeed borrowed from the 'outside', namely, from the Romano-Germanic *droit coutumier*. At the same time, many other countries followed France, also borrowing elements from its code or transplanting it entirely. Evidently, the French code became the template for codification in continental Europe. Aside from any political consideration, not only is comparative law a tool for comparing and contrasting different legal systems to discover similarities and differences, but it also facilitates knowledge-sharing and expertise. To this end, the Napoleonic Code was also meant to represent the maximum example of the best possible codification. Other countries, 'less sophisticated' in legal terms, were compelled to imitate such a legal formant. Therefore, both this way of importing foreign concepts and, *mutatis mutandis*, the activity of 'exporting-importing' the law are termed *legal transplant*.

As said, what we now consider 'outside' is no longer focused on codification but, rather, on economic performance, as exemplified by the three main pillars (or levels) of the new world economic order, namely, facilitating trade, investments, and monetary policies. Even if comparative law interests have changed over time, the goal has always been the same, that is, harmonisation. In the wake of these changes, the legislation of, say, the EU or the USA now acts as the main benchmark outside the law from which developing countries draw inspiration. Traditionally, these countries have fewer liquid capital markets, more bureaucratic administrative systems, and sometimes even a more worrying level of corruption and malpractice that might trigger new economic crises also beyond national borders. Hence, financial stability becomes a common value to be protected; if they are more likely to face unsustainable levels of severe debt, developing countries (such as Argentina or several African states) must change their 'legal outfit'.

Conducted by international organisations and institutions, legal assessments become a new way of making the law from the 'outside'; through it, several jurisdictions are inspired to imitate and adapt their decision-making processes to transnational regulatory frameworks, thus matching the level of performativity suggested through benchmarks and indicators.

3 Indicators as the Factory of Comparative Law

The examples referred to in the previous sections introduce the topic and methodology of this book. As its title suggests, *Global Legal Indicators and Comparative Law: The Factory of Indexes* investigates how the fabrication of new regulatory schemes takes place in the transnational environment, with the aim of fostering, protecting, and securing financial interests. In other terms, it examines how, and to what extent, managing the law from the outside engages with traditional forms of law-making, such as the production of 'publicly made' (or 'state-created') law.[21]

The starting point is the perspective of transnational actors' interests, as well as their attentiveness to fabricating the law that is 'better' to uphold the benefits of the markets. It is not just a matter of comparing jurisdictions – as we said before – to 'pick and choose among their laws'.[22] The cherry-picking is also dependent upon how the law performs economically, which means rankability and politico-legal predictability. At the same time, rankability is related to law-making processes. Hence, it concerns the regulatory environment of each state in the making of new rules. The 'soft power' of indicators holds a particular fascination for countries, inasmuch as their ability to attract foreign investments and stimulate national economic development is evidently determined by the ranking position of the latter.[23]

Managing the law from the outside examines how the interests of the transnational community trigger legal change. The *recherche* of the law that is better at doing business possesses a liberating force that facilitates the harmonisation of laws, the opening of global markets, national territories, and even new legal spaces (such as the digitalised ones[24]), also favouring the smooth flows of goods, capital, and services across national legal systems.

As legal scholars, we are witnessing an epistemological paradigm shift, which affects the very meaning and function of the law.[25] As *comparative* legal scholars, we understand that the soft power of indicators reflects a new methodological trend in comparative legal research. The way indicators are framed, used, and promoted in transnational contexts becomes part of the fabric of economic comfort zones, that is, legal spaces where financial risk inherent to investment and business venture is reduced or made predictable.

As far as comparative law is concerned, three major points deserve to be considered.

The first of these refers to the methodological approach adopted in this book. If its main aim is the examination of the quantitative move towards metrics in the field of comparative law (particularly in transnational contexts), our contribution will be that of comparative legal scholars. To this extent, the quantitative turn triggered by indicators will be assessed by employing the possibilities offered by our discipline.

21 Respectively: David Snyder, 'Private Lawmaking' (2003) 64 Ohio St L J 371, 376; Lisa Bernstein, 'Opting Out of the Legal System: Extralegal Contractual Relations in the Diamond Industry' (1992) 21 JLS 115.

22 Katharina Pistor, *The Code of Capital. How the Law Creates Wealth and Inequality* (Princeton UP 2019) 23. On the concept of 'better law' and the relationships between the law coming from the outside and state law, see Ch 1.2.

23 See Michele Graziadei, 'The Functionalist Heritage' in Pierre Legrand and Roderick Munday (eds), *Comparative Legal Studies. Traditions and Transitions* (CUP 2033) 461 *et seq.*

24 See Nicolini (n 7) 269.

25 This shift is at the core of Jaakko Husa's new edited book, *A Research Agenda for Comparative Law* (Edward Elgar 2024).

The second point refers to the use of indicators in creating transnational regulatory schemes. The Fabric of the Law resonates with the ancillary function of comparative law, that is, providing lawmakers with the knowledge required to frame new laws, unify regulatory ambits, and harmonise regulations. When suggesting how better legislation might be drafted, comparative law engages in conversation with other disciplines also interested in examining the transnational environment. Managing the law from the outside is a cross-disciplinary journey, where finance, socio-legal studies, and econometrics overlap. This book will benefit from disciplines like comparative politics and economics, which provide insights on 'the non-legal context of the law' but are 'less hesitant than comparative law in making legal and policy recommendations based on cross-country comparisons'.[26]

The last point deserving our attention relates to the role of (particularly socio-legal) indicators in transnational communities. These are often made up of a constellation of actors ranging from nation states to international business corporations, usually complemented by 'relatively small numbers of global law firms and advocates, nationally ranked global law schools and academics, and globally networked judges'.[27] It is therefore crucial to ascertain how the 'Factory of Global Legal Indicators' is used within this constellation. The book goes beyond traditional scholarly comparative law; instead of examining convergence and harmonisation of national legislation through indicators,[28] it assumes that the latter are the Fabric of the Law. Intriguing as it is, this perspective evokes the fundamental shift taking place within global governance, where quantitative measurement acts as a driver for delivering a 'plan of [legal] change based upon an imitation of laws', transplants, and borrowings.[29]

Mainstream comparative law usually limits its focus on how global legal indicators impact on domestic law. It is true that the rules thus confected make national jurisdictions coalesce towards the benchmarks set by transnational indicators. The legal outputs of convergence are 'likely to carry much greater weight' than merely state-created law. In terms of financial attractiveness, 'deviation' from the law reflecting transnational legal standards 'will likely prove more difficult than' one might expect.

This predicament, though, is not the whole truth. The 'soft power' of indicators goes above and beyond state actors, also *managing* the laws that make up the private orderings of the transnational constellation. As we shall see,

26 Mathias Siems, 'Bringing in Foreign Ideas: The Quest for "Better Law" in Implicit Comparative Law' (2014) 9 J Comp L 119, 136.

27 Neil Walker, *Intimations of Global Law* (CUP 2015) 42.

28 See, for example, M Graziadei, 'Comparative Law, Transplants, and Receptions' in M Reimann and R Zimmermann (eds), *The Oxford Handbook of Comparative Law* (2nd edn, OUP 2019) 465; Mathias Siems, *Comparative Law* (3rd edn, CUP 2022) 287.

29 Gianmaria Ajani, 'Ruling by Indicators: How the Use of Vague Notions and Quantitative Indicators Facilitates Legal Change' (2017) 23 Cardozo El Bulletin 1, 17. See also David Nelken, 'The Legitimacy of Global Social Indicators: Reconfiguring Authority, Accountability and Accuracy' (2018) 59 Cahiers de Droit 35.

indicators also influence the way transnational private orderings frame their self-regulatory schemes. They are a 'pervasive and important element of contemporary law-making', as well as 'a robust component of commercial and consumer life'.[30] They may also function directly as transnational soft law, also impacting on citizens and firms even if domestic lawmakers remain silent.[31]

3.1 Indicators as Drivers: The Law From the Outside

In academic research, the field of indicators has been widely examined. Scholars with a background in, say, sociology, economics, or comparative law have supplemented a vast literary production, exploring the functions of indicators at various levels of decision-making. Although they cover a host of different issues, cross-disciplinary publications on indicators are predominantly collections written by scholars with sundry backgrounds, where each author explores the topic at stake from their own academic angle.[32] Indicators and their specific features are also dealt with in collections, articles, essays, and chapters.[33]

This partial and incomplete literature review still leaves several research gaps, which our book intends to bridge. As explained in the previous section, this book adopts a comparative law approach, which might be beneficial to re-conceptualising our key research aim, that is, the role of indicators within law-making and convergence.

30 Snyder (n 21) 374.

31 Such as in the case of ESG. See Ch 4.5.

32 See, for example, Kevin Davis et al. (eds), *Governance by Indicators. Global Power Through Quantification and Rankings* (OUP 2012); Richard Rottenburg et al. (eds), *The World of Indicators. The Making of Governmental Knowledge Through Quantification* (CUP 2015); RC Das (ed), *Handbook of Research on Global Indicators of Economic and Political Convergence* (IGI Global 2016); Daniel Oto-Peralía and Diego Romero-Ávila, *Legal Traditions, Legal Reforms and Economic Performance. Theory and Evidence* (Springer 2017); DV Malito et al. (eds), *The Palgrave Handbook of Indicators in Global Governance* (Palgrave McMillan 2018); JG Kelly and BA Simmons (eds), *The Power of Global Performance Indicators* (CUP 2020); SP de Souza, *Designing Indicators for a Plural Legal World* (CUP 2022); Mario Bussani et al. (eds), *Comparative Legal Metrics. Quantification of Performances as Regulatory Technique* (Brill 2023). See also PG Monateri and Mauro Balestrieri, *Quantitative Methods in Comparative Law* (Edward Elgar 2023).

33 Besides Siems (n 28), Ajani (n 29), and Nelken (n 29), see, for example, Ralph Michaels, 'Comparative Law by Numbers? Legal Origins Thesis, Doing Business Reports, and the Silence of Traditional Comparative Law' (2009) 57 Am J Com L 765; AJ Rosga and ML Satterthwaite, 'Trust in Indicators' (2009) 27 Berkeley J Int'l L 253; Francesco Parisi and Barbara Luppi, 'Quantitative Methods in Comparative Law' in PG Monateri (ed), *Methods in Comparative Law* (Edward Elgar 2012); David Restrepo Amariles, 'Legal Indicators, Global Law and Legal Pluralism: An Introduction' (2015) 47 J Legal Pluralism Unofficial L 14; Gerhard Schnyder et al., 'Twenty Years of "Law and Finance": Time to Take Law Seriously' (2021) 19 Socio-Economic Rev 377; David Nelken and Mathias Siems (eds), 'Numbers in an Emergency: The Many Roles of Indicators in the COVID-19 Crisis' (2021) 17 Int J Law Context.; Id., 'Global Social Indicators and Their Legitimacy in Transnational Law' in Peer Zumbansen (ed), *The Oxford Handbook of Transnational Law* (OUP 2021).

Not only are these management tools fostering socioeconomic growth; they also act as performative instruments, contributing to one of the most recent trends in transnational law-making: the idea that good governance of communities and capital is an output-oriented process.[34] The book contributes to the discussion, especially as the good governance debate has tended to focus more on 'the inputs side of the governance question' (i.e. on issues of accountability and transparency), whereas questions about bureaucratic capacity and legal infrastructure have not received the attention they deserve.[35] This has meant paying more attention to indicators as patterns of governance than to indicators as drivers for legal change. In terms of outputs, this is the major consequence of the quantitative turn in comparative law; in terms of change, the soft power of indicators completely reshuffles the relationship between economics and the law. The output-oriented approach thus allows us to understand how, within the transnational constellation, legal regulatory frameworks are outlined within the 'Factory of Global Legal Indicators'.

From a normative point of view, the depiction of indicators as a factory producing the law from the outside is a vivid metaphor of their transformative potential, often resulting from the identification and recognition of legally relevant meanings outside the law. In a time of transnationalism, the law is not an 'input' to codify the capital but, rather, the 'output'. The process whereby indicators identify and recognise meanings outside the law perfectly matches the etymological meaning of the item 'indicator'. The *Oxford English Dictionary* defines it as 'information about a sector, market, or economy'; in supplying such information, it 'directs [our] attention to, something' – in our case, the functioning of communities and markets. Its transformative potential is evidently 'used to predict future outcomes or trends'.[36] As we shall see, this connotation is consonant with the mainstream definition of *indicator* adopted in global studies.[37]

Owing to their factual character, these outside-the-law criteria are often fragmented across the constellation of transnational actors. Dependent as they are upon market fluctuation, they are volatile, and their regulation tends to happen 'without established structures and . . . on *ad hoc* combinations of private actors'. Through their soft power, indicators acknowledge the relevance (and 'social function') of such criteria; with their transformative potential, they promote reforms through legislative outputs that include publicly made legislation, soft law, and self-regulatory instruments. We shall consider this in due course; suffice it here to say that in it lies the very idea of indicators as a factory producing the law from the outside. They encourage harmonisation among

34 See RI Rotberg, 'Good Governance Measures' (2014) 27 Governance 511.

35 Rotberg (n 34) 512.

36 'Indicator' *Oxford English Dictionary* (2021) <www.oed.com/view/Entry/94420?redirectedFrom=indicator#eid> accessed 1 February 2025.

37 See Ch 1.9.

jurisdictions in a cooperative way, thus establishing a common legal meaning, facilitating convergence of laws, and stimulating business and economic development.

In reshuffling the relation between the law and economic performances, legal indicators become 'leximetrics'.[38] This is evident in the field of constitutional law, where global legal indicators make legal systems coalesce towards common/universal standards. Transnational legal concepts such as the rule of law and human rights now express a performance measure referred, *inter alia*, to transnational cross-country influences on human rights and climate change mitigation policies. Through quantitative methods, it is possible to assess the 'quality' of legal systems and rank them, say, on how they implement global indexes, secure predictability on investment returns, and enhance transnational legal frameworks in financial and insolvency practices.

This approach might also reflect on banking and finance law. Indeed, economic indicators in the private sector experiment with cross-border insolvency legislation and legal principles, which convey sustainability as the emerging trend in the new global economic order. The book analyses how a non-legal framework (such as the one rooted in sustainability) has been gradually incorporated inside the new financial architecture. Sustainability is the new 'password' of finance, where new indicators are created to measure the societal impact of an investment (which is, for example, ESG-compliant). Likewise, sustainable-related policies of central banks might constitute a new mandate for monetary policy and financial stability.[39]

These examples are case studies through which the book investigates a new role for the law. Once the efficiency of a legal system becomes its cornerstone, then national reforms are necessary to comply with meanings and legal tools that are implemented at the transnational level. Indeed, constitutional, transnational, and commercial law can no longer be considered 'codes' or preliminary instances of law-making processes – quite the opposite. Firstly, the soft power of indicators encourages countries and transnational actors to arrange their legal frameworks around processes of legal generalisation. Secondly, the reformulation of legal frameworks is achieved by virtue of recognising meanings enshrined in soft law instruments or quasi-legal frameworks, which are shared by the members of the financial community. Thirdly, these act as

38 RD Cooter and Tom Ginsburg, 'Leximetrics: Why the Same Laws Are Longer in Some Countries Than Others' (2003) University of Illinois Law & Economics Research Paper No. LE03–012 <https://ssrn.com/abstract=456520> accessed 1 February 2024; Mathias Siems, 'Taxonomies and Leximetrics' in JN Gordin and WG Ringe (eds), *The Oxford Handbook of Corporate Law and Governance* (OUP 2018). See also KA Kholodilin and Linus Pfeiffer, 'Measuring Unmeasurable: How to Map Laws to Numbers Using Leximetrics' (2021) DIW Berlin Discussion Paper 1933/2021 <www.diw.de/de/diw_01.c.812775.de/publikationen/diskussionspapiere/2021_1933/measuring_unmeasurable__how_to_map_laws_to_numbers_using_leximetrics.html> accessed 1 October 2024.

39 See Ch 1.8.

benchmarks through which legal indicators operate to assess the performativity and efficiency of national legal systems based on how they should address global concerns. In so doing, a new integrative dynamic of the global–local connection is introduced. As said, transnational private orderings frame their self-regulatory schemes in relation to financial services and financial regulation, whose main centre is now located in private international organisations, such as the IMF, INSOL International, the WBG, UNCITRAL, the European Commission, and so on. While some chapters focus more directly on the US and EU experience, they will also cover the functioning of several other international and supranational organisations and agencies. Consequently, the book will be of interest also to non-Western audiences, especially in the field of foreign investment. In all these cases, the law is an 'output' fabricated from the outside.

3.2 *Indicators as a Paradigm Shift in Comparative Law*

Within the transnational community, we are experiencing a new way of manufacturing (and managing) the law from the outside. Both the 'Factory' and the 'soft power' of indicators reflect this methodological trend that characterises comparative legal research. This trend is also substantive, inasmuch as the Factory elicits a further change, which relates to how the law is actually conceived and understood within the transnational community. What lies at the heart of the Factory is a new way of framing regulatory schemes. Our point is this: The Factory and the metaphor of the 'soft power' evoke new mechanisms to allow countries to open up their domestic markets to attract foreign investors. With this focus on the maximisation of profits in transnational environments, the book will assess the most recent developments in comparative law that are based on the constantly evolving economic conditions and competitive requirements imposed by globalisation.

More on this in due course. For what concerns us here, managing the law from the outside permits us to revisit comparative law in our time of globalisation, to assess the processes of legal change triggered by the Factory, and to point out the increasingly 'significant role indicators tend to play in contemporary societies' owing to their being 'integral to the fabric of global governance'.[40]

We are therefore experiencing a new process of knowledge production, which deserves our attention. We all know that comparative law is a way to gain control (and therefore order) the knowledge of the world, and that

40 See, respectively: David Restrepo Amariles, 'Supping With the Devil? Indicators and the Rise of Managerial Rationality in Law' (2017) 13 Int J L Context 465; Alexander Cooley, 'The Emerging Politics of International Rankings and Ratings: A Framework of Analysis' in Alexander Cooley and Jack Snyder (eds), *Ranking the World: Grading States as a Tool of Global Governance* (CUP 2015) 17.

this type of legal mapping conveys a deliberate plan of change, however it is arranged, by way of maps or indicators. The huge transformation we are witnessing operates at both levels, that is, the practical and the epistemological. Staging benchmarks for legal assessment is extremely useful for scientific advancements of comparative law (i.e. the knowledge and understanding of the Factory and its related conception of law-making); at the same time, it is servient to the 'better' legislation required to harvest profits within the state–investor intercourse, is part of the production and the growth of knowledge.

The idea of managing legal change from the 'outside' points to a change that resonates with Thomas Kuhn's idea of *paradigm shift*, which has been deployed to explain the transformative changes in several academic disciplines.[41] The shifts caused by globalisation in general, and the Factory in particular, are indeed remarkable. This is patent, as we shall see, in how the holders of capital peruse comparative-legal nomenclatures (mainly generalisations and functionalism) to promote change in domestic legislation from the outside (Chapter 1). Again, this is apparent in the semantic change affecting several constitutional-legal derivatives (such as government, rule of law, to name just a few) that measure the economic fitness of domestic legislation (Chapter 3).

We shall see that this approach resonates with the scientific state of mind and its effort to mathematise the law in line with the following assumption: Hard science paradigms are 'more' scientific and objective than those practised in social sciences and the humanities (Chapter 2). A thorough application of Kuhn's model leads to considering the Fabric a type of scientific-cum-practical 'revolutionary progress'. What has prompted us to adopt Kuhn's paradigm is its ability to link the different features and stages around which our research on the Factory of the law may be arranged. For our purposes, his paradigm gives consistency to our project, which can be listed as follows: (1) 'the accepted facts', (2) the 'puzzles which remain to be solved', and (3) 'the procedures by which solutions to the puzzles are sought'.[42]

Beginning with 'the accepted facts', Kuhn's paradigm points to the description and explanation of the growth of scientific knowledge. In our case, this is related to the changes triggered by globalisation, which has resulted in a new economic order where the constants are outside the law (i.e. the financial interests to be pursued) and legal tools are manufactured from the outside. The same applies to comparative law, whose goal is the production of knowledge to be used when manufacturing legal solutions that the Factory will subsequently share with state actors. The second stage points to the 'puzzles which remain to be solved', that is, the aims of our scientific endeavours. What we want to explore is how legal knowledge is now produced, more specifically,

41 Thomas Kuhn, *The Structure of Scientific Revolutions* (Chicago UP 1962).

42 For these stages, see RJ Johnston, 'Paradigms and Revolutions or Evolution? Observations on Human Geography Since the Second World War' (1978) 2 Progress in Human Geography 189.

how and why the Factory has been set up, who its main actors are, how the process of legal unification actually manages the law from the outside. Last but not least, we try to explain why this process of legal fabrication from the outside holds a particular fascination when it comes to the fabrication of new legislative outputs and regulatory schemes.

The third stage comprises of 'the procedures by which solutions to the puzzles are sought'. This means pointing to the cooperative intercourse, that is, a new way of manufacturing publicly made law which is likely to generate private (but also public) benefits. Taking place among transnational actors and national jurisdictions, this intercourse turns transnational investors' privately made law into domestic publicly made legislation (Chapter 1). It is therefore based on the soft power of indicators. These are the very source of fascination for state actors; the legal solutions they suggest often take the form of indicators. Indicators are used to carry out massive comparative law surveys to find out which domestic legal solution is better at maximising profits for shareholders. To a broader extent, they convey rankings, that is, 'measures of relative performance because they establish the performance of an organisation in relation to the performance of other organisations'.[43] In sum, indicators enhance the state–investor cooperative intercourse. As Restrepo Amariles correctly argues, global legal indicators rank 'the quality of law and legal institutions across the entire world, particular regions, or selected jurisdictions'. But – we add – they are relevant because, by 'measuring institutional performance', they point to the legal effects generated by the Factory, that is, the ability of legal solutions fabricated from the outside to satisfy the constants and interests of the transnational constellation.[44]

The Factory represents a kind of 'disciplinary matrix', that is, a template, that is useful for explaining how the law is actually managed. It is an instrument, as well as a capacity, for comprehension and synthesising the knowledge of the world. It is not, in Lyotard's words, a *grand narrative* or one of the 'metadiscourses . . . which have provided' the Factory and its related 'ideologies with a legitimating philosophy of history'.[45] If it were the case, this would undermine the relativist tone of our legal research: The soft power of indicators perfectly embeds the empirical character of comparative law, also showing attentiveness to operational rules beyond the written law, inasmuch as they provide the knowledge required in terms of economic performance.

Kuhn's paradigm thus gives consistency to our efforts to identify the contingencies, variables, and operational rules that make up the Factory. And its disciplinary matrix undoubtedly accounts for the complexity of the relations between financial and state actors, as well as for the processes of manufacturing the law that is functional to harvesting benefits within the Fabric. Like

43 Restrepo Amariles (n 40) 472.
44 Restrepo Amariles (n 40) 466.
45 Daniel Chandler and Rod Munday, *A Dictionary of Media and Communication* (1st edn, OUP 2011). See J-F Lyotard, *La condition postmoderne* (Les éditions de minuit 1979).

in Kuhn's 'normal' phases of science, the varieties of actors, methods, variables coded through the law generate a 'cumulative picture of scientific progress'. This picture accounts for the unceasing regeneration of the Factory. And this demonstrates that, at least as an area of legal research, indicators have a 'reasonable chance of solving the puzzle', which also depends on the state–investor cooperative intercourse.[46]

As said, we do not want to undermine the relativist tone of legal research. Our point is this: If the paradigm shift accounts for the remarkable changes prompted by globalisation, some recent events seem to be still explicable in terms of 'normal' (and cumulative) phases of science. Something has changed, indeed. The pandemic, the war in Ukraine, and the insurgence of populist movements across the globe seem to be paving the way to a new wave of nationalism, which might have an impact on how the Factory manufactures its own constant and legal solutions.

4 Manufacturing Global Indicators: The Structure of the Book

Chapter 1 ('Legal Indicators: The Law as an "Output"') provides the normative scenario to the 'Factory of Global Legal Indicators'. Managing the law from the outside raises several issues, particularly when indicators might trigger legal change in discrete fields (such as constitutional, transnational, and commercial law) and at several levels (national, transnational, supranational, or global).

The first issue regards the role of comparative law in the study of legal indicators. Due to its critical (and cross-disciplinary) approach, comparative law is well-equipped in detecting the non-legal variables that trigger such change through their soft power. This is especially true as far as 'numerical comparative law' is concerned. This is also a new way to look at comparative law; it is no longer a science merely comparing legal systems to highlight commonalities and differences. Nor is it a science that identifies a global code by virtue of exporting the law. Traditional comparative methods and their related taxonomies (such as functionalism and universalism) will be re-interpreted to study different legal tools mainly found outside the law, thus supplying the toolkit for fabricating, measuring, and assessing it.[47]

As the Fabric of the Law resonates with the use of comparative law in law-making processes, the second issue concerns how indicators are used as a part of the fabric of transnational legal spaces. The chapter considers the shift in traditional law-making that takes place especially at the state level, thus confirming the idea of indicators as a factory producing the law from the outside.

46 Kuhn (n 41) 92.
47 See Siems (n 28) 41.

The output-oriented approach to legal indicators causes a further shift in how legal definitions are coded. These now reflect a concern that is shared by all the actors of the transnational community, that is, the sustainability and solvency of both public sector and private investors. No wonder, therefore, that the Fabric of the Law manufactures rules that 'can be – and are – made for particular but wide-ranging contexts'.[48]

The process of coding new legal definitions is a remarkable sign of how things have recently been changing. To this extent, Chapter 1 examines patterns for forging definitions, engaging with Hans Kelsen's *Grundnorm*, which he styled as a fact – and as a fact, it is hence outside of the law. Although contravening his entire legal theory of the law as an 'input', Kelsen's argument is particularly relevant to our discussion of legal indicators. A similar assumption is devised in Katharina Pistor's *The Code of Capital*, whose main argument is that capital has been codified for centuries by the law. In her view, 'law is code'. Hence, codification becomes the main instrument through which power and private interests can be protected, even at the cost of infringing on the interests of vulnerable parties, such as Indigenous rights in the era of colonisation.

In sum, the chapter conceptualises the law as an 'output' rather than an 'input', whose ultimate legal source must be detected in non-legal instances, such as indicators. This is our theorisation of indicators as a 'factory of the law' manufactured from the outside.

Chapter 2 ('A Scientific State of Mind: The Onset of Legal Indicators') focuses on the epistemological paradigm underpinning this factory. Firstly, it explains what indicators are, how they are created, and who creates them. Secondly, it examines how these powerful devices measure the efficiency of legal systems. It then considers how indicators allow us to see the world through the lenses of metrics – or, as said, 'leximetrics' – upholding that the quantitative turn in comparative law has been triggered by a well-defined *scientific state of mind* lying beneath comparative legal methodologies.

The chapter then investigates the consequences of leximetrics. We have already noted that, in an output-oriented approach, they turn out to be drivers for legal change, whose transformative potential activates transplants, borrowings, and convergence. This is due to their soft power: Indicators trigger not only changes but also rankings, that is, a new form of law-mapping process that assesses the 'quality' of legal systems according to the standards and benchmarks set by the same indicators. The chapter will thus consider the impact of, among others, some of the world-famous indexes, such as the discontinued World Bank's *Doing Business Reports*, the Democratic Economy Index, and climate change–related benchmarks against which national jurisdictions are measured.

48 DV Snyder, 'Molecular Federalism and the Structures of Private Lawmaking' (2007) 14 Indiana J of Global Legal Studies 418, 435.

This process has twofold consequences: The first one reshapes the relationship between law and economic performances, with its huge impact on classifications. If the ranking of legal systems depends on their performativity, the Western legal tradition is dominant, and within it, common law prevails over civil law, since it ensures elevated economic performances. The second consequence is the semantic shift in the meaning of the legal lexicon. The transformative potential of indicators favours the development of both common financial language and global market regulation. Linguistic and legal changes are thus a projection of the global financial architecture. In terms of policy-making, the chapter suggests indicators be framed by adopting the contextual approach mentioned earlier so as not to lose sight of reality in their real-world assessments.

The normative and epistemological scenarios of Chapters 1 and 2 will find practical application in the subsequent chapters. Chapter 3 ('Legal Indicators and Constitutional Governance') will consider how the Factory of the Law prompted by indicators has clear-cut consequences in terms of constitutional law and governance. The pre-eminence of economic universals results in a noticeable process whereby the public–private divide is often blurred by blending finance and banking legal instruments with constitutional systems. In an output-oriented approach, countries must provide a comfort zone for foreign investments if they wish to survive in a globalised economy.

The chapter examines how indicators have twisted the rule of law into a measurable value-neutral legal concept that secures predictability on investment returns. Indicators are, indeed, part of the laws of probabilities and a form of measuring financial risk. Liberal democracy, as said, has enshrined the new universals of global economic and financial dominance. Since they have built the current global system, only Western liberal democracies are deemed to be compatible with the derivatives of transnational legal communities. The role of indicators is even more apparent as far as the rule of law, human rights, democracy, and climate change are concerned. These encourage countries to arrange their constitutional frameworks around a legal architecture managed from the outside to promote institutional efficiency. We shall see that the rule of law now deals with governance, not with government. Furthermore, it has become the driver promoting good governance. This reflects the shift towards the creation of a global common regulation of international financial relations and markets. It also triggers a shift towards the efficiency rule. Its application requires that the national level be financially responsible *vis-à-vis* financial markets and international investors.

Chapter 4 ('The International Financial Architecture: Financial History and Evolution') upholds that legal indicators are out-of-law managerial tools whereby the law is produced. The chapter illustrates the new world economic order by critically analysing the functions and aims of the WTO, IMF, and WBG. In the global village, the patterns of codification suggested by Kelsen and Pistor no longer take place. Today, as this book assumes, the new architecture of contemporary financial markets – or better, financial systems – is not based on interests coded through the law and vindicated by virtue of the same coding; rather, it is expressly based on sustainability. Decisions are taken at the 'periphery' (the constellation of private orderings which is transnational law) rather than at the apex of a decadent Westphalian state. This is due to the absence of a central planner or supreme architect of the financial system. Daniele D'Alvia has already interpreted sustainability as a (legal) constant in this 'brave new world', where it is measured by specific indicators whose role is to grade the societal impact of an investment.[49] For instance, key performance indicators (KPIs) for ESG are now a compelling reality for corporates, and investors and analysts integrate them into a classic spreadsheet analysis. ESG parameters guide investors' decisions too.

The chapter defines *sustainability* as one of those non-legal meanings lying outside the law that has become legal by virtue of quasi-legal frameworks, such as non-binding and non-enforceable policy statements, guidelines, and soft law instruments. Nonetheless, this non-enforceability can still create a modification of the legal environment, due to the spontaneous compliance and self-imposed regulation practices of market operators.

Yet sustainability pays. Investors are turning away from old models of exploiting natural resources and workers who produce them. There is an increased demand for ethical investing, coupled with easier access to investing in the stock market. With apps like Robinhood, Mint, or eToro, more and more ESG-focused products are delivered to the market, and in some cases, the uptake for these is greater than with traditional exchange-traded funds or index tracker funds. One effect of Covid-19 has been the chance to slow down and consider how we spend our money. The closing of shops and the slowing of industry were a unique opportunity to take stock and reflect on our relentless spending culture, also attending to the environmental and social concerns that this raises.

The new financial architecture is thus based on sustainability, which becomes a (legal) constant rich in meanings also relevant for financial law, insolvency law, sovereign debt relief practices, corporate governance, and environmental law in an out-of-the-law search for non-legal meanings. The codification era has just ended, and the instauration or initiation of the future of (legal) constants and out-of-the-law meanings has just started.

In Chapter 5 ('The Benchmarks of International Insolvency Law'), the starting point is the global pandemic, which saw numerous winners and losers in the business world. Uncertainties are once again dominating the scene at the international level, in the face of economic downturns, wars, inflation, and eroded capital reserves. Both in private and public companies, insolvency could lead to debt restructuring, takeovers and mergers, or closures.

49 See Daniele D'Alvia, 'Legal Constants and the "Constant" Outside of the Law: Mobile Payments in Comparative Perspective Under European Union Law' (2021) 28 Maastricht J Eur Comp 332; and *International Insolvency and Finance Law Legal Constants in Times of Crises* (Routledge 2022).

A modern and progressive insolvency law framework matters. Insolvency law frameworks can help save distressed businesses from a fatal destiny of liquidation. Today, the progressive role of insolvency practices is based on non-insolvency rules or, better, preventing restructuring. At the EU level, we speak of the Restructuring Directive of 20 June 2019. All the 27 EU member states were obliged to implement the European Restructuring Directive by 17 July 2021. Indeed, insolvencies are value-destructive and lower the prospects of a recovery for creditors. The directive made it mandatory for all EU member states to offer a preventive restructuring framework. The latter is an evolved form of commercial law that focuses on hybrid restructuring mechanisms based on a mix of elements ranging from a minimal court-supervised approach to a consistent out-of-court feature centred on private arrangements or workouts.

Yet this new configuration of the law is no longer grounded in a classic conception of insolvency. According to our output-related approach, it might lead to the transformation of the legal meanings and constants outside the law we examined in Chapter 1. Countries around the globe had started to understand the importance of preventing restructuring even before Covid-19, but the appearance of the pandemic has definitively accelerated the process. The modification of national laws is directed by international organisations, rather than national parliaments, through the transformative and soft power of the Factory of Global Legal Indicators. It is within this new role of international practices that nation states seek cooperation and establish consolidated practices and principles to be followed as guidance when enacting new laws.

The chapter considers the importance of this new cooperation at the transnational level in the field of insolvency law frameworks, thus testing the theory of global legal indicators. The EBRD's Core Principles, the World Bank's Principles for Effective Insolvency and Creditor/Debtor Regimes, and the UNCITRAL Legislative Guide to Insolvency Law represent the most vivid examples of this new 'codification' of the law, or better, of its new 'uncodified-codification'.

Again, and unlike in the past, this process has its roots in out-of-law principles transposed and transformed into hard-law provisions at the national level. The establishment of specific insolvency law principles is the direct outcome of continuous discussions encouraged and promoted by international institutions, such as the IMF and INSOL International. In other words, these principles correspond to the practical needs and hurdles that are currently being experienced and reported by national practitioners. Furthermore, the WBG, the EBRD, and other international organisations or multilateral institutional banks have developed specific indicators to measure the effectiveness of insolvency law frameworks. The principles thus settled reflect the best practices in the sector that they are aiming to assess, that is, insolvency law. To this end, pieces of legislation, such as the 2019 Restructuring Directive, can serve as a benchmark.

A modernised insolvency law framework attracts a higher level of capital and investments. At no time has competition mattered so much, and financial innovation and creativity are essential to keep businesses alive and on the market. We might summarise this chapter by saying that, at least in insolvency and financial practices, global indicators matter and help us move towards (and eventually achieve) one of the main aims of comparative law, that is, harmonisation.

In an epoch dominated by the transnational constellation of public actors and private ordering, the law is the result of an unceasing process identification and recognition of constant meanings outside the law. As we will be upholding throughout this book, the 'Fabric' is a new way to look at comparative law, and indicators point to its less-descriptive and more dynamic use. Comparative law should thus be re-interpreted to study different meanings that are mainly to be found outside the law. We shall examine how indicators, soft law, or quasi-legal frameworks act as transnational benchmarks, measuring the performances of domestic legal systems. Once the efficiency of a legal system is under scrutiny, then national reforms are necessary to comply with such new common meanings created outside the law and implemented at the transnational level.

1 Legal Indicators

The Law as an 'Output'

1 Setting the Scenario

The way indicators impact on domestic law-making processes reflects a new trend in comparative legal research, which our book refers to as the 'Factory of Global Legal Indicators'. As stated in the Introduction, indicators foster socio-economic growth, thus playing a pivotal role in managing legal change from the 'outside'. Our main point is that good governance – of both communities and capital – has become an output-oriented process affecting several areas of the law. Among them, this book will focus on constitutional law, international financial regulation, and it will delve as a case study into the global standards adopted under international insolvency law theories and practices. By impacting on them, the 'Factory of Global Legal Indicators' develops into a driver for legal unification-harmonisation in domestic contexts with wider politico-legal implications.

Against this background, this chapter addresses the normative scenario within which the 'Factory' is located. It will look at how law-making is part of the broader externally driven process mentioned earlier. More specifically, it will examine how and why the Factory has been set up, who its main actors are, how the process of legal unification actually works, and last but not least, it will shed light on how indicators have become functional to managing the law from the outside. It will try to explain why their 'soft power' holds a particular fascination when it comes to the fabrication of new 'hard' legislative outputs and regulatory schemes.

Such a 'fascination' is remarkable within the processes of globalisation, which possesses a liberating force facilitating legal harmonisation, stimulating economic development, and promising an 'impending radiant future' to humankind.[1] It does not come as a surprise that fascination is strictly related to such a liberating force: Global markets need new legal spaces to favour the

1 Mikhail Xifaras, 'The Global Turn in Legal Theory' (2016) 29 Can J L Juris 215, 216. No wonder that the very idea of 'development' has to do with 'economic wealth . . . also associated with policies designed to promote economic growth': Mariana Mota Prado and MJ Trebilcock, *Advanced Introduction to Law and Development* (2nd edn, Edward Elgar 2021) 3.

DOI: 10.4324/9781003304333-2

smooth flows of goods, capital, and services across frontiers and national legal systems.[2] Globalisation is fascinating *also* for state authorities, which show a 'readiness' to adopt 'a considerable part of the law' proposed by transnational actors for the regulation of their national public spheres, communities, and markets.[3]

More of this later in this chapter. For now, suffice it here to remember that the main purpose of indicators is to favour the connection with domestic legislation to foster, protect, and secure investors' financial interests. At the same time, they reflect a further interest that is shared by state actors, that is, the improvement of business culture and the attractiveness of their domestic markets to foreign investors. We understand that states 'are not neutral when it comes to whose interests in an asset shall be given priority'.[4] Given the fascination of such regulatory schemes, setting the scenario for the 'Factory of Global Legal Indicators' is of utmost importance.

This scenario revolves around the two expressions we will constantly be perusing: The law is an 'output' managed from the 'outside'. Both lexical items deserve to be examined and re-interpreted in light of comparative law, also taking into account the connotations implied by global legal indicators. Re-interpreting them reflects how the Factory generates law-making processes that cross the public–private divide. Indicators manage the law from the outside by supplying the toolkit for fabricating, measuring, and assessing the law. We shall see that this way of managing the law from the outside resonates with the concept of 'privately made law', where private actors promote the law that they want by engaging with traditional forms of law-making, that is, the production of publicly made 'state law governing economic life'.[5]

2 The Search for Better Legislation

We shall now consider what the law as an 'output' effectively means within the Fabric of global legal indicators. Ours is not an academic exercise in legal linguistics. The quest for the most appropriate connotation of this expression reflects the nature – and we add, the main purpose – of comparative law as an academic enterprise,[6] which is primarily interested in broadening the

2 For more on this fascination, see Matteo Nicolini, *Legal Geography. Comparative Law and the Production of Space* (Springer 2016) Chs 5 and 8.

3 Alan Watson, *Failures of the Legal Imagination* (University of Pennsylvania Press 1988) 87.

4 Katharina Pistor, *The Code of Capital. How the Law Creates Wealth and Inequality* (Princeton UP 2019) 23.

5 See, respectively: DV Snyder, 'Private Lawmaking' (2003) 64 Ohio St L J 371; Jürgen Basedow, 'The State's Private Law and the Economy' (2008) 56 Am J Com L 703, 708. For more on the 'privately/publicly made law' divide, see DV Snyder, 'Contract Regulation, with and without the State: Ruminations on Rules and Their Sources. A Comment on Jürgen Basedow' (2008) 56 Am J Com L 723.

6 See, for example, Günter Frankenberg, *Comparative Law as Critique* (Edward Elgar 2016) 17 et seq.

understanding of legal phenomena across and beyond jurisdictions. It is not merely a matter of comparing and contrasting them; in promoting the advancement of critical legal knowledge, comparative law allows us to grasp 'the truest expression' of the 'essence and potentials' of the fabrication and management of the law from the outside.[7] Any full understanding of this phenomenon entails a full understanding of the underlying principles of the context in which legal-rules-as-outputs are manufactured, that is, the global (and transnational) legal community, as well as its institutions and law-making processes.

From wherever it is managed, the law is (and remains) a human artifact that has always been used to change, complement, and improve legal systems across the world.[8] With its alleged unchangelessness, even divine law, revealed to mankind through Holy Scriptures, requires human legislation to adapt itself to the changes and chances of this fleeting world. This 'strange kind of artifact' is an output used to improve the technical and substantive quality of legislation.[9] Law-making is used to frame 'better' legislation (or pieces of legislation, as the case might be) to match the politico-legal project through which a given community reimagines itself.[10]

What really matters is the way legal outputs are actually framed. To a broader extent, manufacturing 'better' legislation resonates not only with the idea of the law as an output but also with the rationale of comparative law. The idea of enacting 'better' legislation inevitably involves a process of comparison; this occurs when a political community wants to change the law in force because it is deemed unsuitable to reach a given goal, implement a specific policy, or just for the sake of laying down new regulations. The reasons for change usually vary; the law may not be as performative as it ought to be as far as socio-economic development is concerned, it may be considered outdated when it comes to confronting new challenges, or far from preventing or solving conflicts, it triggers unpredictable outcomes, thus deepening internal fractures. A community might thus consider its legal artifacts qualitatively 'inferior' to a 'superior' (and preferable) standard of regulation. An assessment is usually made, and the law currently in force has been compared with (or, which is the same thing, assessed against) this allegedly 'superior' legal benchmark. Seldom is this an abstract ideal type; in the majority of cases, those who draft new

7 Richard Weisberg, *Poetics: And Other Strategies of Law and Literature* (Columbia UP 1992) 227. See VG Curran, 'Dealing in Difference: Comparative Law's Potential for Broadening Legal Perspectives' (1998) 46 Am J Com L 657.

8 On the law as a human artifact, see Luka Burazin, Kenneth Einar Himma, and Corrado Roversi (eds), *Law as an Artifact* (OUP 2018). See also PG Monateri and Mauro Balestrieri, *Quantitative Methods in Comparative Law* (Edward Elgar 2023) 76 and 73 (on the forces underpinning social change).

9 DS Clark, 'Nothing New in 2000? Comparative Law in 1900 and Today' (2001) 75 Tul L Rev 871, 911.

10 Giovanni Tuzet, 'A Strange Kind of Artifact' in Luka Burazin, Kenneth Einar Himma, and Corrado Roversi (eds), *Law as an Artifact* (OUP 2018) 217 and 227 (as a social artifact, 'it exists only in, and for, a society').

legislation draw inspiration from the outside, by way of comparative surveys. Often, the 'superior' standard of legislation is an assemblage of diverse components, usually combined between them and possibly already 'tested' in other legal environments, where they have proved to work satisfactorily.[11]

This process of comparison is nothing else than the 'use of foreign legislation for law making', that is, an ancillary function of comparative law.[12] Since its inception as an academic discipline, comparative law in this 'applied version' has been providing lawmakers with the practical knowledge – *external* to the domestic legal systems, as is evident – required to frame new laws.[13] This practical advice is extremely useful as an 'aid to the legislator'; at the same time, it is relevant at the international/supranational level, where national legal solutions are combined so as to produce the 'best solution' (or 'compromise') when achieving legal unification.[14]

Perhaps Zweigert and Kötz were right when stating that 'good laws cannot be produced without the assistance of comparative law'.[15] Yet a predicament like this hints at legislators making deliberate use of comparative legal methodologies to activate processes of legal change.[16] Taken from the outside, legal benchmarks are probed to draft 'better' legislative outputs, and comparative law helps legislators 'choose the solution which best suits their own legal traditions'.[17]

This *political use of comparative law* reinforces the assumption that the law is not as 'natural' as one might think.[18] Not only is the law an artifact often fabricated drawing suggestions from the 'outside', but the deliberate use of 'superior' external benchmarks is also extremely volatile and may change over

11 Miller terms this type of law-making a 'cost-saving transplant'. See JM Miller, 'A Typology of Legal Transplants: Using Sociology, Legal History and Argentine Examples to Explain the Transplant Process' (2003) 51 Am J Com L 839, 845 et seq.

12 Otto Kahn-Freund, 'On Uses and Misuses of Comparative Law' (1974) 37(1) MLR 1, 12. On the ancillary functions of comparative law, see also Konrad Zweigert and Hein Kötz, *An Introduction to Comparative Law* (OUP 1998) 101, 102.

13 Jonathan Hill, 'Comparative Law, Law Reform and Legal Theory' (1989) 9(1) Oxford J L Studies 101. The applied version of comparative law has been considered inherent to its methodology since the 1900 Congress of Paris: see, for example, Clark (n 9) 833.

14 Mathias Siems, *Comparative Law* (3rd edn, CUP 2022) 4. The best-solution assessment was used when drafting the Principles of European Contract Law (PECL) and the UNIDROIT Principles. See Ole Lando, 'Comparative Law and Lawmaking' (2001) 75 Tul L Rev 1015, 1027.

15 Zweigert and Kötz (n 12) 16.

16 On legislators using 'comparative law as a tool to support a political argument', see FG Sourgens, 'Comparative Law as Rhetoric: An Analysis of the Use of Comparative Law in International Arbitration' (2007) 8 Pepp Disp Resol L J 1, 5. See also Jedidiah Kroncke, 'Law and Development as Anti-Comparative Law' (2012) 45 Vanderbilt J Trans L 477, 545 ('the very messy cauldron of political values and functional solutions that is at the heart of legislative activity makes it . . . compatible with the challenges of comparative law').

17 Zweigert and Kötz (n 12) 16–17.

18 Hill (n 13) 115.

time, depending on political choices; if policies and interests change, so too should the benchmarks.[19] The ancillary function of comparative law, therefore, is both concrete and absolute. It is *concrete* because comparative law surveys are functional to promoting a specific regulatory change, as well as the search for 'better' regulation of societal interests and needs. But it is also *absolute*, inasmuch as the practical use of foreign patterns must represent 'superior' and objective standards of legislation. As said, the patterns chosen are often a combination of legal derivatives already applied in several jurisdictions to regulate concrete issues. Yet the choice of the benchmark 'cannot be achieved by simply conjuring up an ideal law or any topic and hoping to have [the best one] adopted'.[20] The comparative law survey legitimises the proposed legal change. The 'superior' benchmark and the 'best solution' have been chosen because they are perused across jurisdictions, where they have demonstrated that they meet societal needs. It is therefore possible to turn them into the 'model' legislation to be adopted.[21] Their thorough application makes them a 'constant' outside the legal system, offering 'the possibility of a "better model" which . . . must be implemented everywhere else' – evidently also within the legislator's own jurisdiction.[22]

In so doing, the deliberate use of foreign legal derivatives is provided with an 'objective' basis of evaluation, which is the outcome of the traditional – and allegedly 'objective' – methodologies deployed in comparative law, namely, functionalism and generalisations. To promote the adoption of 'superior' external benchmarks, legislators resort to a kind of 'hyper-simplified and stylised version of comparative legal functionalism'; if all legal systems face similar problems, it is possible to 'deal with them . . . through the same set of rules'.[23] Generalisations add the final touches to this process, whereby an idea is, or intended to be, used everywhere, thus favouring the dissemination of legal concepts, irrespective of their social, cultural, and legal backgrounds. Generalisations thus supply the possibility of turning a relative legal solution to a concrete issue into the 'better' constant to be adopted,[24] as well as a universal

19 Indeed, 'the influence of foreign law on legislatures is anything but a temporary phenomenon': see Uwe Kischel, *Comparative Law* (OUP 2019) 25.

20 Zweigert and Kötz (n 12) 24.

21 This is particularly evident in Finland, where comparative surveys of foreign legislation are the starting point of legislative drafting. The surveys have 'to be followed up if government proposal contains solutions that have been influenced by foreign models': Jaakko Husa, *Introduction to Comparative Law* (2nd edn, Hart 2022) 93.

22 Monateri and Balestrieri (n 8) 110.

23 Marta Infantino, 'Quantitative Legal Comparisons: Narratives, Self-Representations and Sunset Boulevards' (2019) 6 J Int'l Comp L 287, 302. On functionalism as the 'yardstick to determine "better law"', see Ralph Michaels, 'The Functional Method of Comparative Law' in Mathias Reimann and Reinhard Zimmermann (eds), *The Oxford Handbook of Comparative Law* (2nd edn, OUP 2019) 379.

24 For further remarks on the theory of legal constants, see Daniele D'Alvia, *International Insolvency and Finance Law: Legal Constants in Times of Crises* (Routledge 2022).

legal device worthy of being disseminated, irrespective of time, place, and legal traditions.

We shall see that the Factory of Global Legal Indicators endorses the same appeal to objectivity as applied comparative law does, particularly when it comes to promoting their own constants outside the law. In both cases (comparative law and the 'Factory' of indicators), objectivisation conceals the political and dispositional use of foreign law when promoting change in domestic legislation.

The question remains why the constant is supposed to exist and to be valid outside the legal system. Mathias Siems provides us with a workable answer: 'Possibly, it matters that all law-makers have a similar aim, namely to increase the wealth of their countries', to boost the efficiency of their respective legal system,[25] to smooth trade and eliminate friction that might cause elevated transaction costs,[26] or to reduce 'legal risks of international business'.[27] Whatever the cause, outside 'there exists a real market for law', to which legislators resort when adopting 'better' legislation, 'if only to "sell" it better' to foreign investors.[28] Usually located outside domestic legal systems, these aim to choose 'the most efficient, but also the least costly, legal system' for maximising their profits.[29]

3 Managing the Law From the Outside as a Form of Cooperation

Dealing with the law as an output managed from the outside, the practical use of foreign legal derivatives navigates what Ralf Michaels and Mathias Siems label 'traditional comparative law',[30] of which it shares the main features: state-centrism, positivism, and formalism.[31] Practical comparative law is *state-centric*, as it assumes that law-making processes using legal patterns

25 Siems (n 14) 37, who refers to Faust Florian, 'Comparative Law and Economic Analysis of Law' in Mathias Reimann and Reinhard Zimmermann (eds), *The Oxford Handbook of Comparative Law* (2nd edn, OUP 2019) 833–34.

26 Monateri and Balestrieri (n 8) 117 et seq.

27 Zweigert and Kötz (n 12) 45.

28 Bénédicte Fauvarque-Cosson and Anne-Julie Kerhuel, 'Is Law an Economic Contest? French Reactions to the *Doing Business* World Bank Reports and Economic Analysis of the Law' (2009) 57(4) Am J Com L 811, 815. See also David Restrepo Amariles and Julian McLachlan, 'Legal Indicators in Transnational Law Practice' (2018) 58 Jurimetrics 163, 174–75.

29 See Horatia Muir Watt, 'Globalization and Comparative Law' in Mathias Reimann and Reinhard Zimmermann (eds), *The Oxford Handbook of Comparative Law* (2nd edn, OUP 2019) 618.

30 See Ralf Michaels, 'Transnationalizing Comparative Law' (2016) 23 Maastricht Journal of European and Comparative Law 352; Siems (n 14) 14 et seq.

31 On 'the ubiquitous (and paradigmatic) hallmarks of mainstream comparative practice in the field', see Pierre Legrand, 'Paradoxically, Derrida: For a Comparative Legal Studies' (2005) 27 Cardozo L Rev 631, 644 ('logocentrism, nomocentrism, objectivity, scientificity, "no-politics", functionalism, "better-law", sembling, and uniformization').

from the 'outside' are the exclusive domains of states. Hence, borrowings and loans are a matter of 'legislation comparée'; *positive law* is, first and foremost, *publicly made law*.[32] Its *formalism* then insulates the law from the contexts where it is applied. This 'bracketing'[33] is functional to concealing the deliberate use of foreign law in promoting legal change, where its political unspoken assumptions are slyly concealed under the 'better legislation' banner. Again, comparative law provides legal reforms with an objective basis for assessing the superior quality of law-from-the-outside within law-making processes.

The 'Factory of Global Legal Indicators' poses new issues as far as the manufacturing of transnational regulatory schemes is concerned. We are not denying the relevance of practical comparative law in areas where indicators suggest legislative action be taken from the outside. Far from it. The Fabric of the Law is still rooted in 'the use of foreign legal patterns for the purpose of producing . . . social change',[34] which confirms their deliberate use in law-making processes. Nor do we maintain that Michaels's tripartite scheme ought to be dismissed; it has to be reimagined, or at least reinvented.[35] Consequently, the quest for 'better' legislation is still the focus of comparative law, even in a time of indicators.

In our time of global legal indicators, something has obviously changed. Being managed from the outside, the law-making process has become less state-centric.[36] The practical use of foreign legal derivatives is now promoted by a further group of actors (namely, multinational corporations and investment funds making up the constellation of the global holders of capital). As we shall see, these seek connections with domestic legal orders to code their own interests through the law either by eliciting 'a fierce regulatory competition between state legal systems in many fields of business law' or through the creation of cross-border and transnational (i.e. non-state-centric) regulatory systems matching their 'private ordering in the name of party autonomy'.[37]

How do the holders of capital apply practical comparative law? The answer to this question lies in the concept of cooperation. Beneath indicators we find the first form of cooperation. To set them up, the holders of global capital

32 See Snyder (n 5) 371.

33 Nicholas Blomley, 'The Ties That Blind: Making Fee Simple in the British Columbia Treaty Process' (2015) 40 Transactions of the Institute of British Geographers 168, 169.

34 Kahn-Freund (n 12) 5.

35 See, for example, Jaakko Husa, 'Traditional Methods' in Mathias Siems and Po Jen Yap (eds), *The Cambridge Handbook of Comparative Law* (CUP 2024).

36 See SE Merry, *The Seductions of Quantification: Measuring Human Rights, Gender Violence, and Sex Trafficking* (University of Chicago Press) 12.

37 Respectively: Restrepo Amariles and McLachlan (n 28) 164; Horatia Muir Watt, 'The Relevance of Private International Law to the Global Governance Debate' in Horatia Muir Watt (ed), *Private International Law and Global Governance* (CUP 2014) 9. On transnational regulatory schemes triggering comparisons of 'forms of regulations across different legal regimes', see VV Ramrai, 'Transnational Regulation' in Mathias Siems and Po Jen Yap (eds), *The Cambridge Handbook of Comparative Law* (CUP 2024) 576.

need the cooperation of several actors. We have traditionally been taught that global law comprises 'a relatively small numbers of global law firms and advocates, nationally ranked global law schools and academics, and globally networked judges'.[38] Yet global legal indicators 'are not made by lawyers. . . . [A]nalysts are mainly political scientists and also include historians, economists and human rights activists'.[39] When suggesting how better legislation might be drafted, the 'Factory of Legal Indicators' makes comparative law conversant with several other disciplines also interested in the transnational environment.[40]

Especially at the state level, this shift in traditional law-making accounts for another cooperative intercourse, which in turn expresses the very idea of indicators as a Factory producing the law from the 'outside'. We said that the law has become less state-centric; with this, though, we do not point to the end of publicly made law. The holders of capital still need national legislation to code, that is, generalise, their own financial interests through the law.[41] Cooperation is therefore a key concept, particularly because it avoids the – political, legal, and accountability-related – risks that are connected to traditional comparative law. Take, for example, legal transplants: In traditional comparative law, their assessment is often a matter of predictable legal outcomes. Certainly, contextual comparative approaches might want to point to the possible rejection of transplants into the recipient country, yet this comparative legal evaluation 'often lacks probability assessments, let alone quantitative measurements of legal risks or of financial implications of legal decisions', which are in turn provided by indicators.[42]

Although indicators retain a state-oriented approach in their comparative law surveys of national legislation,[43] their soft power is based not on the 'superiority' of legislative solutions adopted by a given state donor but on the very purpose of the process of cooperative law-making that they endorse. Like transplants, the need for 'better' legislation reflects the need for selling one's national laws with the aim of attracting foreign investors.[44] Unlike transplants, however, legal change promoted by indicators must also benefit recipients. This is the reason there is no hegemonic, dominant, or superior donor country

38 Neil Walker, *Intimations of Global Law* (CUP 2015) 42.

39 Infantino (n 23) 299. See also KE Davis, 'Legal Indicators: The Power of Quantitative Measures of Law' (2014) 10 Ann Rev L Soc Sc 38, 40.

40 On such a multidisciplinary approach in transnational law, see, for example, Peer Zumbansen (ed), *The Oxford Handbook of Transnational Law* (OUP 2021).

41 See also DM Trubek et al., 'Global Restructuring and the Law: Studies of the Internationalization of Legal Fields and the Creation of Transitional Arenas' (1994) 44 Case W Rsrv L Rev 407, 408 (transnational law comprises 'concrete practices of multiple agents, including lawyers, in a multitude of national "systems"').

42 Restrepo Amariles and McLachlan (n 28) 178 and 198 et seq.

43 Infantino (n 23) 299.

44 See Miller (n 11) 840.

to copy. Under no circumstances do indicators elicit direct competition among national jurisdictions; their supplying an objective basis to socio-legal change is always related to economic growth, thus stimulating competition as regards the best legal devices to be adopted domestically to reach this goal. In this sense, objectivity means that 'the test for the reality created by indicators is . . . functionality'.[45]

Through cooperation, the interests of a given investor are thus able to count as the interest also of the state. This also explains why the way the Factory works cannot be equated to what Dezelay and Garth term 'entrepreneurial transplants'.[46] As Jonathan M. Miller states, this kind of transplants requires an investor 'willing to provide the capital' and a state 'interested in the import, with each guided by what it is able to gain domestically by operating internationally'.[47] Yet under the proposed legal derivative, only the investor managing the law from the 'outside' undoubtedly 'will "reap benefit" from it', and the transplant might be harmful to the recipient country. This departs from what indicators do, inasmuch as the better legislation fabricated from the outside allows 'entrepreneurial activity to flourish . . . accidentally also promoting the wellbeing of the [domestic] society at large'.[48]

4 Private Law-Making and Legal Constants

More on this fruitful cooperation between holders of capital and states later in this chapter. For now, let us focus on the second feature that practical comparative law exhibits within the Fabric of Global Legal Indicators. As noted in the previous section, it maintains that positive law is, first and foremost, ***publicly made law***. Managing the law from the 'outside' entails engaging with different types of rules, which we usually label as outcomes of ***private law-making***.

Perused by David V. Snyder in an eponymous essay, the expression at stake points to a 'pervasive and important element of contemporary lawmaking', which is also 'a robust component of commercial and consumer life'. Private law-making is extremely different from state law: Unlike legislators, private lawmakers are (and remain) private actors; although incorporated in a given country, they operate at a transnational scale,[49] and the law which they

45 Rene Urueña, 'Indicators as Political Spaces – Law, International Organizations, and the Quantitative Challenge in Global Governance' (2015) 12 Int'l Org L Rev 1, 17.

46 Yves Dezelay and BG Garth, *The Internationalization of Palace Wars: Lawyers, Economists, and the Contest to Transform Latin American States* (University of Chicago Press 2002) 7.

47 Miller (n 11) 851.

48 Infantino (n 23) 304.

49 Snyder (n 5) lists 'private legislatures', such as the American Law Institute (ALI), the National Conference of Commissioners on Uniform State Laws (also known as Uniform Law Commission), UNIDROIT, and UNCITRAL. He also refers to the Securities and Exchange Commission (SEC), the NYSE, the NASDAQ, the American Stock Exchange (Amex), the International Chamber of Commerce, corporate banks, credit card associations, and minor rule-makers, such as the Association of Diamond Dealers e la Grain Merchants. See also GR

manufacture is not confined within the precincts of their private orderings. Theirs is privately made law.[50] And privately made law controls 'important segments of lawmaking power, affecting millions who are not group members'.[51]

Privately made law refers to further forms of cooperation taking place among the holders of global capital. The first form of cooperation between private lawmakers confirms that the fabric of legal global indicators does not necessarily require legal transplants; the effects of private law-making in the field of business and finance may indeed be generalised through default rules. Acting as 'gapfillers', Snyder explains, 'privately made law will often displace any publicly made default rules' and is actually put into operation having legally binding effect more than the terms contained in legislation'.[52] This cooperative intercourse discloses an intriguing way of fabricating the law from the outside: Publicly made law is reimagined in a way that best suits private investors' economic interests and their privately made law. It is no longer possible to refute its legal relevance within the legal fabric; nor can we deny its legal character, particularly because this privately made law avoids the – political, legal, and accountability-related – risks connected to positive (i.e. state) business and finance law. Snyder is right when he argues that, 'as far as default rules go, the rules confected by an actor's community or association are likely to carry much greater weight' than that enacted by domestic legislators.[53]

In areas not covered by default rules, privately made law is rooted in another form of cooperation between the global holders of capital. Taken individually, transnational actors aim to maximise *only* their own profits, thus supporting legislation that perfectly matches their own needs. Generalisations of this kind are extremely concrete, and their legislative outputs tend to be 'contingent' and 'selective'; as it solely focuses on the interests of a given investor, it will be likely to increase its financial returns regardless of other investors' and states' interests. Whether we like it or not, this type of 'generalisation simultaneously *suppresses* others'. If we multiply this pattern by all interests that the global holders might want to pursue, contingent-selective generalisations will probably '*extend* . . . in different and potentially conflicting directions',[54] because private law-making 'happens without established structures and depends on

Teubner, 'Societal Constitutionalism: Alternatives to State-Centred Constitutional Theory?' in Christian Joerges et al. (eds), *Transnational Governance and Constitutionalism* (Hart 2004) 16.

50 Snyder (n 5) 374.

51 Snyder (n 5) 377.

52 Snyder (n 5) 407 and 409. See also Avery Katz, 'Taking Private Ordering Seriously' (1996) 144 U Pa L Rev 1745, 1752.

53 DV Snyder, 'Molecular Federalism and the Structures of Private Lawmaking' (2007) 14 Indiana Journal of Global Legal Studies 418, 420.

54 Frederick Schauer, *Playing by the Rules* (OUP 1991) 22. See also A Beckers, 'A Societal Private Law' (2022) European Law Open 380, 384 (institutions and law 'must be understood as containing the seeds for moving in opposite directions').

ad hoc combinations of private actors'.[55] At the same time, they deprive states of the objective basis they require when it comes to implementing the panoply of (often conflicting) legal derivatives managed from the outside. Do we really think that states would be willing to adhere to each of these extremely contingent processes of generalisation? Would they really incorporate pieces of privately made law servient only to investors' entrepreneurial activity, without promoting the well-being of their domestic societies?

What states are likely to accept are generalisation processes where all investor-specific legal derivatives operate *in the same direction*, that is, promoting shared and not mutually exclusive economic growth across transnational and domestic realms. Cooperation among global holders of capital precisely fulfils this function, inasmuch as it makes contingent and selective generalisation processes 'nest within each other in the same direction'.[56] This reinforces the idea that the law is an output manageable also from the outside. The 'society' of transnational economic actors join forces so that they express a 'collective intentionality and shared cooperative activity' necessary for the creation of legal solutions serving their 'social purposes or functions'.[57] The outcome is the generalisation of substantively similar rules. At the same time, individual investors' privately made laws will be prone to their own economic growth and, accidentally, of other transnational actors and state societies.

With such a cooperative intercourse, the global holders of capital supply privately made law with an 'objective' basis of evaluation by reinventing the traditional (and 'objective') comparative-legal methodologies, which are functionalism and generalisations. Unlike contingent ones, comparative law generalisations nest within each other in a common direction, because they are conceived as the 'translation of diverse legal rules into one language'.[58] In so doing, the Factory of Global Legal Indicators can reach the legal uniformity required by its actors. Owing to their fragmentation, economic interests (and their related privately made law) are not 'universal in scope and character';[59] anyway, they are able to develop this quality by way of generalisations, which turn sectional interests into the interest of the whole, and privately made law into the type of 'better' legislation that may pursue those interests.

Turning fragmentation into a coherent whole is the outcome of what Snyder terms 'molecular federalism', that is, a type of cooperative intercourse which 'is more likely to meet different kinds of diverse regulatory needs'.[60]

55 Snyder (n 53) 420.
56 Schauer (n 54) 22.
57 Husa (n 35) 27.
58 See George Mousourakis, *Comparative Law and Legal Traditions. Historical and Comparative Perspectives* (Springer 2019) 8. On generalisations as constitutive features of comparative law, see JH Merryman, *The Loneliness of the Comparative Lawyer* (Kluwer 1999) 491.
59 Matteo Nicolini, 'Methodologies of Comparative Law: Universalistic Approach' in *Max Planck Encyclopaedia of Comparative Constitutional Law* (2nd edn, OUP 2023) at 1–5.
60 Snyder (n 53) 441.

The molecule is a vivid metaphor replicating James Madison's predicament of the USA as a 'compound republic'.[61] Snyder probes the metaphor because it is opposed to the idea of the atom that extends in different and potentially conflicting directions. The molecule, by contrast, 'invokes the idea of a compound because private lawmaking can only occur as a cooperative effort of at least two actors, and usually many more'. In other terms, 'this figure . . . recognizes that even privately made law is a social function'. Likewise, molecular federalism stresses the necessity of cooperation even among economic actors competing with each other: 'The complex of governmental and private relationships . . . can show how different law-making entities . . . influence and react to each other'.[62]

This complex web of relations reflects the presence of a non-legal constant lying outside the law, which is the need to maximise financial returns. We shall examine it in the next section. Suffice it here to say that privately made law is the legal 'output', allowing for its identification and recognition, which exists and is valid outside domestic legal systems. This is not to deny the presence of contingent and selective legal solutions matching investors' individual interests; rather, it highlights their interdependence. Molecular federalism acts as a toolkit of several legal solutions that are often crafted after comparative law surveys. Certainly, each of its tools has usually been invented to fulfil the volatile interests of transnational corporations; if policies and interests change, so too should the tools. Generalisations, as said, necessarily nest within each other in a common direction, thus reconciling the extremely concrete – and often conflicting – interests of the members of the transnational community. What the toolkit makes possible is the fact that legal solutions are comparable (and therefore replicable) all around the world. There is something utilitarian in this process: Each legal solution in the toolkit is the outcome of the 'cooperative effort' among transnational actors. The fabric of global indicators requires this collective effort.

The extensive use of generalisations discloses a further feature of the cooperative intercourse: The holders of global capital are particularly skilled at handling comparative legal methodologies.[63] Together with generalisations, functionalism is servient to reimagining the third component of traditional comparative law in a time of global legal indicators: It slyly brackets corporations' unspoken assumptions to maximise profits under the 'better legislation' banner.[64] Functionalism provides an extremely flexible framework when generalising the

61 'The Federalist No. 51' (James Madison), In Publius, *The Federalist Papers* (Clinton Rossiter ed., The New American Library 1961) 323.

62 Snyder (n 53) 420.

63 See PG Monateri, *Advanced Introduction to Comparative Legal Methods* (Edward Elgar 2021) Ch 5.

64 Functionalism is closely related to universalism: see Jaakko Husa, *Interdisciplinary Comparative Law. Rubbing Shoulders with the Neighbours or Standing Alone in a Crowd* (Edward Elgar 2022) 168–69.

transnational toolbox of legal solutions. As it concentrates on the comparison of the 'particular material and isolated provisions' that make up privately made law, it may help the global holders of capital to highlight the commonalities among their contingent generalisations: Not only are their specific solutions comparable, but they can also 'be understood as providing answers to similar problems', because they all extend in the same direction, that is, allowing entrepreneurial (and state) activity to flourish 'in situations that are supposedly identical'.[65] Owing to such an 'uncomplicated' and 'nondoctrinal' scheme,[66] it also opens up the cooperative intercourse to states. Certainly, comparative law surveys are conducted to demonstrate that investors' privately made laws extend in the same direction; but it also assesses whether the law managed from inside state jurisdictions is already a functional equivalent of the legal benchmarks privately made from the outside. To this extent, they provide a further objective basis stimulating regulatory competition among states, thus outwardly overcoming 'theoretical and practical problems that result from the study of legal systems foreign to the comparatist'.[67] No wonder, therefore, that functionalism accommodates the need for uniformity through the law[68] with the variety of domestic legal traditions, which avoids turning privately made law into a marketplace 'with one legal culture' and an 'extremely impoverished habitat'.[69]

The joint application of generalisations and functionalism is particularly apt to cross the public–private divide in law-making. To a broader extent, the distinction between private and public law-making becomes irrelevant. It is not merely a matter of detecting which legal output managed from the outside is better at pursuing the constant lying outside the law. The issue at stake is now the turning of the maximisation of financial returns into a legal constant that states might be willing to incorporate. It is to the framing of this legal constant outside the law that we shall turn now our attention.

5 The Theory of Legal Constants, and the Constant 'Outside' the Law

So far, we have considered the shift in traditional law-making that takes place through cooperative intercourse, especially at the state level, which conveys the idea of indicators as a factory producing the law from the 'outside'. The output-oriented approach to legal indicators causes a further shift in how legal definitions are coded. These now reflect a concern that is shared by all the actors of the transnational community, namely the sustainability and solvency of both public sector and private investors.

65 Husa (n 35) 23.

66 Respectively: Husa (n 35) 25; Michaels (n 23) 347.

67 Husa (n 35) 25.

68 Muir Watt (n 37) 9.

69 Michele Graziadei, 'The Functionalist Heritage' in Pierre Legrand and Roderick Munday (eds), *Comparative Legal Studies: Traditions and Transitions* (CUP 2003) 114.

The process of coding a new legal definition is a remarkable sign of changing factors. In this regard, we shall start considering patterns used when forging definitions. We shall engage with Hans Kelsen's *Grundnorm*,[70] that is, a concept that he justified as a fact, unavoidably located 'outside' the law. Despite contradicting his entire legal theory of the law as an 'input', Kelsen's argument is particularly relevant to our discussion of legal indicators. A similar assumption is devised in modern terms in Katharina Pistor's *The Code of Capital*, whose main argument is that capital has been codified for centuries by means of the law. In her view, 'law is code'. Hence, codification becomes the main instrument through which power and private interests can be protected, and sometimes their protection even goes against the primary preservation of vulnerable parties, such as in the case of Indigenous rights in the colonisation era.

In a time of transnational private ordering, the law is not the 'input' to codify the capital; rather, it is an 'output', that is, the result of the identification and recognition of constant meanings 'outside' the law. These meanings are often recognised in soft law or self-regulation instruments. Indeed, our book focuses on a new role that comparative law can play in financial crises based on what we define as the 'uncodified' process of the law. Indeed, the Covid-19 pandemic has imposed a dramatic reformulation of the rule of law, giving way to a more flexible and dynamic form of regulation where traditional instances of statute law are unable to provide answers to new legal issues. This also occurred as regards contact-tracing systems, which introduced new forms of surveillance mechanisms in Western democracies (Chapter 3).

It seems that Pistor's theory can be reversed. In other words, today, we may say that the strange artifact, which is law, is 'dead' – at least as far as its traditional processes of legitimacy and law-making are at stake. This is the starting point of our discourse. In a Covid-19 scenario – and, even before it, during the global financial crisis (2007–2010) – we all were (and still are) outside the law (in the traditional connotation). Hence, this has prompted us to re-discover constant(s) outside the law: essentially, commercial common concepts, or other common meanings and concerns that, albeit not necessarily 'legal', are nonetheless shared by several legal systems. In other words, they are uncodified/shared common meanings which are often found in soft law or self-regulation instruments, which means privately made law or, more generally, non-binding legal instruments. Once they are identified, such instruments are used to promote harmonisation processes through which public law-making can subsequently identify the common legal meaning and codify it in domestic legislations. This is a phenomenology that might be defined as the 'uncodified codification' of the law: Any codification process must necessarily start from an uncodified and outside-the-law identification of (legal) meaning(s).

70 Hans Kelsen, *General Theory of Law and State* (The Lawbook Exchange 1945).

Within the 'Factory', the law is conceived differently from Pistor's way: It is not the 'input' which codifies the capital or construes financial assets but, rather, the 'output' – that is, the result of the identification and recognition of constant meaning(s) outside the law. This is also a new way to look at comparative law. It is not merely a science whereby different legal systems – or, in Pistor's terms, different codifications – are compared in order to highlight commonalities and differences, as well as to identify a global code by virtue of 'exporting the law'. Following in the steps of, say, Sacco's 'legal formants' or Watson's 'legal transplants', this comparison of laws is still rooted in traditional comparative law. By contrast, comparative law must be re-invented and re-interpreted to study different meanings that are mainly to be found 'outside' the law. This is what we define as *legal constants*. In mathematical terms, it is a negative expression where the inputs, that is, the constant(s), are always outside the law and become legal provided they are identified and recognised throughout the legal systems.

This way of thinking paves the way for an in-depth exploration of the 'uncodified codification' of the law, connecting concepts imposed by new market realities to, say, new insolvency (privately made) law frameworks that not by chance promote business restructuring and out-of-court proceedings. Publicly made law is no longer at the centre of the system, which is now decentralised, as is also decentralised the new emerging form of decentralised and centralised finance that challenges traditional finance. To this end, even direct listings are no longer directed by underwriters or financial intermediaries, that is, the key actors that Pistor identified as closer to the apex of the 'legal theory of finance'.[71] Today, the apex is located in the peripheries, and the world has irremediably changed. Indeed, this predicament makes us re-imagine the law with its core objectives and intimate meanings as the starting point – objectives and meanings that sometimes push the 'legal' boundaries to build up new integrated and harmonised legal or quasi-legal systems. For example, alternative ways of investing represent different models of financing, either in the form of virtual currencies (e.g. Bitcoin) or in the form of cash shell vehicles and unconventional acquisition models (e.g. special-purpose acquisition companies). In both instances, the law does not play any substantive role in the form of state regulation, and financial markets appear – for the first time – to be 'democratised' rather than liberalised through regulation and cross-border rules.

In sum, a legal constant is the result of the interpretation and construction of different meanings that are derived from legal systems or privately made legal toolkits nesting within each other within the Factory – or more precisely, from the comparison of two or more legal systems, decisions, or legal toolkits manufactured from the outside. Specifically, the interpreter is

71 Katharina Pistor, 'A Legal Theory of Finance' (2013) Paper Number 13–348 Columbia Law School – Public & Legal Theory Working Paper Group, 13.

focused on finding a constant 'outside' the law to which regulators, judges, lawyers, scholars, and lawmakers assign a legal meaning, so that we can speak of legal constant(s) where the 'legal' refers to the subsequent identification of a non-legal concept recognised as a common meaning for one (or more) legal system, as well as one (or more) decision or toolkit. Indeed, a legal constant cannot be construed only as a common legal element to be discovered while studying different legal systems. The concept under scrutiny is not simply based on the idea that a legal institution exists (in terms of either functionalism or structuralism) in two or more legal systems.[72] Far from it. A *legal constant* is the constant meaning derived from the interpretation of different legal institutions, and it is usually identified as the only meaning that can relate to (and justify) the comparison between two or more different laws, principles, or judgements.

Meaning is the ultimate objective of legal analysis in comparative law, as well as within any national or domestic system. For instance, interpretation is the core activity that judges carry out in every legal system to solve a dispute; it is also the main legal activity that lawyers undertake to defend their clients by providing judges with alternative qualifications of the relevant facts and/or provisions. For this reason, the act of indissolubly associating comparative law with the comparison of different legal systems is unsatisfactory. Most of the time, the comparison being carried out is directly related to the study of different meanings, through which different legal constant(s) can be discovered by examining either legal transplants or legal formants. In view of this, legal transplants and legal formants represent 'working tools' for the interpreter useful to identify the constant meaning(s) outside the law that have eventually been incorporated into the legal system.

72 For instance, the right of one party to terminate a contract is a right that is usually present in many different legal systems, namely, under English common law as well as civil law countries, such as Italy, France, Germany, and so on, but the mere fact that this element exists in more than one country does not make it a legal constant. In this light, it can be considered only a simple common element that has mainly a descriptive function. To provide the reader with another example, divorce exists in more than one legal system, such as under English Common Law, in civil law countries, and in some cases also under Islamic Law. The termination in contract law as well as the divorce in family law are considered in this instance as a common element of the law that is present and exists in one or more legal systems, but it is not a legal constant. Indeed, a legal constant can be appreciated in the research of a common legal meaning that is mainly identified by a constant meaning outside of law to which jurists, judges, scholars, and lawmakers give a legal status. For instance, in mobile payments as an alternative payment system, a constant meaning outside of the law can be identified. Such meaning deeply relates to mobile payments and qualifies the legal recognition of such constant meaning outside of law as a legal constant. In this specific example, the payment function is seen as a constant outside of the law to which, for example, the European legislation as well as judgements of the European Commission are granting a legal status to protect several public interests, such as consumer protection, technological network safety, and so on.

6 The New Legal Theory of Finance Through the Lenses of Legal Constants

In her *Code of Capital*, Katharina Pistor makes the claim that finance is legally constructed, which means that it does not stand 'outside' the law. To uphold her assumption, she makes the case that financial assets are disciplined by legal rules and regulations. Although this can vary from jurisdiction to jurisdiction, the legal enforcement of financial commitments is present in every jurisdiction and can influence the scope of the entire financial system. In other words, without legal enforcement, contractual promises cannot be honoured, and the capital outflows or inflows between jurisdictions cannot be effective. For this reason, market participants often design financial instruments that are not in conflict with the rules existing in different jurisdictions. It means that contract law plays a major role in contemporary financial markets, and that contractual rules are able to provide financial operators (as well as the financial industry) with new contractual devices, which – according to Pistor – in turn seek legal 'vindication of private coding efforts by a court of law'.[73]

In claiming legal vindication, financial operators can try to mitigate uncertainty and prevent volatility of liquidity. In her reasoning, liquidity is not a free asset, and when the future shows a scarcity of liquidity, the refinancing of financial commitments becomes more challenging. This is because every financial system is inherently unstable, and the exercise of discretionary powers to enforce legal commitments can bring about a new theory of political economy of finance.

Pistor's conception of liquidity is borrowed from Bernanke.[74] From this perspective, liquidity is connected to the ability to sell any asset for other assets or cash at will. In a business re-organisation procedure, we might think of carve-out merger and acquisition (M&A) transactions and the dismissal of business-related going concern (i.e. the selling of an asset for cash). In respect of financial markets, we can also imagine any secondary market where the investor sells financial instruments (these being derivatives, bonds, or stocks) to second-hand investors. In sovereign debt restructuring practices, these take the form of, say, an exchange offer (or a debt-for-debt swap), but they might also take place through the use of an internal collective action mechanism (if included in the debt instrument).[75]

73 Pistor (n 4) 43.

74 Ben Bernanke, 'The Great Moderation' (20 February 2004) Federal Reserve <www.federalreserve.gov/boarddocs/speeches/2004/20040220/defaul.htm> accessed 16 December 2024.

75 Historically, collective action clauses (CACs) derive from the failure of the IMF's proposal for a sovereign debt restructuring mechanism (SDRM), perhaps the best-known attempt to create a multilateral sovereign debt framework in the early 2000s. The private creditor community actively lobbied creditor-hosting governments and debtor states against the SDRM by presenting an alternative, more market-friendly approach to debt restructuring: CACs. CACs benefit private creditors by allowing them to remain in control of their loans to debtors

To this end, Pistor defines 'liquidity shortage' – namely, the impossibility of finding second-hand investors willing to buy financial assets – as one of the main triggers of financial crisis. Rather than underpinning money creation processes, she specifically claims that uncertainty undermines the possibility of obtaining new financing – and therefore it qualifies liquidity shortage in terms of crisis. Consequently, if financial assets are legally constructed, the law directly contributes to the instability of finance. The main example that is brought to the attention of the reader is the case of sovereign debt. The law of the issuer (i.e. the law of the country that is borrowing money from investors through a Eurobond[76]) matters; at the apex of the financial system, the law is much more flexible in comparison to the periphery (the contractual terms and conditions of a bond prospectus or the offering memorandum or circular). It is indeed more elastic than at the periphery because the survival of the entire system is at stake, and discretionary powers to enforce legal commitments can be limited to save the system. At the periphery, by contrast, the law is less elastic, and default can result in involuntary exit. If we agree with this vision, we must consequently admit that the survival of the system is determined at its apex.

States, financial intermediaries, and financial institutions are in greater proximity to the apex. Hence, they are also more likely to benefit from a relaxation of the rules or a suspension of the full force of the law. A direct example can be seen in sovereign debt contracts whose enforceability is doubtful, or at least elastic. States' assets cannot be seized and liquidated, and only assets located overseas can be frozen (if ever). In other words, a state cannot be subject to liquidation as would happen in the event of private distressed companies; these might indeed be liquidated if they do not find a viable alternative to restructure their finances. Furthermore, sovereign governments that owe debt to many foreign creditors can choose which creditors to favour when making payments by implementing a *de facto* seniority structure of sovereign debt.[77] Essentially, the state issuing sovereign debt can 'escape' legal obligation by changing the

during crises. In contrast, a multilateral sovereign debt framework would be capable of overriding debt financing contracts, imposing a stay on creditor litigation, and brokering a debt restructuring under the auspices of a defined framework, to the detriment of private creditors.

76 A *Eurobond* is a type of international bond that is issued in a currency different from the currency of the country or market in which it is issued. It is a debt instrument used by corporations, governments, or international organizations to raise capital in global markets. For example, a bond denominated in US dollars but issued in European or Asian markets would be considered a Eurobond. Eurobonds are not confined to Europe despite their name; they are a global financial tool that provides issuers access to diverse investors and facilitates cross border capital flow. These bonds are typically unsecured, issued in bearer form, and often traded in high denominations. Their flexibility and broad appeal make them a preferred choice for financial institutions seeking funding across international borders.

77 Matthias Schlegl, Christoph Trebesch, and MLJ Wright, 'The Seniority Structure of Sovereign Debt' (May 2019) Research Division Federal Reserve Bank of Minneapolis – Working Paper 759 1.

law or altering the order of priority of payments. However, financiers have been able to sue their own sovereigns for default. The Brady Plan in the 1980s was the turning point for sovereign debt litigation,[78] and today's investors in sovereign debt markets differ from a handful of major syndicated commercial banks prior to the Brady Plan.

The growth of secondary sovereign bond markets and transferability of bonds has opened up access to a wide range of new investors, including professional sovereign debt litigants. These are distressed debt funds that have taken advantage of a business opportunity presented by the secondary market in the absence of a sovereign bankruptcy regime to operate a business model based on sovereign litigation. They have been labelled 'vulture funds', as they acquire defaulted (or nearly defaulted) sovereign debt at a significant discount from their issue price on the secondary market. Their view is premeditated, inasmuch as they aim to hold out[79] from a restructuring and to litigate for the debt's full face value with interest and delay penalties, and subsequently pursuing the debtor country's assets to realise the full value of the claim.[80] They sue sovereigns in multiple jurisdictions in order to seize sovereign assets to satisfy their court judgements.

Under the threat of potential litigation, states try to pay the majority of debt most of the time in the hope that this can more easily enable them to access further financing through capital markets and official sector intervention. The litigation risk has exponentially escalated due to the fact that sovereigns frequently issue debt to foreign investors. The latter have brought arbitration proceedings against the state once it defaults on its external debt.

Arbitration is also the field that allows us to make some preliminary reflections on soft law. Historically, the contractual right to choose soft law as the governing law has been narrowly restricted to arbitration. For instance, the Uniform Commercial Code provides the closest US non-arbitration precedent, allowing parties to vary its provisions by choosing soft law promulgated by intergovernmental authorities, such as UNCITRAL or Unidroit, or to trade codes, such as the Uniform Customs and Practice for Documentary

78 The Brady Plan involved exchanging outstanding commercial bank loans for bonds to relieve the emerging market debt crisis of the late 1980s and early 1990s. See Ch 5.3.

79 Holdout litigation has proliferated since courts have explicitly upheld the vulture funds' business model of the late 1990s. In *Elliot Associates v Republic of Peru* (1998), the US Court of Appeals dismissed Peru's champerty defence on the grounds that Elliot's principal intent was to be paid in full and that Elliot's litigation was incidental and contingent on Peru's non-performance of obligations under the contract. Champerty prohibited the purchase of debt with the intent and for the purpose of bringing a lawsuit. The court rejected the champerty defence even though it was clear that, at the time of buying Peru's debt, Elliot, a vulture fund, would have known that Peru would not be able to pay in full. Vulture funds then lobbied in NY legislature in 2004 to amend the NY Judiciary Law 489 so as to prevent the defence of champerty from arising for any debt purchases above $500,000.

80 Julian Schumacher and others, 'Sovereign Defaults in Court' (2018) ECB Working Paper 2135 17.

Credits. The Hague Principles on Choice of Law in International Commercial Contracts also favour the right of parties to choose 'rules of soft law' that 'are generally accepted on an international, supranational or regional level as a neutral and balanced set of rules' (Art. 3).

It seems that international commercial, financial, and other business transactions are increasingly conducted under 'soft law' rules, which are non-state rules that may be aspirational or reflect best practices but are unlikely to be legally enforceable in the foreseeable future. The attraction to soft law is focused on the fact that it does not need governmental validation or consent. Nonetheless, it is undeniable that the law still plays a vital role in shaping the enforcement of legal obligations. The law and the power that is exercised by the state can effectively change the level of enforcement and vindication. By contrast, soft law can be seen as a reliable methodology to provide parties with friendly regulatory frameworks that are seen as a non-mechanical form of regulation. Indeed, parties tend to spontaneously adhere to soft law frameworks rather than hard law, which is often perceived as a sort of external imposition. For this reason, it has sometimes been said that soft law is harder than hard law.[81]

This dynamic evolution of regulatory regimes has contributed to the exponential growth of hybrid models of regulation. For instance, this has occurred as far as swaps and derivatives contracts are concerned. Indeed, the International Swaps and Derivatives Association (ISDA) has played a major role in the rise of derivatives by creating standard contracts and adapting them to different legal systems around the world.[82] In other words, the ISDA was formed to develop templates for derivative instruments that would be enforceable in multiple jurisdictions. This is a direct example of the critical role that the law is playing in shaping the future, and indirectly in allowing private organisations discretionary powers to determine market practices. This is, according to Pistor, the establishment of a central planner that can exercise its authority and power in order to influence the legal environment. The central planner can be a public entity, such as the state, or a private organisation, such as the ISDA, whose objective is to ensure that critical pieces of legislation validate the contracts it sponsors.

81 Francis Snyder, 'Soft Law and Governance: Aspects of the European Union Experience' in Luo Haocai (ed), *The European Union Experience* (Peking University Press 2009).

82 ISDA is a global trade organisation that represents participants in the derivative market. Established in 1985, ISDA aims to foster safe and efficient derivatives trading and risk management practices worldwide. It plays a pivotal role in the standardization, regulation, and documentation of over-the-counter (OTC) derivatives transactions. One of ISDA's key contributions is the development of the ISDA Master Agreement, a standardised legal framework that governs derivatives transactions between counterparties. This document reduces legal uncertainties, simplifies negotiations, and facilitates the netting and collateralisation of obligations, thus reducing systemic risk. ISDA also develops guidelines to promote financial stability and innovation in derivatives markets. Its work ensures greater transparency, legal clarity, and operational efficiency for market participants.

The same example can be found in sovereign debt, with the International Capital Market Association (ICMA),[83] which in 2014 published a new standard of the *pari passu* clause for inclusion in the terms and conditions of sovereign debt securities, as well as an updated version of the aggregated collective action clauses for the terms and conditions of sovereign notes.[84] A very good example of the application of those principles comes from the final restructuring deal that Argentina reached with its foreign bondholders in early August 2020 in the form of a bond exchange offer which was approved overwhelmingly by its foreign bondholders. The tortuous negotiating process lasted several months and came after Argentina had defaulted on its sovereign debt in late May 2020 for the ninth time in its history. On the issue of CACs, prominent professors around the world wrote open letters to express their strong support for Argentina's negotiating position.[85] Specifically, those professors claimed that CACs based on aggregated voting across multiple series of bonds should be incorporated in the new bonds, as opposed to CACs that contained a requirement for series-by-series voting (a position that was favoured by certain bondholders). This is because aggregated CACs became the market standard, as embodied in the model promulgated in 2014 by the ICMA, and earlier-generation CACs based on series-by-series voting essentially only strengthened the hand of potential holdout creditors. Those are standard contractual terms that ensure the legal enforcement of financial obligations.

As Pistor points out, the critical and central role of law in financial contracting is reflected in this, that is, that every financial intermediary desiring to issue a new financial instrument employs lawyers to check its compliance with laws and regulations. This practice also gives rise to so-called regulatory arbitrage, namely, a practice through which financial innovation is (in Pistor's parlance)

83 ICMA is a global trade association that serves the capital markets by promoting transparency, efficiency, and resilience in international debt securities markets. Founded in 1969, ICMA acts as a bridge between market participants, including issuers, intermediaries, investors, and regulators, to support a well-functioning and integrated global financial market. ICMA is best known for its role in setting industry standards, such as the ICMA Primary Market Handbook, which provides guidelines for issuing debt securities, and the Global Master Repurchase Agreement, a standardized document for repo transactions. These frameworks ensure legal and operation consistency across markets. The association also plays a vital role in fostering sustainable finance, advancing regulatory dialogue, and providing education and training for market participants. Its work is instrumental in enhancing market integrity and facilitating cross-border capital flow.

84 International Capital Markets Association, 'Standard Collective Action and Pari Passu Clauses for the Terms and Conditions of Sovereign Notes' (2014) <www.icmagroup.org/Regulatory-Policy-and-Market-Practice/Primary-Markets/primary-market-topics/collective-action-clauses/> accessed 7 July 2021.

85 Joseph E Stiglitz, Edmund S Phelps, and Carmen M Reinhart, "Restructuring Argentina's Private Debt Is Essential" (6 May 2020) <www.project-syndicate.org/commentary/argentina-sovereign-debt-restructuring-private-creditors-by-joseph-e-stiglitz-et-al-2020-05> accessed 13 June 2021.

made rule-compliant. In other words, for every legal enforcement of obligations, we might find ways to 'escape those obligations.

What really matters is the nature of power that is exercised and the interests that are protected. For any protected interest, there are many unprotected ones that cannot find reasonable satisfaction, such as in the case of foreign investors and the external debt of a sovereign state. In such cases, the law creates a 'global hierarchy of finance' where transactions can take different forms depending on parties and their importance in the financial ecosystem. Law matters also as regards the position of different actors within the hierarchy, and therefore, it is not possible to conceive of 'unregulated' financial markets. Indeed, as we said, the increasing role of non-state actors (ISDA, ICMA, etc.) is a direct confirmation – at least in Pistor's eyes – that financial markets are based on a system of law where the hierarchy of financial market operators is determined by private actors, organisations, states (i.e. the actors that are close to the apex). Likewise, these actors establish the legal enforceability of financial instruments. In light of this, a legal theory of finance can effectively determine a new paradigm of political economy. This traditional thinking of financial markets provided by Pistor has been further developed in her latest book, *The Code of Capital*,[86] where she argues that capital has been codified for centuries by means of the law. In her view, the 'law is code'.

As can be seen, financial markets are complex entities – or, better, complex systems. This means that they are open systems that communicate with their environment, but they do not operate the other way round (so-called operation closure). This idea is challenging, and it gives rise to a new role for law-making where the system itself might develop and enact its own regulation. The idea of fragmented knowledge is Ladeur's central point of assertion to recognise the end of a centralised stock of knowledge administrated by the state. As opposed to a Westphalian model of legislation mentioned earlier, modern society is characterised by the 'a-centric' creation of order, and no central planner is contemplated within this new globalised framework.[87] For Ladeur, this means recognising society as a 'network of networks' (a term he borrowed from Eli M. Noam).[88] In other words, society is no longer based only on hierarchical forms of power but on heterarchical relationships aimed at creating a spontaneous process of cooperation, rather than individualism. For this reason, one side-effect of this cooperation is the establishment of a collective order which is the product of self-organisation behaviours in society. Consequently, the law becomes merely a secondary instrument of integration that is no longer supported by its traditional authoritative legitimacy as a form of

86 Pistor (n 4).

87 Karl-Heinz Ladeur, 'The Financial Market Crisis – A Case of Network Failure?' in PF Kjaer, Gunther Teubner, and Alberto Febbrajo (eds), *The Financial Crisis in Constitutional Perspective: The Dark Side of Functional Differentiation* (Hart Publishing 2011) 78.

88 Eli M. Noam, *Interconnecting the Network of Networks* (The MIT Press 2001).

mediation of consensus. Furthermore, the law has a political connotation that is embedded into super-structures, such as states' constitutions (Chapter 3).

Rather than being undermined by uncertainty, financial markets are underpinned by it. To this end, uncertainty is also the trigger that has changed the role of the law. As we have been upholding throughout this chapter, today the law is the 'output' rather than the 'input' in the absence of a central planner. This new connotation is the direct product of uncertainty. The lawmaker cannot predict the future or control uncertain events; especially if financial innovations are growing fast as a symptom of market regeneration, the law cannot keep pace. For this reason, uncertainty is not only determining a new formation of structures within financial systems by virtue of autopoiesis but also a new codification process through which uncodified common meanings by virtue of interpretation are found inside non-legal words, legal provisions, or decisions that are the results of new heterarchical relationships. Once they are agreed at the international level, those forms of cooperation and common meanings are embedded in hard law provisions of national legal frameworks (for instance, the reform of national insolvency frameworks based on the insolvency law assessments of international organizations or multilateral institutions at international level). By contrast, hard law provisions are incorporated at the same international level (e.g. the Restructuring Directive), and the same occurs when quasi-legal frameworks are embedded in soft law instruments (the UNCITRAL Model Law on Cross-Border Insolvency). This is the new role of legal constants; (legal) constants, rather than the law, are the unique instances of the new uncodified codification process of the law.

7 Coding Constants From the 'Outside' With Global Legal Indicators

As seen in the previous sections, ours is a time of transnational private orderings and privately made law. This has brought about a huge change in law-making processes, also impacting on how the law is conceived within the 'Factory of Global Legal Indicators'. This change is patent in our conceptualisation of the law-as-an-artifact in terms of an 'output' managed from the outside.

The way wealth is distributed in societies supplies us with a suitable example of this change. Its distribution has traditionally been the domain of publicly made law. As a 'powerful social ordering technology', the law has been instrumental in acting as the 'input' to codify and control 'the levers for the distribution of wealth in society'.[89] This has also meant finding an equipoise between individuals' substantive equality and private groups' interest in maximising their financial investments.

No wonder, therefore, that 'the control and accumulation of resources . . . was and remains' the organising theme within political communities, as well as

89 Pistor (n 4) 17, 19.

a 'key element of political tension'.[90] In *The Code of Capital*, Katharina Pistor vividly explains the tension between the law as an input as far as the redistribution of wealth and the maximisation of profits are concerned. Her main argument is that, with the right legal coding, any type of assets (i.e. any 'object, claim, skill, or idea') can be turned into capital and thereby increase their propensity to create wealth for its holder(s). In so doing, the legal coding has also set constraints on private actors. Pistor's assumption is the following: Within the state–global holders intercourse, transnational actors are also keen on considering state law – and for what concerns us here, also traditional-practical comparative law – as the 'input' for codifying their assets as capital. If we understand her correctly, the law as an input is rooted in a generalisation process that always has an 'objective' basis when it comes to perusing comparative law in its applied version and providing lawmakers with the practical knowledge – *external* to domestic legal systems, as is evident – required to frame 'better' legislation. Within this scenario, publicly – not privately – made law supports investors' entrepreneurial activity. As the input is still framed at the domestic level, it focuses on the whole set of interests at stake and is likely to increase investors' and state communities' interests alike.

In dealing with global legal indicators as a management tool to assess the performance of domestic legal systems, we have adopted a quite different stance. Privately made law favours alternative forms of generalisations, which are contingent and selective. Within this scenario, the law is no longer the 'input' to codify the capital. By contrast, it is now the 'output' of law-making processes where 'publicly made law is often designed to bow to private agreements and thus to privately made law'.[91] Indeed, private interests tend to gain control over the distribution of wealth by placing 'the law . . . firmly in the service of [their] capital'.[92] We also saw that this kind of law-making is aimed at identifying and recognising constant meanings outside the law. Revolving around the unceasing quest for maximising profits, these non-legal instances require a legal constant to achieve this goal, which we detected in the toolkit of several diverse legal solutions that make up molecular federalism. Used to establish a common legal meaning to be subsequently codified in domestic legislations, this toolkit is often crafted after comparative law surveys which take the form of out-of-law managerial tools – that is, the indicators – which are the instruments whereby the law is produced.

The 'legal' qualification of a non-legal concept may thus become a common meaning for one or more legal systems, eventually being incorporated into domestic jurisdictions. This occurs through the cooperative intercourse between holders of capital and states. When coding their constant through

90 Fritjof Capra and Ugo Mattei, *The Ecology of Law: Towards a Legal System in Tune with Nature and Community* (Berrett-Koehler Publishers 2015) 53.
91 Snyder (n 53) 428.
92 Pistor (n 4) xi.

state law, the holders of capital seek a connection with the public sphere. Theirs are not merely interested in blurring the divide between privately and publicly made law.[93] The connection poses substantive questions: The very idea of the law is indeed challenged owing to the fact that we imagine 'any part of [it] . . . as no longer being traceable back to' the state as 'a legitimate lawmaking authority'.[94] States and private orderings are extremely different entities of the cooperative intercourse. The former ones represent the general interests of their communities, whereas the holders of capital are private sectionalities propagating, through contingent generalisations, their own interests at several scales and in different legal orders.

8 Connecting With the Public Sphere

How does this connection take place? This section supplies us with a theoretical explanation, which can be traced back to the remarkable 'fascination' of globalisation. Legal scholars do usually praise global law, as well as its 'aesthetic consequences' and 'sublime effects'.[95] It does not come as a surprise that, with their privately made law, globalised markets need the reopening of domestic legal spaces to favour the smooth flows of goods, capital, and services across frontiers and national legal systems. This reopening of territories does not mean rubbing borders out of maps; it solely requires a connection with the transnational actors making up the legal spaces of globalisation. The holders of global capital make 'use of it . . . on the basis of an underlying logic and with the help of the knowledge and technical expertise', that is to say, of a 'system' in the form of what we have styled as molecular federalism.[96] We have also said that they have experimented with new ways to generalise their interests (and their privately made law) by promoting legal changes in national spaces so that the latter incorporate the legal constants that best achieve their goals. As a result, their legal space impacts on how political communities arrange their organising themes.

But how does this process actually occur? How is it possible that the holders of global capital have infiltrated the public sphere and contributed to manufacturing domestic legislation in accordance with their own interests? Again, in *The Code of Capital* (2019), Katharina Pistor provides us with a possible answer, arguing that globalisation holds a particular fascination *also* for states. The prospect of benefitting from capital gains is 'more likely to find [states'] blessings than claims that assert self-governance or seek to ensure environmental sustainability'.[97]

93 See Muir Watt (n 29) 610.

94 Peer Zumbansen, 'Transnational Law: Theories & Applications' in Peer Zumbansen (ed), *The Oxford Handbook of Transnational Law* (OUP 2021) 8.

95 Heather Hugues, 'Aesthetics of Common Law – Domestic and International Implications' (2007) 67 La L Review 690, 696.

96 Henri Lefebvre, *The Production of Space* (Donald Nicholson-Smith tr, Blackwell 1991) 11.

97 Pistor (n 4) 23.

Per se, the allure of globalisation does not trigger changes in domestic normative spaces. Something more is required. The forces of capital seek a connection with the public sphere, which is usually drawn by suggesting a renovated 'morally eligible foundation on which' communities might 'organise their practical affairs'.[98] What is shared is the maximisation of profits for shareholders, capital investors, and asset owners, which is part of the organising theme within political communities. In the public sector, private investors' concerns meet 'that of public finance and the income and solvency of state'.[99] In so doing, the interests of transnational actors turn out to be the interests of the whole community.

The connection revolving around public finance concerns is as old as the relationship between capital and states. In fact, ***public finance*** refers to the management of a government's revenues, expenditures, and debts to achieve economic stability and growth. Financial markets, in turn, are platforms where financial instruments (such as bonds, stocks, and derivatives) are traded. The interplay between public finance and financial markets is crucial when it comes to funding government activities and shaping broader economic conditions. As we all know, governments nowadays rely on financial markets to raise funds for public projects and cover budget deficits. To this end, they issue financial instruments (such as sovereign bonds), which investors purchase. These bonds are traded on domestic and international markets, linking public finance to their own dynamics.

The connection revolving around public finance took place at the very onset of the modern nation state. In constitutional history, for example, the establishment of the Bank of England (1694) tackled the 'dramatically increased rate of growth in public finance' by resorting to national debt and other 'means of state funding through new kinds of long-term and short-term loans'.[100] And this connection is still more alive than ever. Take for example how investors in financial markets react to governments' fiscal policies, such as tax reforms or spending plans. If such policies are perceived as unsustainable, it can lead to a loss of confidence, higher borrowing costs (through higher bond yields), and challenges in raising funds. Direct examples of this understanding can be found in the gilt (i.e. government bonds) turmoil in the UK when, in autumn 2022, the then Chancellor of the Exchequer Kwasi Kwarteng announced a series of expansionary fiscal measures, ***inter alia***, supply-side policies and tax

98 R Mullender, 'Context, Contingency and the Law of Negligence (or from Islands to Islands of Time)' (1997) 29 Bracton L J 23, 25. On how economic actors penetrate the public sphere, see also John Braithwaite, *Markets in Vice, Markets in Virtue* (OUP-Federation Press 2005) 9.

99 Richard Hoyle, 'Introduction: Aspects of the Crown's Estate, c. 1558–1640' in Richard Hoyle (ed), *The Estates of the English Crown 1550–1640* (CUP 1992) 1.

100 See ME Turner, *Enclosures in Britain 1750–1830* (Macmillan 1984) 36; JM Neeson, *Commoners: Common Right, Enclosure and Social Change in England, 1700–1829* (CUP 1993) 15 et seq.; Julia Rudolph, *Common Law and Enlightenment in England, 1689–1750* (The Boydell Press 2013) 131.

cuts. Markets reacted negatively, with the 30-year gilt yield spiking 120 basis points over three days. This instability was primarily triggered by the government's 'mini-budget' reform (a public finance strategy), which proposed substantial unfunded tax cuts and increased borrowing, leading to a loss of investor confidence and movements in gilt yields. The rapid rise in gilt yields had a pronounced effect on pension funds employing liability-driven investment (LDI) strategies.[101] These strategies often involve the use of derivatives to hedge against interest rate movements, requiring collateral to be posted when yields rise.

The sudden increase in yields led to substantial margin calls, forcing pension funds to sell gilts to raise liquidity, thus further exacerbating the decline in gilt prices and creating a self-reinforcing cycle of forced sales and falling prices. At that time, the Bank of England (i.e. the central bank of the UK) was forced to step in and purchased long-dated gilts to ensure proper market functioning. This action aimed to restore orderly market conditions and alleviate pressures on pension funds. The Bank of England's intervention helped calm the markets, and gilt yields gradually returned to more stable levels. The 'mini-budget' reform is today a key example that vividly illustrates the connections between public finance strategies and the sentiment of the market. Investors value predictability in fiscal policy. Sudden and unvetted policy changes – like those in the mini-budget – unavoidably create uncertainty, which is detrimental to investor sentiment. Transparent communication about fiscal strategies helps maintain confidence and mitigate market over-reactions. While pro-growth fiscal policies are essential, they must be balanced with fiscal sustainability. Policies that ignore this balance risk spooking investors, as in 2022 in the UK. Hence, the adverse reaction of the market highlighted the importance of aligning fiscal strategies with prevailing market expectations. Clearly, when governments appear disconnected from economic realities or fail to acknowledge debt implications, they lose credibility with investors. To this end, the 'mini-budget' proposed unfunded tax cuts and significant borrowing, signalling to investors a lack of fiscal discipline. This perceived fiscal recklessness

101 *Liability-driven investment* (LDI) is an investment approach primarily used by pension funds and insurance companies to manage their assets in a way that aligns with their future liabilities. The goal of LDI is to minimise the risk of mismatches between the fund's obligations (liabilities) and the performance of its assets. The starting point is analysing the timing and size of future liabilities, such as pension payments. These are often long-term and sensitive to changes in interest rates or inflation. LDI strategies use financial instruments like government bonds (gilts), inflation-linked securities, and derivatives to hedge against risks, particularly interest rate and inflation risks. When interest rates fall, liabilities often increase due to discount rate changes. By holding bonds or derivatives that increase in value when rates fall, the strategy ensures the asset values rise alongside liabilities. Specifically, to maintain liquidity while hedging liabilities, LDI strategies often involve leverage. This allows funds to hold other return-seeking investments while still managing liability risks through derivatives like interest rate swaps. LDI portfolios are actively managed to adjust for changes in liabilities or market conditions.

prompted concerns about the UK's ability to manage its debt sustainably. At the same time, it led to a sharp depreciation of the British pound, as investors doubted the government's ability to maintain macroeconomic stability. The currency decline reflected broader concerns about the UK's attractiveness as an investment destination.

Likewise, the re-election of Donald Trump in 2024 significantly influenced financial markets, echoing the 'Trump Trades' phenomenon observed during his initial presidency in 2016. Investors swiftly adjusted their portfolios in anticipation of the policy directions of the prospective administration, leading to notable market movements. Specifically, major US stock indices – including the Dow Jones Industrial Average, S&P 500, and NASDAQ – reached record highs in equity markets in the aftermath of the election. This surge reflected investor optimism regarding anticipated tax cuts and deregulation, which were (and are) expected to stimulate corporate profits and economic growth in the near future. In bond markets, the prospect of expansive fiscal policies has raised expectations of increased government borrowing, leading to a sell-off in US government bonds and a corresponding rise in yields. We might say that investors are bracing for potential inflationary pressures resulting from policies of the prospective US administration. In particular, investors are positioning themselves by anticipating policy shifts, including (1) tax reforms (the new Trump administration proposed corporate tax cuts to enhance after-tax earnings for companies, prompting increased investment in equities, particularly in those sectors poised to benefit from reduced tax burdens), (2) deregulation (plans to roll back regulations in sectors such as finance and energy have enhanced investor confidence, leading to sector-specific rallies as markets anticipate a more business-friendly environment), and (3) trade policies reflecting the Trump administration's stance on trade, including potential tariffs, which have introduced a degree of caution. Industries reliant on global supply chains are closely monitoring developments, as protectionist measures could impact profitability.[102]

As can be seen, the connection between public finance and private capital and markets' sentiment is clear today as it was at the very onset of the modern nation state. This connection elicits a further reflection on how holders of capital are able to pursue their interests through legislative law-making processes, promoting their own legal constants from the outside, that is, the 'superior' benchmark whose application across jurisdictions is demonstrated by indicators. Their thorough application makes them a 'constant' outside the legal system, which states incorporate, thus creating 'the law that was wanted' by the holders of capital.[103] These infiltrate the public sphere and indirectly act as

102 Daniele D'Alvia, 'Why Donald Trump's Election Win Fueled a Stock Market Surge' *The Conversation UK* (20 November 2024) <https://theconversation.com/why-donald-trumps-election-win-fuelled-a-stock-market-surge-243949> accessed 7 December 2024.

103 Watson (n 3) 87 and 96.

legislators of national communities; their constants outside the law are turned into domestic legislation, inasmuch as this enforces their interests as if they were *the* organising theme of communities. In other words, they act *strategically* and code, that is, generalise, their own interests through the law. This is, as William Twining puts it, a truly 'sophisticated models of law reform': Through indicators, the constant outside the legal system is able to 'find space in the government's legislative programme, be approved and amended in a (preferably democratic) legislative process, enacted, promulgated, explained to key actors, and provision made for implementation'.[104] This connection accounts for the generalisation of private actors' interests through the law and the preservation of the capital–nation state nexus. In other words, it is the basis upon which the out-of-law managerial tools, which are the indicators, are used to fabricate the law from the 'outside'.

9 Legal Constants Through Managerial Tools

From what we have been saying so far, indicators supply the objectivisation required to promote the main goal of the global holders of capital, namely, the connection with state law-making to turn privately made law into domestic publicly made legislation. In other terms, the Factory of Global Legal Indicators is servient to reimagining the third component of traditional comparative law, namely, legal formalism.

As said, the ultimate legal source for indicators is traceable back to the non-legal instance, which is the maximisation of investors' profits. Once this is identified as the constant meaning outside the law, it is necessary to supply it with the right legal coding, that is, with the legal 'output' that best suits transnational actors' interests. This is precisely what indicators are supposed to do. The search for constant meanings outside the law is often recognised in privately made law, such as self-regulation instruments. For what concerns us here, they are embedded in indicators, which establish a prospective legal meaning to be subsequently codified at the domestic level. The law thus becomes a legal constant reflecting the need for harmonisation across jurisdictions.

Their proliferation in recent years is the major consequence of the quantitative turn in comparative law, which we shall examine in the following chapter. No wonder that indicators reshuffle the relation between economic performances and the law.[105] In this lies their soft power, which, as J. S. Nye's eponymous essay states, 'occurs when one' actor 'gets other countries to *want* what it wants'.[106] Through molecular federalism, transnational private sectionalities propagate, and therefore generalise, their own interests at several scales and in

104 William Twining, *General Jurisprudence: Understanding Law From a Global Perspective* (CUP 2009) 253.

105 See Ch 2.

106 JS Nye, 'Soft Power' (1990) 80 Foreign Policy 153, 166.

different legal orders. These generalisation processes permit sectional interests to apply what Günter Frankenberg terms 'strategic comparison'.[107] Strategic comparison also points to Nye's 'ability to set the political agenda and determine the framework of debates in a way that shapes others'. To this extent, indicators are indeed 'intangible power resources . . . so that other countries develop preferences or define their interests in ways consistent with' their own.[108] In numerical comparative terms, the common law matches the criteria adopted by the forces of capital, which revolve around the idea of elevated economic performances measured through numeric indicators. How the connections work is far from being dysfunctional; in a case of conflict between economic and non-economic interests, the former interests prevail by virtue of their coding through transnational law. States do want the law that is wanted from the outside because of 'social pressure' and 'influence State behavior'.[109] If they do not comply, their failure will be visible in 'next iteration of the index' with all 'the reputational consequences of their next rating or ranking'.[110]

The idea of 'soft power' is a vivid metaphor that helps us grasp how indicators turn the law into an output managed from the outside; but the connection among investors, national public spheres, and domestic law-making also requires an explanation. The transformative potential of indicators is functional to enacting 'better' legislation, with the aim of attracting investments from the outside; this is precisely what indicators do, that is, they have turned transnational actors' non-legal instances into *the* interests of the whole community.

The process whereby indicators favour incorporation of these non-legal instances into domestic public spheres matches the meaning of the same lexical item 'indicator', to which we have already made reference in the Introduction. Etymologically, it derives from the Latin 'indicātor' (from the verb 'indicāre', English 'to indicate'). According to the *Oxford English Dictionary*, it 'points out, or directs attention to, something', also serving 'to indicate or give a suggestion of something' for what matters here, the legal constant outside the law to be incorporated. From an economic angle, an *indicator* is '[a] variable, index, etc., which is considered to provide information about a sector, market, or economy'. In supplying such information, it 'is used to predict future

107 See Günther Frankenberg, 'Critical Comparisons: Re-Thinking Comparative Law' (1985) 26 Harv Int'l L J 411.
108 Nye (n 106) 167–68.
109 See JG Kelley and BA Simmons, 'Politics by Number: Indicators as Social Pressure in International Relations' (2015) 59 Am J Pol Sc 59 55; Urueña (n 45) 8: 'If the indicator proves consistent and reliable enough, and a certain State's low score is publicized enough, that State could be brought around to implement measures that are in line with the normative vision of the organization'. See also Ramrai (n 37) 576, according to whom 'the law can have an influence or claim obedience across polities'; and KE Davis, 'The Role of International Organizations in the Production on Metrics' in M Bussani, S Cassese, and M Infantino (eds), *Comparative Legal Metrics. Quantification of Performances as Regulatory Technique* (Brill 2023) 308.
110 See Kelley and Simmons (n 109) 9.

outcomes or trends'. Its main derivative – 'economic indicator' – is even clearer in this direction: The *OED* styles it as '[a] statistic used to gauge or predict economic performance'.[111]

This definition is replicated in the *OECD* definition of *indicator*. This is styled 'a quantitative or a qualitative measure derived from a series of observed facts that can reveal relative positions (e.g. of a country) in a given area', which can also 'point out the direction of change across different units and through time . . . identifying trends and drawing attention to particular issues'. The definition at stake is also consonant with the practical use of comparative law, since it highlights their helpfulness 'in setting policy priorities and in benchmarking or monitoring performance'.[112]

Akin definitions may be found in several scholarly writings. Take for example the definition provided by K. E. Davis, Benedict Kingsbury, and S. E. Merry and perused in several scientific publications. According to them, an *indicator* is 'a named collection of rank-ordered data that purports to represent the past or projected performance of different units'.[113] In its legal variant, it is used to carry out massive comparative law surveys to find out which domestic legal solution is better at maximising profits for shareholders, capital investors, and asset owners – and which, by contrast, ought to be altered to match the benchmark.[114]

In the field of comparative law, both definitions bring about conspicuous implications. Firstly, indicators evoke the idea of measurement. Indeed, they make it possible to measure the quality of the law across jurisdictions, with the aim of comparing them on mathematical terms. Bearing in mind that they outline a quantitative frame to assess reality, they uphold the idea of 'Turn[ing] Law into Numbers',[115] allowing us to see the world through the lenses of metrics – or, better said, 'leximetrics'.[116] Leximetrics is consonant

111 See, respectively: 'indicator' and 'economic indicator' *Oxford English Dictionary* (2021) <www.oed.com/view/Entry/94420?redirectedFrom=indicator#eid> accessed 29 April 2024.

112 OECD, *Handbook on Constructing Composite Indicators. Methodology and User Guide* (OECD 2008) <https://www.oecd.org/en/publications/handbook-on-constructing-composite-indicators-methodology-and-user-guide_9789264043466-en.html> accessed 1 July 2024.

113 KE Davis, Benedict Kingsbury, and SE Merry, 'Introduction: Global Governance by Indicators' in KE Davis et al. (eds), *Governance by Indicators. Global Power Through Quantification and Rankings* (OUP 2012) at 6. The definition is used by, among others, Kelley and Simmons (n 109) 56.

114 See, for example, Davis (n 39) 38; Restrepo Amariles and McLachlan (n 28) 167. Merry measuring the world indicators 84; M Arslan, 'Differentiating and Connecting Indicators: The Quality and Performance of Law in the World Bank's Doing Business Project' (2020) 16 Int J L in Context 17, 20; Davis, Benedict Kingsbury, and SE Merry (n 113) 4.

115 Mathias Siems, 'Measuring the Immeasurable: How to Turn Law into Numbers' in Michael Faure and Jan Smits (eds), *Does Law Matter? On Law and Economic Growth* (Cambridge: Intersentia 2011) 115–36.

116 See, for example, Mathias Siems, 'Taxonomies and Leximetrics' in JN Gordon and W-G Ringe (eds), *The Oxford Handbook of Corporate Law and Governance* (OUP 2018); Malcom Langford, 'The Turn to Metrics' (2012) 30 Nordic J Hum Rts 222; KA Kholodilin

with the idea of benchmark, which styles the model of 'better' legislation that practical comparative law takes from the outside. Indicators inevitably involve a process of comparison, pointing to the legal constant outside the law that has been considered suitable to reach the goal of maximising economic and financial returns within the state–investors cooperative intercourse.

By providing *the* benchmark (the legal constant) outside the law, national legislators thus might want to consider whether their legislation is qualitatively 'inferior' or 'superior' to the standard of regulation which is preferable also in terms of privately made law (and the underlying interests). If there is 'something of public concern and political relevance, which is *worth measuring in the first place*',[117] this is indeed non-performative legislation. Evidently, as indicators 'foster commensuration, or the comparison of different entities according to a common metric',[118] which assesses 'the deviation from the reference standard', therefore engaging 'with status and reputation by leveraging comparative information among peers'.[119]

Secondly, through indicators, the comparative law survey legitimises the proposed legal change, thus providing the objective basis to which the applied version of comparative law has aways aspired through the deliberate use of foreign legal derivatives. Again, this basis is the outcome of the 'objective' methodologies of functionalism and generalisations. Indicators generalise legal constants (or, which is the same thing, investors' privately made law and preferred legal solutions), avoiding the flaws generated by contingent generalisation. They extend in (or point to) the same direction, that is, performative rules maximising profits. At the same time, policymakers may use indicators to assess whether their domestic legislation is already a functional equivalent of the legal benchmarks (privately) made from the outside.

10 The 'Soft Power' of Indicators

Last but not least, metrics embedded in indicators 'successfully [combine] scientific objectivity with normative authority of some sort, winning agreement from both expert and non-expert publics'. Indicators have a twofold identity: On the one hand, they are normative tools; on the other, their intrinsic value lies in how they measure reality, making themselves subject to real-world tests.[120]

---

and Linus Pfeiffer, 'Measuring Unmeasurable: How to Map Laws to Numbers Using Leximetrics' (2021) DIW Discussion Paper 1933 <www.diw.de/de/diw_01.c.812775.de/publikationen/diskussionspapiere/2021_1933/> accessed 30 April 2024.

117 William Davies, 'Spirits of Neoliberalism. "Competitiveness" and "Wellbeing" Indicators as Rival Orders of Worth' in Richard Rottenburg et al. (eds), *The World of Indicators. The Making of Governmental Knowledge Through Quantification* (CUP 2015) 285.

118 Kelly and Simmons (n 109) 9.

119 Respectively: Balestrieri and Monateri (n 8) 71; Kelley and Simmons (n 109) 9.

120 Davies (n 117) 285. On indicators as instruments whereby 'legal texts are mapped into real-valued indices', see Kholodilin and Pfeffer (n 116) 3.

Their normative character is what turns them into the objective basis for fabricating domestic legislation. According to Davis and Siems, they indeed both have 'law-like' functions and effectiveness; these authors' starting point is the 'perceived legitimacy' of indicators.[121] If we understand their arguments correctly, legitimacy must be understood, in Weberian terms, as a 'social action . . . guided by the belief in the existence of a legitimate order'.[122] As for indicators, their belief lies in their being a generalisation which transnational actors are attentive to extend in the same direction, with the aim of fabricating the law that is 'better' to harvest the benefits of the market. As said, the 'outside' is now focused on economic performance in terms of facilitating trade, investments, and monetary policies, yet to fulfil this function, the effectiveness of indicators is rooted in their seeming law-like devices. The use of numbers to present the benchmark seems to secure 'neutrality and generality', also ensuring 'correct and unambiguous transmission of information'.[123] This neutrality is precisely the kind of soft power that makes up their legitimacy and compels 'individuals subject to measurement – namely the addressees – . . . to acknowledge [their] results and to use them as a basis for taking action'.[124]

At the same time, we have said that their intrinsic value lies in how they measure reality. Yet Kelley and Simmons remind us, 'Information is not neutral; it is powerful, and its use is often *purposive*'.[125] In disclosing which is the preferred benchmark maximising the benefits of the markets, indicators carry out comparative legal assessments, allowing us to evaluate, through numbers, the performativity (and the quality) of several legal systems, which are therefore ranked as superior or inferior as regards the benchmark incorporating the constant outside the law. In so doing, they perfectly embed the empirical character of comparative law; indeed, they show attentiveness to operational rules beyond the written law, inasmuch as they provide the knowledge required in terms of economic performance.

It does not come as a surprise, then, that their use is widespread across jurisdictions and among transnational actors. As far as the latter group is concerned, their combining objectivity and real-world assessments are also particularly apt to accommodate the *political use of comparative law* with the unspoken assumptions of external investors. Markets and interests are extremely volatile

121 Davis, Benedict Kingsbury, and SE Merry (n 113) 22 and Siems (n 14) 368, 370. See also Mathias Siems, David Nelken, 'Global Social Indicators and the Concept of Legitimacy' (2017) 13 Int J L Context 436.

122 Max Weber, 'The Protestant Ethic and the Spirit of Capitalism' in *Economy and Society* (University of California Press 1968) 81.

123 Matti Rissanen, 'Standardisation and the Language of Early Statutes' in Laura Wright (ed), *The Development of Standard English 1300–1800: Theories, Descriptions, Conflicts* (CUP 2000) 120. On indicators and their 'ostensibly neutral, technical and ultimately market-facilitating conception of law', see Tor Krever, 'Quantifying Law: Legal Indicator Projects and the Reproduction of Neoliberal Common Sense' (2013) 34 Third World Q 131, 132–33.

124 Krever (n 123) 144.

125 Kelley and Simmons (n 109) 56.

and change over time; if investors' policies and interests change, so too should the benchmarks. Indicators exhibit an impressive flexibility: The presentation as numbers is particular fitting for the purpose of incapsulating new non-legal instances, constants, and meanings proceeding from external factors, such as political and economic ones. As TC Halliday puts it, 'indicators reinforce voices for the portability of global norms'; in comparative legal terms, this means norms crafted as 'model laws that may be slotted into national statute books with a minimum of fuss and disruption'.[126] This predicament reflects the fact that the data to be 'prioritised' (that is, used to frame the indicator) and 'downplayed' (and therefore deliberately omitted from it) are not chosen after a 'random' process – quite the contrary. The process is selective in nature and follows 'criteria that are external to the phenomena being described', that is, a new economic interest or a new type of investment.[127] In other terms, they 'measure not simply reality but the gap between reality and the ideal, between performance and the standard'.[128]

The change in their numerical form does not affect the stability of indicators, because these are adaptable to new economic interests that still extend in the same direction and fulfil the same function even better than they used to do under the previous numeral version of the benchmark. Whatever change they take, indicators are able to reframe new constants outside the law. A new legal change is therefore required. 'Fascination' and states' financial concerns will secure compliance with them. Functional, as it is, to maximising financial returns, the new legal constant outside the law will be incorporated into the system as the output fabricated from the outside through unceasing cooperative intercourse between states and investors.

126 TC Halliday, 'Legal Yardsticks: International Financial Institutions as Diagnosticians and Designers of the Laws of Nations' in KE Davis et al. (eds), *Governance by Indicators. Global Power Through Quantification and Rankings* (OUP 2012) 214.
127 Urueña (n 45) 2.
128 David Restrepo Amariles, 'Supping with the Devil? Indicators and the Rise of Managerial Rationality in Law' (2017) 13 Int J L in Context 465, 467.

2 A Scientific State of Mind

The Onset of Legal Indicators

1 The 'Soft Power' of Indicators and Its Epistemological Background

As seen in the previous chapter, ours is a time of transnational private orderings, privately made law, and legal-institutional changes. We have styled this transformation – which is particularly marked – the 'Factory of Global Legal Indicators', inasmuch as it represents a true challenge to the state as *the* legitimate law-making authority.[1] The law is – and remains – a human artifact. Far from being only the preserve of domestic legislators, it has become the 'output' of private lawmakers, and its ultimate legal source is often rooted in non-legal instances, such as global legal indicators.[2] With their combination of objectivity and real-world assessment, these are particularly apt to accommodate the political use of comparative law with the goals of external investors.

We find the main consequence of this transformation in the way the law is conceived and understood. This has become an 'output' often 'manufactured' from the outside. The cornerstone of our theorisation lies in the 'soft power' of indicators as a form of law-making and cooperative practice, that is, an expression grasping the idea that indicators govern the fabrication of the law from the outside. As explained in Chapter 1, if states follow 'the "best-practice" law recommendations' suggested by indicators, they may improve their 'scores and rankings'.[3] The cooperative intercourse takes place among transnational actors and extends over national jurisdictions, turning transnational investors' privately made law into domestic publicly made legislation. The holders of global capital are the major force of the whole process; in making up the

1 This is also true at the international/supranational level, as well as the transnational one. See Mathias Siems, *Comparative Law* (3rd edn, CUP 2022) 322 et seq.; Alicia Pastor y Camarasa, *Transnational Constitution Making. External Actors, Expertise, and Democratic Transition* (Routledge 2024).

2 KE Davis, 'Legal Indicators: The Power of Quantitative Measures of Law' (2014) 10 Ann Rev L & Soc Sc 48.

3 M Arslan, 'Differentiating and Connecting Indicators: The Quality and Performance of Law in the World Bank's Doing Business Project' (2020) 16 Int J L in Context 17.

DOI: 10.4324/9781003304333-3

drivers of the transnational community, they are the 'cosmopolitan agents of change'.[4]

This predicament discloses a further feature of the cooperative intercourse: Transnational investors carry out massive comparative law surveys, rank, and order legal systems according to their economic performances and attractiveness vis-à-vis financial investors. Once they have found the legal solution that is better at maximising their profits, they usually tend to generalise its 'diffuse model laws' to 'shape . . . national policies'.[5]

The use of such an output-oriented approach is a remarkable sign of this time of globalisation. Against this background, indicators are the major changing factor, connecting transnational private orderings and domestic publicly made legislation. For what specifically concerns us here, they establish a prospective legal meaning to be subsequently codified at the domestic level. In Chapter 1 we saw that they reconcile an interest that is shared by transnational investors and state actors, namely, the maximisation of profits through the improvement of business culture and the attractiveness of domestic markets.[6] This concern triggers a connection between capital and the public sphere; not only does it provide the theoretical explanation for the soft power of indicators, but it also accounts for the fascination that, through indicators, transnational economic actors exert on states.

Besides this theoretical explanation, we understand that something more is required when it comes to justifying the proliferation of the indicators in recent years. Albeit pivotal to understanding their soft power, the theoretical explanation solely explains why the Factory is fascinating for states. Yet collecting real-world data on legal systems, creating benchmarks, and delivering rankings have become fascinating *also* for other actors. Besides investors and policymakers, indicators have drawn the attention of academics. Although it was originally an area of research for political scientists and economists, legal quantification through indicators has recently stirred interest among legal practitioners and lawmakers,[7] as well as international donors, who might want to 'ensure that their donations are not misused' by recipient countries.[8] The audience can be widened even further, so as to encompass 'a broader network of institutions which support' the use of indicators.[9] It is perhaps

4 Anna Beckers, 'A Societal Private Law' (2022) 1 European L Open 380, 384.

5 Arslan (n 3) 17.

6 See KE Davis, Benedict Kingsbury, and SE Merry, 'Indicators as a Technology of Global Governance' (2012) 46 Law Soc Rev 71, 89.

7 Arslan (n 3) 20; see also KE Davis and MB Kruse, 'Taking the Measure of Law: The Case of the Doing Business Project' (2007) 32 Law & Social Inquiry 1095, 1096.

8 KE Davis, 'The Role of International Organizations in the Production on Metrics' in Mauro Bussani, Sabino Cassese, and Marta Infantino (eds), *Comparative Legal Metrics. Quantification of Performances as Regulatory Technique* (Brill 2023) 309.

9 See also Mathias Siems, David Nelken, 'Global Social Indicators and the Concept of Legitimacy' (2017) 13 Int J L Context 436, 445.

such wide acceptance (not to mention use) that has led to stress the 'law-like' character of indicators, as well as their 'proclaimed bindingness . . . reflected in the mutual expectations of the relevant community'.[10]

The reference to the 'relevant community' is fitting for our purposes, as it likens their soft powers to the context within which they are applied. What is striking is that their 'proliferation' is not a one-way process (from investors to states);[11] it also operates the other way around (from states to investors). State–investor intercourse exhibits a kind of 'recursivity'. A 'set of three cycles' turns the law into an output manufactured from the outside. And these cycles constantly interact. There are thus 'recursive cycles' of national 'lawmaking and law implementation', 'iterative' cycles of global '*norm*-making', and a third cycle lying at their crossroads, where 'national experiences influence global norm making and global norms constrain national lawmaking, in an asymmetric but mutual fashion'.[12]

Recursivity reflects a further feature of the Factory, that is, the production of knowledge useful for framing better legislation. It is as if all the aforementioned actors have joined a transnational epistemic community, whose major consequence is a new way of conceiving, understanding, and manufacturing the law. This epistemic community revolves around the knowledge produced through indicators and subsequently exchanged and coded through 'a quantitative metric'.[13] States, drafters of indicators, consumers, NGOs, and investors alike peruse a common (and universal) mathematical grammar comprising 'measures, standards and rankings of the quality of law and legal institutions across the entire world'.[14] These actors all contribute to establishing a 'performance culture' which is 'dominated by targets, benchmarks, indicators, and league tables'.[15]

In this chapter, the focus is on the epistemological paradigm that lies beneath (and percolates through) the Factory. This paradigm is related to the

10 Oren Perez, 'Fuzzy Law: A Theory of Quasi-Legal Systems' (2015) 28 Can J L & Jurisprudence 343, 355.

11 Some scholars use the terms 'invasion' and 'explosion' to point to their massive use. See Amanda Perry-Kessaris, 'Prepare Your Indicators: Economics Imperialism on the Shores of Law and Development' (2011) 7 Int J L in Context 401, 406; Niels Petersen and Konstantin Chatziathanasiou, 'Empirical Research in Comparative Constitutional Law: The Cool Kid on the Block or All Smoke and Mirrors?' (2021) 19 Int J Const L 1810.

12 TC Halliday and BG Carruthers, 'The Recursivity of Law: Global Norm Making and National Lawmaking in the Globalization of Corporate Insolvency Regimes' (2007) 112 Am J Sociology 1135, 1138. See also TC Halliday, 'Legal Yardsticks: International Financial Institutions as Diagnosticians and Designers of the Laws of Nations' in KE Davis et al. (eds), *Governance by Indicators. Global Power Through Quantification and Rankings* (OUP 2012) 211 et seq.

13 Siems and Nelken (n 9) 436.

14 David Restrepo Amariles, 'Supping with the Devil? Indicators and the Rise of Managerial Rationality in Law' (2017) 13 Int J L Context 465, 466.

15 William Twining, *General Jurisprudence: Understanding Law from a Global Perspective* (CUP 2009) 254.

steady rise of 'calculative practices' and the massive 'use of quantification' in the form of metrics and indicators.[16] The predicament is also valid for comparative law. Not only are indicators used to measure the fitness of domestic legislation, but they also suggest which legal constant is likely to 'generate public as well as private benefits'.[17] There is, we argue, a *scientific state of mind* upholding quantification in comparative law, which affects the way knowledge is produced through indicators, thus supplying the 'epistemological authority' required to measure the efficiency of legal systems. This quantitative turn in comparative law has become so 'powerful that it can determine even how we allow ourselves to imagine the world'.[18]

2 'Mathematising' the Law

In his handbook *Comparative Law*, Mathias Siems introduces the chapter on 'numerical comparative law' with a lengthy quotation from the renowned British mathematician William Thomson, 1st Baron Kelvin (1824–1907). The quotation reads as follows:

> When you can measure what you are speaking about, and express it in numbers, you know something about it, when you cannot express it in numbers, your knowledge is of a meagre and unsatisfactory kind; it may be the beginning of knowledge, but you have scarcely, in your thoughts advanced to the stage of *science*, whatever the matter may be.[19]

Lord Kelvin's predicament epitomises the spirit that is shared by the transnational epistemic community within the state–investor cooperative intercourse. It is a way of seeing, understanding, and grasping the world intellectually, which we style the *scientific state of mind*. It has been percolating through comparative legal studies in the last few decades.[20] We met an example of such mentality when examining the idea of legal constants which evokes the negative

16 Richard Rottenburg and SE Merry, 'A World of Indicators: The Making of Governmental Knowledge Through Quantification' in Richard Rottenburg et al. (eds), *The World of Indicators. The Making of Governmental Knowledge Through Quantification* (CUP 2015) 3. On the rising interest in the quantification of legal phenomena, see Twining (n 15) 253.

17 Davis (n 8) 309.

18 See BS Hammond, 'Scriblerian Self-Fashioning' (1988) 18 The Yearbook of English Studies 108, 113.

19 Siems (n 1) 207 quoting William Thomson Baron Kelvin, 'Electrical Units of Measurement' in *Popular Lectures and Addresses*, vol 1, *Constitution of Matter* (MacMillan & Co 1889) 73–74. See also RK Merton, DL Sills, and SM Stigler, 'The Kelvin Dictum and Social Science: An Excursion into the History of an Idea' (1984) 20 J Hist Behav Sci 319.

20 This way of seeing a world is also a way of constituting its reality. See Rene Urueña, 'Quantitative Forms of Legal Governance' in Mathias Siems and Po Jen Yap (eds), *The Cambridge Handbook of Comparative Law* (CUP 2024) 598 et seq. See also later in this chapter, Sections 7 and 8. See also Bernhard Grossfeld and EJ Eberle, 'Patterns of Order in Comparative Law:

expression used in mathematics and the very idea of quantitative research and methods, which have become 'increasingly fashionable among academics'.[21] Traditional approaches to comparative law have then started to be challenged: Quantification renders traditional legal comparison 'outdated';[22] qualitative assessment ought to be replaced by several exercises in legal metrics, owing to its being a superior methodology associating 'modernity with a belief in rationality'.[23] Finally, some advocate 'stronger interdisciplinarity between economics and comparative law'.[24] Whatever the case may be, quantification has led to 'a growing field of empirical legal studies, applying statistical methods to legal questions'. A vast array of scientific outputs now employs quantitative approaches: Mathias Siems classifies them under the umbrellas of 'counting facts about law', 'coding law . . . based on mechanisms which translate . . . legal rules into numbers', and 'conducting survey about the law'.[25]

Are we, comparative lawyers, reproducing the spirit of hard sciences? We like to think that we now share a common 'standard scientific model of knowledge and cognition' with, say, mathematicians or physicists.[26] Consequently, we assume that these methods are universally valid across jurisdictions and disciplines, because they are based on the transformative force of numbers; as a matter of common sense, numbers are essentially neutral and objective items that 'mathematise' the law and make the 'relationships . . . between concepts' 'transparent'. At the same time, they possess the ability 'to describe, measure and judge an ever-wider range of social life', which means making them evidence-based and empirically verifiable, turning 'complex and abstract features of legal rules and systems into quantitatively expressed scores'.[27] In

Discovering and Decoding Invisible Power' (2003) 38 Tex Int'l LJ 291, 294, who number numbers among the legal formants.

21 Francesco Parisi and Barbara Luppi, 'Quantitative Methods in Comparative Law' in PG Monateri (ed), *Methods of Comparative Law* (Edward Elgar 2013) 306. See also PG Monateri, *Advanced Introduction to Comparative Legal Methods* (Edward Elgar 2021) 109 et seq. As Monateri puts it, they have 'infiltrated the legal field to the point of becoming boring': PG Monateri and Mauro Balestrieri, *Quantitative Methods in Comparative Law* (Edward Elgar 2023) 101. For an examination of this scientific state of mind through the lenses of law and literature, see Matteo Nicolini, 'Praising the World "by Geometrical Terms": Legal Metrics, Science and Indicators in Swift's *Voyage to Laputa*' (2019) 13 Pólemos 327.

22 See, for example, Mathias Siems, 'The End of Comparative Law' (2007) 2 J Comp Law 133, who lists four challenges to comparative law: 'the disregard', 'the complexity', 'the simplicity', and its 'irrelevance' in a converging/global legal reality.

23 See Markus Müller-Chen et al., *Comparative Private Law* (Dike 2015) 94.

24 Ralf Michaels, 'Comparative Law by Numbers? Legal Origins Thesis, Doing Business Reports, and the Silence of Traditional Comparative Law' (2009) 57 Am J Com L 765, 792.

25 Siems (n 1) 180–81.

26 JB Harley, 'Deconstructing the Map' (1986) 26 Cartographica 1. See also Zachary Elkins, Tom Ginsburg, 'On Disruption and Leximetrics: A Reply to Niels Petersen and Konstantin Chatziathanasiou' (2021) 19 Int J Const L 1835, 1837, according to whom in 'the presumed hierarchy of knowledge generation across academic disciplines . . . physicists are at the top of the heap'.

27 Respectively: Perry-Kessaris (n 11) 401 and 410; Arslan (n 3) 17.

sum, these processes 'produce public, authoritative knowledge that makes them appear legible to outsiders'.[28] Indicators are thus 'quantitative tools that are public and easily available with a regular periodicity', also able to assess legal fitness of states from a comparative perspective.[29] They provide a 'simple quantification and mathematical evaluation methods' to be applied in comparative law studies; they then supply 'legible and user-friendly data to make informed recommendations on the legal risks in different countries', suggesting how the adoption of 'better' legislation from the outside may positively impact on national economic performances.[30] Through indicators, numbers become crucial when assessing domestic policies, which are '*worth measuring in the first place*'.[31]

We are 'measuring the immeasurable', then, through a *quantitative frame* that is able to 'turn law into numbers'.[32] But what made this shift possible? From an epistemological perspective, the *scientific state of mind* embeds a fideistic attitude, according to which (even legal) progress and economic development can be achieved only through quantitative methodologies. We shall consider this in the next section, when tracing the origins of quantification in law. For now, suffice it here to highlight how numbers and indicators help us *de-code* the complexity of the world's legal systems and, at the same time, establish a prospective legal meaning (the constant outside the law) to be subsequently *coded* through the law at the domestic level.[33] They give us the illusion of simplicity; de-coding is made possible through their transparency (they are 'easy to communicate'), their 'objectivity' (they make us feel part of the hard science community), and alleged neutrality.[34] The way indicators code the constant outside the law depends on how they are able to position a given jurisdiction in their proposed ranking. In case of a state's bad performance in terms of legal fitness, they immediately indicate whether states might direct their policies, and which direction they ought to follow to improve, through these powerful devices, the efficiency of legal systems.

28 Wendy Espeland, 'Narrating Numbers' in Richard Rottenburg et al. (eds), *The World of Indicators. The Making of Governmental Knowledge Through Quantification* (CUP 2015) 56.
29 Urueña (n 20) 595.
30 Arslan (n 3) 20.
31 William Davies, 'Spirits of Neoliberalism: "Competitiveness" and "Wellbeing" Indicators as Rival Orders of Worth' in Richard Rottenburg et al. (eds), *The World of Indicators. The Making of Governmental Knowledge Through Quantification* (CUP 2015) 285.
32 Mathias Siems, 'Measuring the Immeasurable: How to Turn Law into Numbers' in Michael Faure and Jan Smits (eds), *Does Law Matter? On Law and Economic Growth* (Intersentia 2011). See also Mathias Siems, 'Numerical Comparative Law: Do We Need Statistical Evidence in Law in Order to Reduce Complexity' (2005) 13 Cardozo J Int'l & Comp L 521, 523–28 for a variety of examples in which the law is turned into numbers.
33 On indicators as tools making comparison 'easy', see Espeland (n 28) 61.
34 KE Davis, Benedict Kingsbury, and SE Merry, 'Introduction: Global Governance by Indicators' in KE Davis et al. (eds), *Governance by Indicators. Global Power Through Quantification and Rankings* (OUP 2012) 18.

3 Enduring Indicators: 'Legal Origins' for 'Doing Business'

When examining quantification in law, we usually refer to two events that demonstrate how pervasive indicators have become in comparative legal studies: the *legal origins thesis* (LLSV, or LLS, as the case may be[35]) and the *Doing Business Reports* (DBRs). According to Ralf Michaels, both are 'the most important development' comparative law has witnessed in the last few decades.[36] We will not indulge in their repetitive accounts. Our scope is more limited; we assume that both developments are a symptom of the *scientific state of mind* shared by the transnational epistemological community populating the Factory of Global Legal Indicators.

LLVS assumes that, in every jurisdiction, there is a natural causal connection between how legal institutions are arranged and how economic development is boosted. Here is the syllogism for this theory: If legal institutions matter to economic growth and 'are a function of the origins of the legal system', then 'legal origin impacts economic growth'.[37] Needless to say, this 'firm relationship' between law and economic performances is probed through 'empirically observable variables, through mathematical regression' and indicators – which is nothing else other than the power of numbers mentioned earlier.[38] The quantitative methods applied in LLSV have allowed scholars to assess the 'quality' of legal systems, ranking them, for example, on how they actually protect foreign financial investors. In their famous essay *Law and Finance*, LLSV measured and ranked 49 national legal systems as regards the quality of shareholder and creditor protection regulation. Depending on whether or not they protected minority shareholder rights and remedial creditor rights, each country was scored '0' or '1'.[39] What is striking is the outcome of the

35 The acronyms reflect the authors' initials of the papers. All of them are economists: Rafael La Porta and others, 'Legal Determinants of External Finance' (1997) 52 J Finance 1131; 'Law and Finance' (1998) 106 J Pol Econ 1113; Rafael La Porta et al., 'The Economic Consequences of Legal Origins' (2008) 46 J Econ Lit 285; Rafael La Porta, Florencio Lopez-de-Silanes, and Andrei Shleifer, 'Law and Finance After a Decade of Research' in GM Constantinides, Milton Harris, and Rene M Stulz (eds), *Handbook of the Economics of Finance* (Elsevier 2013), Volume 2, Part A. See also Michaels (n 24) 768. See Gerhard Schnyder, Mathias Siems, and RV Aguilera, 'Twenty Years of "Law and Finance": Time to Take Law Seriously' (2021) 19 Socio-Economic Review 377 (the authors conducted a literature review of 56 articles between 1997 and 2017, which they consider 'the core' of LLVS). See also Simon Deakin and Katharina Pistor (eds), *Legal Origin Theory* (Edward Elgar 2012); Guangdong Xu, *Does Law Matter for Economic Growth? A Re-examination of the 'Legal Origin' Hypothesis* (Larcier-Intersentia 2014); Nuno Garoupa and Carlos Gómez Ligüerre, *Legal Origins and the Efficiency Dilemma* (Routledge 2016).

36 Michaels (n 24) 765. Michael's predicament is shared by Siems (n 22) 144 and Marta Infantino, 'Quantitative Legal Comparisons: Narratives, Self-Representations and Sunset Boulevards' (2019) 6 J Int'l Comp L 287, 288.

37 Michaels (n 24) 769.

38 Monateri and Balestrieri (n 21) 107.

39 Rafael La Porta et al. 1998 (n 35) 1127–1138. Enforcement was measured differently, considering 'estimates of "law and order" in different countries compiled by private credit risk

comparative survey: Within the common-law family, both shareholder and creditor protections were always 'higher', 'stronger', and 'better' than in the (French and German) civil legal family. Legal origin matters, then; 'countries whose legal rules originate in the common-law tradition tend to protect investors considerably more than the countries whose laws originate in the civil-law, and especially the French-civil-law, tradition'.[40] This difference is then turned into the following causal connection: Common law boosts economic development more than civil law.

Based on figures, numbers, and counting, such types of measurements were widely used by, among others, Katharina Pistor, Simeon Djankov, and Lutgart van den Berge. All of them replicated LLSV's patterns in several fields of research, particularly as regards legal transplants and corporate governance.[41] LLSV has thus changed the (qualitative) approach to the comparative study of legal families. Measuring the law is not functional to establishing genealogies among families which share a common historical ancestor – far from it. Quantitative legal assessments demonstrate that a given legal tradition (i.e. the common law) is better at protecting investors, owing to its intrinsic qualities; in terms of legal origins and performativity, common-law legal solutions are better than those elaborated within the civil law and deserve to be spread across the globe when manufacturing the law from the outside.[42]

LLSV theories are often interwoven with the second major event mentioned earlier, that is, the release of the DBRs in 2004 by the International Finance Corporation (IFC), that is, a part of the World Bank Group.[43] The reports were intended to be issued annually to demonstrate a further causal connection between the law of a given jurisdiction and its foreign investment attractiveness. This was a way of measuring, *inter alia*, 133 state legal systems by quantifying five business activities,[44] as well as 'the "success" of legal reform projects', particularly in countries experiencing transition from authoritarian regimes to democratic economic liberalism.[45] The reports were not confined to

agencies for the use of foreign investors interested in doing business in the respective countries'. Rafael La Porta et al. 1998 (n 35) at 1140. See Siems (n 39) 524.

40 Rafael La Porta et al. 1998 (n 35) 1138.

41 For further details, see Siems (n 32) 525–26.

42 Siems (n 1) 236.

43 For further remarks on the international financial architecture and the World Bank, see Ch 4. According to Schnyder, Siems, and Aguilera (n 35), the DBRs drew on the LLVS 'regarding shareholder and creditor protection, while extending its logic to legal rules related to taxation, electricity, construction permits, cross-border trade and public procurement'.

44 These were: '(1) starting a business; (2) hiring and firing workers; (3) enforcing a contract, (4) getting credit, and (5) closing a business': Davis and Kruse (n 7), 1097. The subsequent instalments increased the number of states, and the activities related to business to be measured and quantified to create the ranking. On DBRs measuring and comparing 'the "ease of doing business" in more than 130 countries worldwide', see Twining (n 15) 253. See also Davis and Kruse (n 7), 1097 et seq.

45 Twining (n 15) 253.

describing the legal fitness of several domestic jurisdictions. Theirs was a true imaginative leap, as they effectively established one of the key mechanisms of the Factory assembly line. As an aggregate of legal metrics – that is, real-world data collected and 'used to measure the performance of legal norms'[46] – they pointed to legal constants outside the law that had been considered suitable to reach the goal of maximising financial returns within the state–investor cooperative intercourse. Like the LLSV, the Factory relied on the correlation between common law and its origins to stimulate economic growth. In so doing, they mimicked the regression we have found in LLSV: '[T]he quality and the performance of law are positively correlated'; to put it more stylistically, 'the quality and the performance go hand in hand'.[47]

This originated a ranking system capable of exerting an incredible soft power, the thorough application of which made the DBRs a true 'constant' outside the legal system. Many countries adopted the law that was wanted from the outside to improve their legal fitness; their soft power was also rooted in social pressure, which was visible in the 'next iteration of the index' with all 'the reputational consequences of their next rating or ranking'.[48] To put it bluntly, 'the recommendations in the DB reports [were] too important to be ignored'.[49] No wonder several countries accepted to have their laws changed from the outside, even though these changes triggered reforms that, at first sight, seemed patchy and erratic. As Siems and Nelken uphold, to quickly climb the ranking, countries complied with the DBR indicators, it being 'irrelevant' that 'the remainder of their legal system' remained 'unchanged'.[50]

This last predicament is illuminating, inasmuch as it replicates the major criticism used to challenge Leibniz's theory of law. Regardless of the fact that his legal theory was considered complete and consistent, the way he applied 'the naturalistic science of his time' to the law 'led him . . . to piecemeal investigation, to the detailed study of the part rather than the whole'.[51] Likewise, the vagaries of the reforms mentioned earlier are a form of piecemeal legislation manufactured from the outside. It is no coincidence, we add, that the same objection can be raised to both Leibniz and indicators, since both were

46 Davis (n 8) 306–7. See also Marta Infantino and Mauro Bussani, 'Rule by Metrics. Performance, Quantification, and the Law' (2023) 11 European Journal of Comparative Law and Governance 187, 192–93.

47 Arslan (n 3) 18 and 24.

48 JG Kelley and BA Simmons, 'Politics by Number: Indicators as Social Pressure in International Relations' (2015) 59 Am J Pol Sc 55, 56. The most important example is Georgia; by complying with the DBR indicators, it rapidly rose in the ranking as one of the better places to do business around the world. See also Krever (n 67) 145 Akonor Di Kwame, 'Africa and IMF Conditionality: The Unevenness of Compliance, 1983–2000' (Routledge 2012) 163; KJ Havnevik (eds), *The IMF and the World Bank in Africa: Conditionality, Impact and Alternatives* (Scandinavian Institute of African Studies 1987).

49 Davis and Krause (n 7) 1114.

50 Siems and Nelken (n 9) 441.

51 Huntington Cairns, 'Leibniz's Theory of Law' (1946) 60 Harvard L Rev 200, 201.

(and are) influenced by the scientific state of mind in their 'algebraic approach' to legal phenomena.[52]

This, however, is just one of the manifold arguments raised against the idea that legal origins (and legal metrics) matter as far as law and economic development are correlated. We all know that both the LLVS and the DBRs were harshly criticised by legal scholars.[53] When the World Bank Independent Evaluation Group (IEG) released its review on the DBRs in 2022, indeed, three major flaws were exposed. Several indicators were 'of little value' inasmuch as (1) they merely focused on the black-letter law, disregarding the operational rules making up the 'business experience'; (2) they were arbitrarily 'construed'; and (3) several real-world data embedded in indicators were not 'particularly relevant to the ultimate intended beneficiaries', namely, 'small and medium-sized firms in developing countries'.[54]

More on such arguments later in this chapter, when we shall assess some critical features displayed by indicators. What we want to highlight here is that their soft power was hard to die. We know that the aforementioned allegations completely discredited the DBRs: Not only were they fiercely attacked by civil law legal scholarship,[55] but several independent reviews also found irregularities in the way they contributed to setting up the Factory, such as states' 'improper influence', ranging from pressure to change scores to consulting arrangements with the experts drafting the indicators.[56] Or which is worse, there had been changes in the methodology to allow some countries (such as India) to raise or several others (e.g. Chile) to fall in the rankings. And changes, it goes without saying, were politically and ideologically motivated.[57] Our point is this: Although the DBRs were discontinued in 2021, the change brought about by them and the LLSV was 'enormous' and 'groundbreaking' even in terms of comparative law.[58] In establishing a causal connection

52 Monateri and Balestreri (n 21) 29.

53 See, among others, Siems (n 32) 528 (according to whom 'the division into common law and civil law is not useful in terms of comparative corporate law'); Schnyder, Siems, and Aguilera (n 35) 378 (LLSV 'does not take law seriously' and 'fails to have a clear theoretical understanding about the impact of law on economic outcomes').

54 World Bank, *The Development Effectiveness of the Use of Doing Business Indicators*, Fiscal Years 2010–20 (Independent Evaluation Group 2022). Quotations are from Davis (n 8) 320.

55 See Fondation Henry Capitant, *Les droits de tradition civiliste en question. À propos des Rapports* Doing Business *de la Banque Mondiale*, Vols 1 and 2 (Société de Législation Comparéé 2006). For further references, see Bénédicte Fauvarque-Cosson, A-J Kerhuel, 'Is Law an Economic Contest? French Reactions to the *Doing Business* World Bank Reports and Economic Analysis of the Law' (2009) 57 Am J Comp L 811, 816 et seq. (French reactions) and 820 et seq. (the critical analysis deployed by the *Association Henri Capitant*).

56 Davis (n 8) 320.

57 SP de Souza, *Designing Indicators for a Plural Legal World* (CUP 2022) 20–21.

58 Respectively: Michaels (n 24) 765; DF Vagts, 'Comparative Company Law – The New Wave' in RJ Schweizer et al. (eds), *Festschrift für Nicolas Druey zum 65. Geburtstag* (Schulthess 2002) 604.

between economic development, investment attractiveness, and the law, their legacy suggests that the 'law still matters'. A predicament like this reconciles (the deliberate use of) comparative law with the purposes of transnational finance actors, through the 'objective' use of its traditional methodologies, such as functionalism and generalisations.[59] Indicators generalise legal constants (or, which is the same thing, investors' privately made law and preferred legal solutions), avoiding the flaws generated by contingent generalisations. They extend in (or point to) the same direction, that is, performative rules maximising profits.

It does not come as a surprise that, after the DBRs were discontinued, the World Bank released new sets of metrics, such as the *Worldwide Governance Indicators* (WGI) in 2022 and the *Business Ready* (B-READY) in 2024. In particular, the B-READY takes the 2021 remarks by IEG into account. As stated in the Concept Note, not only does B-READY seek 'a balanced approach when assessing the business environment', but it also ponders the 'ease of conducting a business and broader private sector benefits', the balance 'between regulatory framework and public services, between de jure laws and regulations and de facto practical implementation', that is to say, how publicly made law may be helpful when manufacturing the law from the outside.[60]

Despite such criticism, indicators are here to stay.

4 The Scientific State of Mind and the Onset of Indicators

Released by the World Bank, the B-READY represents a new set (and a new wave) of social global indicators. The very fact of their being published despite all the criticism towards the DBRs confirms what we have been saying so far, that is, that the use of metrics in law is a practice deeply embedded in our transnational legal environment. This predicament is also complemented by what Schnyder, Siems, and Aguilera note as regards LLSV: LLSV uses the label 'legal origins' because it reflects the notion of 'regulatory style', and therefore, 'legal origins are . . . less malleable and more stable over time'. In sum, they satisfy the 'scientific' test in legal studies: What is stable is indeed the independent variable that gives consistency and stability – and therefore can be measured. Saturated as it is, with the idea of measurement, this predicament peruses indicators to satisfy our unquenchable thirst for quantification.[61] This,

59 See Mathias Siems, 'Legal Origins: Reconciling Law & Finance and Comparative Law' (2007) 52 McGill L J 55. Objectivity as a legacy of functionalism and generalisations define *indicators* as political spaces: see Urueña (n 20) 596. This is patent in how DBRs impacted in the field of comparative law. See Arlsan (n 3) and Davis (n 8).

60 Word Bank, BEE Concept Note (2002) <https://thedocs.worldbank.org/en/doc/2250b12dfe798507f7b42064378cc616-0540012022/original/BEE-Concept-Note-December-2022.pdf> accessed 19 July 2024.

61 Schnyder, Siems, and Aguilera (n 35) 381.

we argue, is nothing else than a further demonstration of how the scientific state of mind pervasively percolates the current state of legal affairs. At the same time, quantification through measurement explains why indicators are here to stay: The act of mathematising the law goes above and beyond all recent and contingent exercises in legal metrics.

If we broaden our perspective and adopt a historical posture towards the scientific state of mind, we realise that indicators have been manufactured and widely perused long before the first LLSV article, which was published in 1998. For example, the use of indicators had already been attested in the 1980s, when the World Bank released its 'Country Policy and Institutional Assessment' (CPIA), which annually measures the quality of borrowing countries' policies and institutions.[62] Likewise, the Organisation for Economic Co-operation and Development (OECD) has been developing indicators since the early 1990s; take for example the OECD Indicators of Employment Protection.[63] Several indexes date back to the 1970s, when private actors produced them to sell 'information about country risk profiles . . . for profit'. The Index of Economic Freedom is even older, as it was released in the 1950s.[64]

The post–Cold War era promoted 'peace and security, freedom and the rule of law', but it did so by fostering legal change to support economic development. Fukuyama's 'end of history' thus started with a new narrative: The global village had to be established 'from the economic ground up'.[65] There was widespread belief in the strong correlation between 'better' legislation

62 The CPIA applies 16 criteria, which are 'grouped in four clusters: (a) economic management; (b) structural policies; (c) policies for social inclusion and equity; and (d) public sector management and institutions'. See Word Bank, 'Country Policy and Institutional Assessment' <https://databank.worldbank.org/source/country-policy-and-institutional-assessment> accessed 17 September 2024. The CPIA is also used by the Word Bank's International Development Association (IDA) to manage development funds among borrowing countries. The IDA Resource Allocation Index (IRAI) is, indeed, based on the CPIA. The IRAI and portfolio performance together constitute the IDA Country Performance Rating (CPR). See also Krever (n 67) 154–47.

63 See Monateri and Balestreri (n 21) 73. On the OECD Indicators of Employment Protection <www.oecd.org/en/data/datasets/oecd-indicators-of-employment-protection.html> last update May 2022, see Siems (n 1) 236 and Mathias Siems, 'Bringing in Foreign Ideas. The Quest for Better Law in Implicit Comparative Law' (2014) 9 J Comp L 119, 126. On how steady use of numeric representation has been developed since the 1980s, see Rottenburg and Merry (n 16) 6.

64 Katharina Pistor, 'Re-Construction of Private Indicators for Public Purposes' in KE Davis et al. (eds), *Governance by Indicators. Global Power Through Quantification and Rankings* (OUP 2012) 167. On how steady use of numeric representation has been developed since the 1980s, see Rottenburg and Merry (n 16) 6. On early human rights assessments in the 1980s, see AnnJanette Rosga, ML Satterthwaite, 'Measuring Human Rights: UN Indicators in Critical Perspective' in Kevin Davis et al. (eds), *Governance by Indicators: Global Power Through Quantification and Rankings* (OUP 2012) 298.

65 SJ Rosow, 'Globalisation as Democratic Theory' (2000) 29 Millennium 27, 29. On the end of history, see Francis Fukuyama, *The End of History and the Last Man* (Free Press 1992).

and economic development,[66] which was decisively patent in the semantic shift undertaken by the concept of rule of law. We shall examine this shift in Chapter 3; suffice it here to remember that the rule of law originally encompassed a set of constraints on political power to protect individuals' rights and freedoms. In the post-communist era, it underwent a huge transformation, as it was turned into a driver promoting good governance and elevated economic performances. The rule of law became measurable and quantifiable because it perfectly matched the 'new world order' announced by US President George Bush in the aftermath of the end of the Cold War. It is an outcome of neoliberalism, the World Bank's and the WTO's policies, as well as an output of the new institutional economics (NIE) movement.[67] Its performative use was facilitated by the *scientific state of mind*:[68] Again, progress and economic development could be achieved through the quantitative measurement of legal fitness.

If we go back in time, we find further expressions of this *scientific state of mind*, which demonstrates how this attitude is rooted in our transnational community. The process whereby the law was mathematised is older than indicators. On the one hand, the advent of computing machines in the 1960s made legal quantification more and more viable: Projects such as Lee Loevinger's jurimetrics and Marvin Frenkel's legal cybernetics became feasible because computing would align legal reasoning 'to the accuracy of numerical science' and its related scientific state of mind.[69] On the other hand, the 1960s and the 1970s witnessed a steady use of inferential statistics and regression analysis combining law and development.[70] This marked a new era which we usually style 'empirical comparative law': The law (or its variants: legal origins, common law, transnational law) was (and still is) 'either the dependent variable ("what explains law?") or one of the independent variables ("does law matter?") of the regression analysis'.[71]

66 The economic school of thought known as NIE established a correlation encompassing also 'institutional quality'. Mariana Mota Prado and MJ Trebilcock, *Advanced Introduction to Law and Development* (2nd edn, Edward Elgar 2021) 34.

67 Tor Krever, 'The Legal Turn in Late Development Theory: The Rule of Law and the World Bank's Development Model' (2011) 52 Harvard Int L J 287. See also Perry-Kessaris (n 11) 401: The WB Group 'has, for at least twenty years, campaigned for foreign direct investment'.

68 Alvaro Santos, 'The World Bank's Uses of the "Rule of Law" Promise in Economic Development' in David Trubek and Alvaro Santos (eds), *The New Law and Economic Development: A Critical Appraisal* (CUP 2006).

69 Monateri e Balestrieri (n 21) 58. See RV De Mulder, Kees van Noortwijk, and Lia Combrink-Kuiters, 'Jurimetrics Please' (2010) 1 Eur Journ L Technology: 'Jurimetrics is the empirical study of the form, the meaning and the pragmatics (and the relationships between those) of demands and authorisations issuing from state organisations with the aid of mathematical models and using methodological individualism as the basic paradigm for the explanation and prediction of human behaviour'. Lee Loevinger, 'Jurimetrics – The Next Step Forward' (1949) 33 Minn L Rev 455; M Frankel, *Criminal Sentences: Law Without Order* (Hill and Wang 1973).

70 On regression analysis in empirical legal research, see Lee Epstein and AD Martin, *An Introduction to Empirical Legal Research* (OUP 2014) 173 et seq.

71 See Siems (n 1) 159.

Bearing in mind the correlation between law and economic development, this form of regression became the reality also for legal scholars. Among several projects carried out in the 1970s,[72] there was the SLADE Project promoted by Stanford Law School.[73] William Twining highlights that, within this project, the aforementioned correlation was probed empirically, as it surveyed the legal institutions of Chile, Costa Rica, Italy, Mexico (subsequently replaced with Colombia), Peru, and Spain to ascertain combinations between the law, legal change, and development.[74] The project was probably the 'tail end' of the broader 'law and development' movement, with its idea that legal solutions and constants could be manufactured from the outside and imported into underdeveloped countries. Such constants would be exported from the West in a sort of post-colonial attempt to control the economic development of Latin America and former European colonies in Africa. We find here the same recursivity which percolates all the successive waves of law and development, such as the 'Washington Consensus' of the 1980s, the 'good governance approach' to the rule of law brought about by the World Bank in the 1990s, the LLSV, and the DBRs. What mattered most was to influence legal change in recipient countries with development aids going hand in hand with the legal constants fabricated from the outside and the soft power of indicators.

5 Inferential Correlations That Mathematise the Law

If we go further back in time, we realise that the scientific state of mind has always been rooted in a mathematical approach to the study of the law, also percolating the history of the Western legal tradition. The correlation between numbers and the law was originally more methodological and less empirical. Take the study of quantitative methods in the seventeenth century. Partly due to the effects of Cartesian philosophy,[75] they originated in France with an immediate resonance in the common-law world. John Locke, among others, made use of mathematical techniques in his *Essay Concerning Human Understanding* (1689): He inferred 'from self-evident propositions, by necessary consequences, as incontestable as those in mathematics', the very 'measures of right and wrong', and the politico-legal foundations of the body politic.

72 Siems (n 1) 159.

73 Twining (n 15) 251. For accurate accounts of the projects, see Pierre Legrand, 'John Henry Merryman and Comparative Legal Studies: A Dialogue' (1999) 47 Am J Com L 3. See also the following articles by John Merryman: 'Law and Development Memoirs I: The Chile Law Program' (2000) 48 Am J Com L 481; 'Law and Development Memoirs II: SLADE' (2000) 48 Am J Com L 713; 'SLADE: A Memoir' in Laurence Friedman and Rogelio Pérez-Perdomo (eds); *Legal Culture in the Age of Globalization* (Stanford UP 2003)

74 According to Twining (n 15) 252, 'the indicators were bunched around four categories – legal institutions, legal actors, legal processes, and resources consumed'.

75 See, for example, Gerd Buchdal, 'The Relevance of Descartes's Philosophy for Modern Philosophy of Science' (1963) 1 The British Journal for the History of Science 227.

Thomas Jefferson did the same when writing the US Declaration of Independence.[76] Theirs was an 'abstract-deductive' approach with long-lasting applications. In the nineteenth century, both John Austin's analytical jurisprudence and Christopher Columbus Langdell's case method were influenced by (and perhaps based upon) the 'idea that law can be reduced to a set of first principles, on the order of mathematical axioms'; likewise, and thanks to 'the use of deductive method, these principles [could] yield all necessary consequences'.[77] Monateri and Balestreri go even further back in time, likening the English Reformation, mathematics, and the common law. Leonard Digges, Francis Bacon, Arthur Hopton, and even William Petty predate Descartes's methodological battle and mathematical approach to the law.[78] On the European continent, mathematising the law also encompassed Leibniz and Wolff – even the Thibaut–Savigny dispute about codification had a geometric flavour.[79]

As is evident, the scientific state of mind revolves around the relationship of law and mathematics. Yet we understand that something more is required to mathematise the law, that is, the presence of an inferential regression. Mathematics is useful because it can deductively demonstrate something or – which is the same thing – predict something. As the economist Deirdre McCloskey puts it, 'odd as it sounds, most of mathematics has nothing to do with actual *numbers*'. Maths has to prove deductively; peppering her argument with irony, McCloskey wittily affirms that numbers (and now computers) are used to probe 'back-of-the-envelope tests of hunches on the way to developing what the mathematicians are pleased to call a real proof of such amazing facts as: $e^{\pi i} + 1 = 0$'. To which she adds: '[A]nd therefore God exists'. With their *inductive* and *empirical* approach, quantification and numbers (McCloskey styles them the 'how much') are functional to demonstrate the *deductive* and *theoretical* 'why': 'Accept the premises and you have accepted the Theorem. *Quod erat demonstrandum*' is demonstrated.[80] Through down-to-earth numbers,

76 John Locke, *An Essay Concerning Human Understanding* (PH Nidditch ed, Clarendon Press 1975) IV. iii. 18. See also SA Kenton, 'Mathematical Foundations of Constitutional Law' (1979) 52 Mathematics Magazine 223, 224. ('The form of the Declaration is Euclidean in nature, starting with a list of axioms and concluding in a proof based on these axioms.')

77 MH Hoeflich, 'Law & Geometry: Legal Science from Leibniz to Langdell' (1986) 30 Am J Legal History 95, 96. Akin impacts characterised the first half of the twentieth century. See Michael Geminani, 'Mathematics as Background for the Study of Law' (1979) 86 American Mathematical Monthly 697. Perry-Kessaris (n 11) 404, reminds us of the studies of Ronald Coase, according to whom, in transaction costs economics, 'businesspeople could reduce their costs by adopting different legal forms. . . . Social interactions could now be regarded as costs, and law as cause or an effect of them'.

78 See BJ Shapiro, *Probability and Certainty in Seventeenth-Century England: A Study of the Relationships Between Natural Science, Religion, History, Law, and Literature* (Princeton UP 1983); BJ Shapiro, 'Law and Science in Seventeenth Century England' (1969) 21 Stan L Rev 727.

79 Monateri and Balestreri (n 21) 40–45.

80 Deirdre McCloskey, *The Secret Sins of Economics* (Prickly Paradigm Press 2022) 9–10.

evidently, not through theological exercises. Mere coincidence or not, this is the same scientific approach (and correlation) we find in seventeenth- and eighteenth-century England, where fervent Anglicans measured the 'incommensurable', trying to reconcile geometry, mechanism, and the Holy Spirit. Descartes had separated the three of them by interrupting the *continuum* between the subject and the object, which had been part of the Aristotelian metaphysics; nonconformists and Baconians added fuel to the fire; Newtonians' anti-Trinitarian beliefs inflamed the debate by attempting to mechanically demonstrate the existence of God.[81]

In our case, the relation between the law and numbers is certainly far more prosaic but nonetheless intriguing. The causal correlation is there: The soft power of indicators favours legal fitness through better legislation. And better legislation means attracting foreign investors, which are the majority shareholders of the Factory of Global Legal Indicators. Theirs is probably a way of theorising and an attempt to validate their hunches, that is, the adoption of a given legal device that will maximise their profits. They do this through the odd combination of 'two activities, qualitative theorems and statistical significance'.[82]

Yet there is a huge difference between statistical regression and its significance in the realm of the law. As Petersen and Chatziathanasiou explain, whereas lawyers 'typically have a deterministic understanding of causality', 'social scientists have a probabilistic understanding' of it, which is expressed in 'general regularities', that is, 'whether the presence of a factor *X* makes the occurrence of a factor *Y more likely*'. The example they supply regards the relationship between democracy and economic performance, which we will revisit in Chapter 3. In our legal (i.e. deterministic) understanding of causality, we assume that democracy 'has a positive effect on economic performance'. Or that, which is the same thing, liberal democracy is the form of government that does boost economic growth and development. But in probabilistic terms, as the factor Y, democracy merely makes 'economic growth more likely', inasmuch as 'some autocracies' might 'have a higher level of economic growth than many democracies'.[83]

Petersen and Chatziathanasiou's predicament resonate with the idea, which is particularly familiar to common lawyers, of 'predictability'. The main assumption is that, if states adopt the legal constants proposed by indicators, economic growth will necessarily follow. It is the predictability – not the probability – triggered by a given legal system which is at the heart of the scientific

81 R Wahl, 'Cartesian Rationalism' (1991) 27 Colby Quarterly 100; Stefano Ercolino, *The Novel-Essay, 1884–1947* (Palgrave Macmillan 2014). On Newtonians' anti-Trinitarism, see Gregory Lynall, *Swift and Science. The Satire, Politics and Theology of Natural Knowledge, 1690–1730* (Palgrave MacMillan 2012) 122–30.

82 McCloskey (n 80) 41.

83 Petersen and Chatziathanasiou (n 11) 1812. On the causal connection between legal institutions, the rule of law, and economic development, see Krever (n 67) 132.

state of mind. Is it possible to forecast its development? Does the law matter? Does it boost financial returns? Are there patterns of development that might be suggested to recipient countries to create the most suitable legal environment for financial investments? To various degrees, the issue is always the same: Is the law 'either the dependent variable ("what explains law?") or one of the independent variables ("does law matter?")'? In measuring our strange kind of artifact, which is the law, we come across geometry, mechanism, and the (not-so) Holy Spirit, that is, the basic features of the scientific state of the legal mind, which are still capable of explaining the soft powers of global social indicators.

6 Framing an 'Audit Culture' for Legal Fitness

In the previous section, we maintained that the scientific state of mind is rooted in two major features. To be more accurate, it combines, as Deirdre McCloskey upholds, 'two activities', namely, 'qualitative theorems and statistical significance'. In 1897, Oliver Wendell Holmes Jr. already grasped the way in which the law is mathematised in economic terms: 'For the rational study of the law the black-letter man may be the man of the present, but the man of the future is the man of statistics and the master of economics'.[84]

As the theorem is a hunch to be demonstrated through measurement and quantification, numbers become pivotal. Particularly in the case in which the assumption coincides with the conclusion. Our hunch ('legal origins and better legislation do bring about legal fitness') indeed equals what has to be inferred from quantitative analysis ('legal origins and better legislation do bring about economic development and financial attractiveness'). In other terms, 'legal fitness' is a state of being that brings 'economic development and financial attractiveness'. This is what global social indicators aim to do by manufacturing the law from the outside.

We need data to demonstrate the theorem. Transnational corporations rely on such a requirement when justifying how and to what degree legal devices manufactured within the global Factory have been able to maximise financial returns. It is a continuous exercise in measurement. Corporations' accounts and performances are periodically scrutinised and inspected both *directly* (through auditors) and *indirectly*, that is, ascertaining whether states have effectively adopted the constant meanings outside the law as embedded in indicators, thus maximising their profits and *accidentally* promoting the well-being of domestic societies.

Being a theorem, legal fitness is a qualitative concept: In a world which is – socially, geopolitically, and economically – in a constant state of flux, its demonstration requires proof. Data (i.e. numbers) must be systematically collected and processed to validate it and avoid the volatility in both qualitative

84 Oliver Wendell Holmes Jr, 'The Path of the Law' (1897) 10 Harvard L Rev 457.

research and statistical inference. In terms of figures, a rise (or, which is worse, a decline) in the dissemination of the constants will not be read statistically (the change in factor *X* makes the occurrence of a factor *Y* ***more likely***) but in a legally deterministic way; hence, the decline in the use of the proposed legal constants (factor *X*) will make the drop in commerce and profits unavoidable (occurrence of factor *Y*).

Indicators reflect this sorrowful state of affairs. Owing to legal determinism, their compilers and users struggle to demonstrate, ***on a periodical basis***, the following correlation: the law (either as an independent or a dependent variable) always causes the economic flourishing of investors – and, incidentally, of state communities. No wonder that William Twining terms this the 'audit culture' with its sets of 'measurable objectives, and targets, standards and indicators expressed in quantitative terms'. 'Auditing is nowadays a lifestyle', Amariles argues[85]; and all the major producers and perusers of indicators (the World Bank, the IMF, and the European Bank for Reconstruction and Development – EBRD, to quote just a few) have therefore 'increasingly placed emphasis on implementation and monitoring of impact' of their indicators.[86]

We are not denying that states are part of the audit culture. Due to the pressure caused by the reputational consequences of iterating indexes, countries are held accountable and must explain why they are dropping or improving in the rankings as a consequence of their having (not) adopted the legal constants suggested by indicators. The audit culture is interested in states' legal fitness, economic performances, and financial attractiveness. An increase in profits certifies that legislation manufactured from the outside is effective, and domestic jurisdictions have dutifully complied with the indicators.

A predicament like this elicits an alternative reasoning. What would happen if states' failure to comply with indicators was due to the underperformance of the proposed legal constant? In this event, underperformance would cause a non-reception of the constant and a flaw in the Fabric. With a legal and deterministic approach, states may object that indicators propose a legal solution that is unable to reach the desired goals (the economic flourishing of investors and, incidentally, of state communities). Consequently, they 'will be less accepting and convinced by . . . forms' of accountability not grounded, say, in 'performance indicators, rankings, benchmarking and/or audits and more deliberative forms of account-giving'.[87] If an indicator witnesses a ***decline*** in the

85 Amariles (n 14) 474.

86 Twining (n 15) 257. See Michael Power, ***The Audit Society: Rituals of Verification*** (OUP 1997); Rottenburg and Merry (n 16) 20. See also Courtenay Parleea and Melanie Wiber, 'Whose Audit Is It? Harnessing the Power of Audit Culture in Conditions of Legal Pluralism' (2015) Journal of Legal Pluralism and Unofficial Law 47, 96; Cris Shore and Susan Wright, 'Governing by Numbers: Audit Culture, Rankings and the New World Order' (2015) 23 Social Anthropology 22.

87 Johanna Mugler, 'By Their Own Account: (Quantitative) Accountability, Numerical Reflexivity and the National Prosecuting Authority in South Africa' in Richard Rottenburg et al. (eds),

ability of a given legal constant (factor *X*) to boost economic growth, then the constant will experience a drop in attractiveness, making profits ***unavoidably fall*** (occurrence of factor *Y*). This might generate a sense of distrust in the soft power of indicators.

This deterministic inference may disrupt the cooperative intercourse fabricating the publicly made law suitable for private investors' economic interests. To a broader extent, this poses a question of the reliability and longevity of indicators. The issue replicates what we examined in Chapter 1 as regard concrete, contingent, and selective generalisations. Like in the case of narrowly tailored legislation, single indicators run the risk of focusing on a specific correlation ('a specific legal device triggers an increase/decrease in attractiveness'), regardless of the interests of investors and states. If we multiply this pattern by all interests that the global holders might want to pursue, contingent-selective indicators can be disproved by negative economic performances. As their soft power depends on *ad hoc* combinations of benchmarks and deterministic correlation, the inability of the proposed legal solution to reach the desired goals deprive indicators of the objective basis they require to implement the panoply of legal constants and derivatives managed from the outside.

The cooperative intercourse adopts a variety of measures to sidestep this problem. The first one tends to reduce the degree of concreteness, contingency, and selectiveness of indicators. This results in the majority of indicators being drafted by international and transnational institutions that surpass investors' and corporations' individual interests. Indicators become part of the broader governance of the Fabric, thus 'ensuring [their] permanence and longevity'. Institutions such as the World Bank, Transparency International, and Freedom House, to name just a few, 'all generate copious amounts of narratives around the data and the indicators that they produce'.[88]

A second measure regards the 'aggregation' of indicators to 'measure the same concept in the same units' as a 'reasonable way of both mitigating and estimating the amount of measurement error associated with an indicator'. As is evident, this measure is important inasmuch as it strengthens the legal-deterministic correlation between constants and economic growth (both generating profits), thus serving 'as a means of both enhancing and checking the reliability' of indicators.[89]

A third measure relates to the 'explosion' of indicators. It is important that the legal-deterministic correlation between constants and economic growth be promoted by more than one indicator. Their multiplication is therefore functional to generalising the correlation and establishing a solid cooperative intercourse between states and transnational economic actors. Like social

---

The World of Indicators: The Making of Governmental Knowledge Through Quantification (CUP 2015) 77.

88 de Souza (n 57) 118.

89 Davis (n 2).

norms, also the 'optimal content and scope' of indicators depend 'on how many people are already following' them, 'and what other competing norms are available'. This is a further declension of the state–investor intercourse; we might say that, as indicators 'entail some amount of coordination, they become more valuable as more people use them'. Each actor of the transnational constellation 'who decides whether to follow a norm . . . imposes a positive externality on all who use it', and therefore accrues indicators' legitimacy.[90] To a broader extent, we might say that this process reflects the production of generalisations: states are more prone to accept indicators that, in a given area of law, operate *in the same direction*, which means promoting a correlation in both transnational and domestic realms. Multiplying indicators related to, say, shareholders' protection or bankruptcy precisely fulfils this function, thus reinforcing the correlation and the idea that the law is an output manageable from the outside. This allows indicators to nest within each other in a common direction; the Factory thus reaches the legal uniformity required by its actors and their constants. This is patent in the case of the rule of law; as Mila Versteeg and Tom Ginsburg demonstrate, four indicators (WB's World Governance Indicators project [WGI], the Heritage Foundation, Freedom House, and the World Justice Project) 'are remarkably similar to each other'. It might be argued, they add, that 'one could draw the inference . . . that the four indices indeed capture the essence of the' rule of law 'and that the observed similarities suggest that they are all valid proxies of the underlying concept'.[91] Nothing could be more misleading; they are similar because, by nesting within each other *in the same direction*, they fit into the 'Factory' and reach its desired ends. Again, sectional interests are turned into the interest of the whole, and privately made law into the type of 'better' legislation that may pursue those interests.[92]

A further measure that complies with the 'audit culture' aims to circumvent the risks inherent to the law economic growth correlation. Indicators endorse the idea of longevity and persistence of their own iterations; 'and so', Andrew Farlow says, 'unmeasurable "uncertainty" [is] made measurable, in the shape of "risk"'.[93] We all know that we can skip risk by changing indicators in their subsequent iterations: This usually takes the form of updating numbers and figures, adding/reducing benchmarks, altering composite indexes,

90 Avery Katz, 'Taking Private Ordering Seriously' (1996) 144 U Pa L Rev 1745, 1750 quoting RD Cooter, 'Decentralized Law for a Complex Economy: The Structural Approach to Adjudicating the New Law Merchant' (1996) 144 U Pa L Rev 1643.

91 Mila Versteeg and Tom Ginsburg, 'Measuring the Rule of Law: A Comparison of Indicators' (2017) 42 Law Soc Inquiry 100.

92 Indeed, the use of indicators 'implies acceptance of certain goals by the policy maker': Jack Brand, 'The Politics of Social Indicators' (1975) 26 The British Journal of Sociology 78, 79.

93 Andrew Farlow, 'Financial Indicators and the Global Financial Crash' in Richard Rottenburg et al. (eds), *The World of Indicators. The Making of Governmental Knowledge Through Quantification* (CUP 2015) 223.

and changing methodologies.[94] In all these cases, we circumvent risk because, in changing the assumptions of indicators, we do not change the correlation but reinforce it through a kind of 'political activism through numbers'.[95]

It is indeed ingenious to think that indicators are 'transparently calculative reasoning based on seemingly impersonal and unambiguous data-objects'. This assumption is favoured by the fact that, like in the case of the DBRs, these 'can be reviewed and argued about openly'. Together with its being 'regularly counted and measured' – and, we add, accounted – its 'objective thing-ness seems more plausible, and its integration in decision-making and policy all the more credible'.[96] The soft power of indicators also lies in this credibility, which makes them applicable with regularity at every stage of the complex process which is the Fabric of the law from the outside. Yet regularity cannot be only thought out but must also be 'lived' and applied by those who populate the state–investor intercourse. However expressive of contingent and sectional interests, their regularity generates the validity and effectiveness of the constant lying behind privately made law, because it responds to the need to reiterate solutions and legal rules where the promotion of the interests at stake requires it. Take for example the Index of Economic Freedom, which has been upholding 'the formidable positive relationship between economic freedom and progress' for the last 30 years, with the aim of demonstrating 'the extent of an economy's openness to global investment or trade'.[97]

Hence, transnational law is a laboratory where a variety of negotiating tools are created to satisfy the wide range of interests of the relevant legal community. If the rule of recognition is linked to the nature of the interests, their effectiveness regularity will depend on their ability to satisfy them, because of the changing market trends and the production and retail policies of economic actors. Unsurprisingly, indicators 'can be – and are – made for particular but wide-ranging contexts'.[98]

94 For example, the EBRD Legal Indicator Survey used socio-legal surveys (1997–2002) to evaluate domestic corporate insolvency laws and rank them on an ordinal scale. In 2002, it undertook 'a country-by-country analysis of law-on-the-books in 27 states' where it operated', using a five-point scale of compliance with EBRD norms. In 2004, it changed its methods again, asking lawyer to 'report on how well they actually worked in practice'. In any case, 'criteria were quantified and represented in the graphs, which combined comparisons across major issues within an area of substantive law and cross-country comparisons'. Halliday (n 12) 184 et seq.

95 Rene Urueña, 'Indicators as Political Spaces: Law, International Organizations, and the Quantitative Challenge in Global Governance' (2015) 1 Intn'l Organizations LR 1, 11.

96 Nehal Bhuta, 'Governmentalizing Sovereignty: Indexes of State Fragility and the Calculability of Political Order' in KE Davis et al. (eds), *Governance by Indicators: Global Power Through Quantification and Rankings* (OUP 2012) 144.

97 The quotations are from the Heritage Foundation, 'Index of Economic Freedom – 30th Edition' <www.heritage.org/index/> accessed 24 September 2024.

98 DV Snyder, 'Molecular Federalism and the Structures of Private Lawmaking' (2007) 14 Indiana J Global Legal Studies 418, 435.

7 'Making Lists for Years': Drafters and Aims of Global Legal Indicators

The quotation used for this section heading is particularly fitting. Readers can find it in the first lines of Nehal Bhuta's *Governmentalizing Sovereignty: Indexes of State Fragility and the Calculability of Political Order* (2012). There, Bhuta reports a conversation with a USAID official taking place in a food court in Washington. The topic was state fragility/instability rankings,[99] which reflects the anxiety caused by subsequent iterations of the same index – or the creation of new indicators and indexes – within the contemporary 'audit culture'. A true cause for concern, we add. Longevity, persistence, and iterations depend upon indicators, whose basic assumption ('a given legal constant *does* trigger economic growth') is deterministically confirmed. Making lists, rankings, adding (and revising) benchmarks, and making indicators nest into each other in a common direction increase the sense of anxiety that percolates the Fabric of global legal indicators. It is important neither to lose face nor to weaken their soft power.

With its vivid image of actors anxiously compiling rankings, the quotation leads us to consider two further features of the Fabric of global legal indicators, namely, their drafters/users and the process for their production. It is not our intention to supply our readers with a comprehensive list (and its related taxonomy) of all the actors involved. Our scope is limited: As indicators cannot fail when pointing to the 'correct' (i.e. performative) legal constant from the outside, it is apparent that what really matters is how all actors act and react. As Johanna Mugler puts it, indicators have become 'so pervasive and influential that they become synonymous with the measured phenomenon itself', or – which is probably worse – 'they indicate . . . some aspect of reality' and 'are constitutive of this reality [and] influence what people take to be real'.[100]

As for their drafting, de Souza provides us with a three-state process of creation. The first one is *conceptualization*: The indicator is given a name and an identity, and the 'categories of measurement and tools for analysing data' are developed. What de Souza clarifies is that this stage requires a clear understanding of both the world and how it ought to be changed: '[I]n this step, there is a theory of social change backing it'. The second step is labelled *production*: Concepts and data are correlated and 'thereafter presented and packaged in an accessible manner'.[101] Drafters are involved in their production, so to speak, also because, within the Fabric, its actors have become 'all postmodernists now'.[102] Let us clarify what we mean by this. Being postmodernist means that they 'are quite aware . . . that all reality is "constructed" and that there is

99 Bhuta (n 96) 132.

100 Mugler (n 87) 77.

101 de Souza (n 57) 29.

102 RF Blomquist, '"A Fascination without Scruples": American Popular Culture and Its Corrosive Impact on the Law' (2001) 32 Cumberland L R 165, 174.

no such thing as "ideal truth" or no such thing as "objectivist rationality"'.[103] In sum, we all know that the soft power of indicators causes all reality to be *constructed*; at the same time, we are unconsciously persuaded that the whole of our life must adapt to this constructed reality. In a postmodern society, the problem of persuasion is a 'burden we all bear'.[104]

This is particularly apparent as far as the *use* of indicators (i.e. de Souza's third step) is concerned. A further point ought to be clarified here. Although it is widespread, the distinction between *drafters* and *users* of indicators is not as clear-cut as one might expect.[105] Indicators are often drafted also by private entities (which we might want to consider as consumers).[106] In addition, we might think that users are mainly investors, multinational corporations, or even NGOs – the last ones are interested, as usual, in criticising economic imbalances and huge inequalities emerging from rankings.[107] International financial institutions (IFIs), by contrast, count as their drafters. To tell the whole truth, IFIs are as concerned as all the other actors with preserving the soft power of indicators. They safeguard the correlation between legal change and economic power for the sake of prestige. At the same time, their economic interests must nest into those of all other actors and in the same direction. Maximising their profit is, for example, part of the IMF, WB, EBRD, Asian Development Bank (ADB), and African Bank Development Group (AfDG) mission, which indeed aims to achieve sustainable growth and prosperity – primarily those of their contributors, whose member quotas are the primary source of their funding.

The circle is virtuous or vicious according to how member countries perform economically. Several conditionalities are usually appended to loans – and state-funded development agencies do the same (the UK's Department for International Development, Germany's Deutsche Gesellschaft für Technische Zusammenarbeit (GTZ), UNDP, Canada's International Development Agency (CIDA), USAID, and EuropeAid). Conditionalities usually require the adoption of legal constants manufactured from the outside and endorsed by their indicators as driver for economic boost.[108] The desired goal, as seen, is the economic flourishing of investors – but to a higher degree, also of state communities. If the correlation witnesses a *decline* in the ability of a given legal constant (factor *X*) to boost economic growth, not only will IFIs experience

103 RK Sherwin, *When Law Goes Pop: The Vanishing Line Between Law and Popular Culture* (The University of Chicago Press 2000) 220–21.

104 Blomquist (n 102) 176.

105 For a comprehensive list of indicators arranged after the drafters/users divide, see Siems and Nelken (n 9), 439.

106 See, indeed, Pistor (n 64), 167: the first generation of indicators was indeed compiled by 'private producers' for private consumers.

107 See Tatu Vanhanen, 'A New Data Set for Measuring Democracy, 1810–1898' (2000) 37 J Peace Research 251. Usually, NGOs use criticise indicators by using . . . indicators, such as the World Press Index <https://rsf.org/en/index> and the Global Slavery Index <www.walkfree.org/global-slavery-index/>.

108 Bhuta (n 96) 133.

some difficulties in having the debt repaid, but the same constant will also experience a drop in attractiveness, making profits ***unavoidably fall*** (occurrence of factor ϒ). Take for example the WB and AfDG Country Policy Institutional Assessment (CPIA): They assess (every year, the WB; every two years, the AfDG) the quality of policies and the performance of institutional frameworks in several countries (the AfDG, in the 54 African countries). They monitor those states that often receive conditional concessional loans through several macroeconomic management criteria.[109] These countries are 'assigned a rating from 1–6 for each of these elements, and this is aggregated into an overall score'. Thus ranked, countries 'falling below a certain score may become ineligible for further concessional loans due to a failure to improve their policy and institutional scores under the rating'.[110] This is consonant with what Andrew Farlow states as regards credit ratings: To avoid the failure of the Fabric, 'ratings also discipline' private actors and states:

> The lower a country's credit rating, the harder for that country to access financial markets to roll-over its debt, and the higher its costs of borrowing, and the more likely it will try to avoid being in such a situation in the first place.[111]

Furthermore, if indicators drop and the failure is caused by the adoption of the law manufactured from the outside and endorsed by indicators, then impoverished communities might generate a sense of distrust in their soft power. Impoverishment will also affect institutions, inasmuch as the maximum amount of loans members can obtain, their voting rights, and their share in the general allocation of special drawing rights all depend on state economic growth.

Hence, it is difficult to draw a line between drafters and users of indicators. All of them are so deeply implicated in the co-production of the Fabric that they have become postmodernists by necessity. In a kind of circular

109 The WB CPIA comprises the following areas: (1) economic management, (2) structural policies, (3) policies for social inclusion and equity, and (4) public sector management and institutions. See <https://datacatalog.worldbank.org/search/dataset/0038988> accessed 21 September 2024. As for the AfDB CPIA, the scoring is assigned using the results of a questionnaire with 18 criteria, grouped into five clusters (coherence of economic management, coherence of structural policies, degree to which policies and institutions promote equity and social inclusion, quality of governance and public sector management, and degree to which the regulatory framework is enabling infrastructure, development, and regional integration). See <https://cpia.afdb.org/> accessed 21 September 2024. It is worth noting that the WB and the AfDB release the Annual Harmonized List of Fragile Situations: see <www.worldbank.org/en/topic/fragilityconflictviolence/overview> accessed 21 September 2021.

110 Bhuta (n 96) 146. On the CPIA as an exercise in assessing 'the governance performance of its borrowers . . . to allocate aid to its poorest members', see Michael Riegner, 'Governance Indicators in the Law of Development Finance: A Legal Analysis of the World Bank's "Country Policy and Institutional Assessment"' (2016) 19 J Int Ec L 1.

111 Farlow (n 93) 229.

justification, they promote a reality to be constructed, in which they are eventually caught up. At the same time, they are therefore *aware* that the reality they co-construct is nothing else than their core mission, not an 'ideal truth' or a sort of 'objectivist rationality'.

If there is neither 'ideal truth' nor 'objectivist rationality', their being caught up by the soft power of indicators conveys 'how actors make sense of this world'. It is as if they were asking themselves, 'Is our intervention making an impact? Is this the impact we want?'[112] The impact they tend to attain, it goes without saying, is the maximisation of profits.

Drafters and users alike make a political use of comparative law when promoting the 'better' legislation manufactured from the outside. This political use reinforces the assumption that, as an artifact, the law cannot be reduced to a neutral set of rules to be 'understood and applied without reference to immediate economic, social, or political needs'.[113] Legal devices should be assessed, taking into consideration that their full understanding entails a full understanding of all the variables – and contexts – that affect them. The law is not an empty box – quite the opposite. The way it is manufactured and produced within the Fabric pragmatically enriches and influences it.

Per se, they appear as value-neutral, but when it comes to their application, 'quantitative measurement [is] an alternative source of legitimisation' which delivers a deliberate 'plan of . . . change based upon an imitation of laws' and legal constants imported from the outside.[114] Indeed, quantitative methods allow scholars to assess the legal systems *qualitatively* and rank them, say, on how they actually implement the rule of law or protect foreign financial investors.

8 Creating a New Reality by Producing Indicators

In an output-oriented approach, indicators turn out to be drivers for legal change, whose transformative potential activates huge transformations within domestic jurisdictions. The process is more complex and nuanced than that taking the form of transplants, borrowings, and convergence. By mathematising the law, the scientific state of mind helps transnational actors code their preferred constants through state law, allowing them to seek a connection with the public sphere. What is at stake is certainly the vanishing line between privately and publicly made law; at the same time, the whole process poses substantive questions. In upholding the correlation between better legislation, legal fitness, and economic growth, we accept that states are neither the sole legitimate law-making authorities nor the true repositories of well-being

112 Respectively: Espeland (n 28) 57; Rottenburg and Merry (n 16) 2.

113 See BW Frier, 'Autonomy of Law and the Origins of the Legal Profession' (1989) 11 Cardozo L R 259.

114 Gianmaria Ajani, 'Ruling by Indicators: How the Use of Vague Notions and Quantitative Indicators Facilitates Legal Change' (2017) Cardozo Electronic Bull 1, 17 and 1.

and economic progress; this now lies in cooperative intercourse, where private orderings act as the new providers of 'public goods in the market for law'.[115]

Through their soft power, indicators are therefore able to outline a new reality which is managed through rankings, that is, a new form of law-mapping process that assesses the 'quality' of legal systems according to the standards and benchmarks set by the same indicators. More on this in due course. Let us focus on the regulatory character of indicators here, which is servient to the interests of the actors of the Fabric, whether they are drafters, users, or both.

Owing to their law-like allure, they indeed seem to be 'value-neutral'.[116] If the neutrality of the law is enshrined in legal texts, documents, and statutes, indicators' neutrality lies in numbers and in the 'mathematical turn in law'.[117] Whatever form they take, indicators convey 'invisible powers',[118] impose a new sense on the world, and ultimately co-produce reality. We may term this power 'ideology' or the pursuit of 'interests'. Honestly, there is nothing ideological in these processes; there is only the need to make the constructed reality which transnational actors promote – and in which they are eventually caught up – meaningful and useful to them. If indicators convey an ideology, this is an admixture of 'political and normative choices' related to the concrete goals of the actors of the Fabric.[119]

We might still want to use the term *ideology* to define the purposes of the Fabric, provided that this term encompasses all agencies which try to influence the content of domestic legislation from the outside. What indexes do is probably closer to *implicatures*, that is, the interpretation of meaning that linguists work out in pragmatics, when they 'ask what is hinted at by an utterance in its particular context, what the sender's "agenda" is'.[120]

In identifying and understanding how indicators are drafted and used, the first thing we can do is to focus on the purposes they aim to attain. This purposive approach is apparent in Monateri and Balestrieri, who grasp the point when substantiating the following taxonomy of indicators for – we add – our 'audit culture'. In the *Quantitative Methods in Comparative Law*, they differentiate indicators according to their function. Thus, we have (1) *explanatory*

115 Talia Fisher, 'Privatization of Legal Institutions' in Avihay Dorfman and Alon Harel (eds), *The Cambridge Handbook of Privatization* (CUP 2021) 188.

116 Tara Smith, 'Neutrality Isn't Neutral: On the Value-Neutrality of the Rule of Law' (2011) 4 Washington U Jurisprudence Rev 49, 51. See also MH Kramer, *Objectivity and the Rule of Law* (CUP 2009) 101–86. On indicators' neutrality, see Pistor (n 64) 166.

117 David Restrepo Amariles, 'Legal Indicators, Global Law and Legal Pluralism: An Introduction' (2015) 47 J Legal Pluralism and Unofficial L 9, 14.

118 Grossfeld and Eberle (n 20) 291

119 Urueña (n 95) 3. See also Pistor (n 64) 179 and Diego Giannone, 'Political and Ideological Aspects in the Measurement of Democracy. The Freedom House Case' (2010) 17 Democratization 68.

120 Patrick Griffiths, *An Introduction to English Semantics and Pragmatics* (Edinburgh UP 2006) 7. See also Andrei Marmor, 'The Pragmatics of Legal Language' (2008) 21 Ratio Juris 423.

indicators, which 'prove a theory through the correlation of two or more variables'; (2) *policy indicators*, whose aim is to 'measure the impact of social and public intervention measures'; and (3) *ranking indicators*, whose soft power orders 'the efficiency of political or legal institutions according to business opportunities'.[121] As we have been maintaining throughout this book, every indicator is, to various degrees, explanatory, because in the correlation lies the scientific state of mind; indicators are, indeed, a mix of qualitative theorems and statistical significance.

If all indicators are explanatory, we can focus on the other two categories (policy indicators and ranking indicators). Monateri and Balestrieri's taxonomy overlaps with Halliday's distinction between 'dicators' and 'indicators'.[122] If we understand Halliday correctly, whereas *indicators* point to the 'calibration of legal systems' – that is, 'the development and application of legal yardsticks across the nations of the world' to demonstrate the performativity of legal change promoted from the outside[123] – pre-indicators mathematise the 'state of the art' across jurisdictions in terms of policy design and action in the areas, say, of water sanitation, poverty, education, and so on. They *directly* assess the presence/lack of a policy (and its performativity), thus *indirectly* pointing to a process of legal change to be undertaken to improve the system: It is the 'theory of social change backing' indicators to which we made reference when discussing de Souza's three stages in developing indicators. In ranking countries in a given policy field, these indicators are probably a good example of implicatures. UN indexes are pre-indicators. Take the Human Development Index (HDI) or the Global Multidimensional Poverty Index (MPI). The latter gathers data from 110 developing countries (which means 6.1 billion people), with the aim of providing 'insights into the lives of poor people, their deprivations and how intense their poverty is', as well as 'to inform and accelerate efforts to end poverty in all its forms'.[124] What we infer from pre-indicators is that eradicating poverty and boosting individual freedom are drivers for well-being and, indirectly, for economic growth. They point to the environments within which investors operate. That is why these indicators are often complemented by surveys, such as the World Bank Enterprise Survey (WBES), where business owners, managers, accountants, and human resource managers are asked to answer questions related to countries' business environments (e.g. access to finance, corruption, infrastructure, competition, and performance). Evidently, pre-indicators point to policy and legal reforms functional to setting up favourable contexts for the Fabric of the Law.

121 Monateri and Balestrieri (n 21) 71.
122 Halliday (n 12) 202.
123 Halliday (n 12), 180 and 202.
124 UN Development Programme, '2023 Global Multidimensional Poverty Index (MPI)' at 1 <https://hdr.undp.org/system/files/documents/hdp-document/2023mpireporten.pdf> accessed 27 September 2024.

The attempts to contain the pandemic has triggered, *inter alia*, a new type of pre-indicators, that is, the so-called computational indicators, to which we add the Global Health Security Index (GHSI) prepared by the Johns Hopkins Center for Health Security, the Nuclear Threat Initiative, and the Economist Intelligence Unit.[125] These were created by using the data harvested through contact-tracing apps (CTAs) and usually complemented with data collected from the Internet of things, or other 'traditional sources of epidemiological surveillance, such as call centres, hospital records, emergency-call registries, passenger information' and several other 'national health indexes'.[126] These data were 'shared with government actors and other third parties, solely for purposes relating to efforts to understand or combat COVID-19'. These are indeed policy indicators inasmuch as they were (and still are) used for policy purposes, such as epidemiological surveillance (the well-known 'test–trace–isolate (TTI) tryptic', for example), 'risk prediction and epidemiological models'.[127]

Both pre-indicators and indicators leave a profound mark on the law and the way we conceive it. Not only do we accept that privately made law counts as publicly made law, but we also see the world through the lenses of indicators and metrics – or, as said, 'leximetrics'. It is, we might say, an alternative way of re-narrating the role of the law.[128] This is even more problematic as regards epidemiological apps and pre-indicators, in terms of both our right to privacy and data protection[129] and freedom of movement. Not only were they used to implement pandemic-mitigation restrictions (PMRs), but they also seem to accelerate the mathematising process in law through a form of '*law* into technologies'. Restrepo Amariles uses this expression to point to the process 'where legal prescriptions are collapsed into mathematical models',

125 See <https://ghsindex.org/> accessed 20 December 2024. See John Harrington, 'Indicators, Security and Sovereignty During COVID-19 in the Global South' (2021) 17 Int J L Context 249, 251, who also reminds us that some indicators were already set up in the 1990s. See the Global Public Health Intelligence Network (GPHIN) and the Global Outbreak Alert Response Network (GOARN) accessed 20 December 2024. A comprehensive list of indicators can be found in Marta Infantino, 'Hazards and Fallacies of Social Measurements: Global Indicators in the Pandemic' (2021) 17 Int J L in Context 168, 169–74.

126 David Restrepo Amariles, 'From Computational Indicators to Law into Technologies. The Internet of Things, Data Analytics and Encoding in COVID-19 Contact-Tracing Apps' (2021) 17 Int J L Context 261, 265.

127 Hannah Alsdurf et al., 'COVID White Paper. arXiv', Cornell University (2020), at 15 <https://arxiv.org/abs/2005.08502> accessed 19 December 2024

128 See Espeland (n 28) 60. See also Mathias Siems, 'Taxonomies and Leximetrics' in JN Gordon and W-G Ringe (eds), *The Oxford Handbook of Corporate Law and Governance* (OUP 2018). On indicators as a form of leaving marks on how we conceived of the law, see Perry-Kessaris (n 11), 409, 411, and 408 for leximetrics turning legal systems in a 'as if' market game. See also Urueña (n 95) 605; Davis (n 8) 306.

129 Amariles (n 126) 263–64 highlights that, by installing the app, each phone is assigned a unique ID, and data are transmitted to public authorities, often making use of Bluetooth handshake, GPS, Google, and Apple's Exposure Notification (GAEN), or MIT SafePaths.

which means that the law is no longer 'defined by statutes and other formal legal sources'. Far from being 'soft mechanism of surveillant control',[130] the apps and the indicators they generate become 'a hard form of social control whereby rules intended to guide behaviour are explicitly embedded in the [algorithmic decision system] and enforced through the app'.[131] Restrepo Amariles is quite right when stating that this intermingling of privately made digital devices and publicly related security/surveillance/epidemiological concerns and policies is undermining the rule of law as a mechanism putting bridles on politico-economic power. It is a way of blurring the divide that responds to the need to reiterate solutions and legal rules manufactured from the outside. It is, again, a question of how constants become part of publicly made legislation, thus infiltrating the public sphere.

No wonder, therefore, that this alternative way of narrating and understanding the law perfectly matches comparative law. Like in comparative law, indeed, 'the essence of quantification systems is commensuration and comparison' according to a 'principle of similarity so that things can be grouped together, counted and calculated', to create taxonomies and benchmarks.[132] Indicators such as B-READY and WBES (or the discontinued DBRs) compare issues arising in business contexts across jurisdictions. In addition, indicators collect real-world data, which is consonant with comparative law as an empirical discipline, whose 'problem-based approach' is 'the starting point of a comparative analysis'.[133] Indicators then go hand in hand with the scientific state of mind, inasmuch as leximetrics allows the scientific state of mind to percolate through comparative legal studies. Consequently, facts and spirit (i.e. moral-social values and political choices) are incorporated into quantitative approaches. Indicators make moral and ethical modes of evaluation compatible with technical-utilitarian rationalism; furthermore, they have an intrinsic value: As they measure the reality, they are subject to real-world tests. The same holds true in the realm of law: Indicators are powerful devices when it comes to measuring the efficiency of legal systems.

9 Reconstructing Reality in Comparative Law

In identifying and understanding how indicators are used, a further feature deserves to be assessed, that is, how indicators construct – or reconstruct – legal reality. As Malike Arslan reminds us, they reappraise an old idea: It is possible 'to evaluate legal rules based on the extent to which their outcomes achieve societally valuable' ends. She specifically mentions Jeremy Bentham, who claimed that the 'quality of laws should be measured according to the

130 Karen Yeung, '"Hypernudge": Big Data as a Mode of Regulation by Design' (2017) 20 Information, Communication & Society 118, 129.
131 Yeung (n 130) 129.
132 Rottenburg and Merry (n 16) 12.
133 Siems (n 1) 32.

"principle of the greatest happiness of the greatest number"'.[134] Perhaps the biggest difference is that indicators assess the quality of legal systems ***quantitatively***, whereas the Benthamites peruse a qualitative benchmark ('the greatest happiness of the greatest number'). But the Factory also narrows the scope of utilitarianism, inasmuch as the law, as an output managed from the outside, promotes the adoption of a legal constant, which always causes the economic flourishing of investors – and, only incidentally, of state communities. Whas is societally valuable here is the maximisation of profits through managerial tools, reflecting both a 'managerial rationality in law' and 'power and authority' shifting from countries to non-democratically accountable global actors.[135]

In so doing, the transformative potential of indicators assigns real-world assessment a further function. In the Introduction, for example, we made reference to legal mapping as a traditional transformative device in comparative law, a cultural-cum-political competence encouraging legal change. We also saw that probing benchmarks for legal development is still part of the Fabric. In our globalised world, we still map legal systems or – which is the same thing – we use cartography to arrange indicators, display data, benchmarks, and optimal constants. As is evident, this reinforces the correlation and the social pressure to conform with the law manufactured from the outside.

There is nothing decorative in this mapping. Indexes, such as the Corruption Perception Index (CPI), the Rule of Law Index, the Press Freedom Index, or the Global Democracy Index, 'illustrate the point that an instrumental part of cartography (and more broadly of scientific practice) is ideology'; and the joint application of thematic mapping and GIS creates a hierarchy of colours and jurisdictions within maps.[136]

In all these Indexes, countries are coloured to reflect their rank and democratic outlook in terms of shades of yellow and red (CPI), green and red (RLI and PFI), blue and red (GDI). The redder the country, the less democratic it is; the darker yellow, green, and blue the recipient, the more democratic it is. The possibility of clicking on this map allows us to ascertain whether a country comports with the indicators making up the index, which also reflects an additional pattern of normalisation within the Global Democracy Index. The map is objectivised both in geographical and comparative law terms: We compare and contrast countries according to the assigned scores. The Fabric uses it in order to frame a legal cartographic discourse: the soft power of these indicators embeds the 'various "interests" of those who make and use them, rather

134 Arlsan (n 3) 22, quoting Jeremy Bentham, *An Introduction to the Principles of Morals and Legislation* [1879] (Clarendon 1996) 5

135 Respectively: T-H Cheng, 'Power, Authority and International Investment Law' (2005) 20 Am Univ Int L Rev 465, 469; Restrepo Amariles (n 14) 465.

136 JW Crampton, *Mapping: A Critical Introduction to Cartography and GIS* (Wiley Blackwell 2010) 70. See <www.transparency.org/en/cpi/2023> (CPI); <https://worldjusticeproject.org/rule-of-law-index/> (Rule of Law Index); <https://rsf.org/en/index> (PFI) accessed 27 September 2024.

than reflections of the environment'.[137] Or to be more precise, like explanatory indicators, these assess policies by creating their own environment, even in relation to climate change policies.[138]

Whatever projection is chosen for representing the world, the cartographical representation is no longer limited to technicalities for recording and storing information. It is intuitive that, through these indexes, legal imaginative geographies of transnational actors promote the change in national logical spaces, whose decision-making processes must adapt to the interests of transnational actors to code their own interests through the law. The relationship between spatial technologies (cartography, remote sensing, and GIS, just to quote a few) and globalisation leaves a further mark in the remarkable story of indicators – that is, the propaganda of global interests relegating the representation of the earth to a purely decorative role.[139] The GIS represents indexes whereby countries are said to be more or less democratic than others; it also outlines systems according to their economic performances. And probably, economic and financial actors now advocate for new representational tools.

It does not come as a surprise that the ranking of legal systems depends now on their performativity, which is rooted, according to La Porta et al., in their legal origins.[140] With its four 'legal origins' (i.e. English common law, French law, German law, and Scandinavian civil law), the *Western legal tradition* is therefore dominant; within it, *common law* prevails over *civil law* because the former is decisively 'more protective of outside investors than the laws of civil law'.[141] Although civil law systems have demonstrated their ability to secure a shareholder and creditor protection regulation higher than common law jurisdictions, the latter are said to ensure more elevated economic performances. Measured, as they are, through numerical indicators, legal systems now fall under 'numerical comparative law'. As legal systems can be measured through numeric indicators, it is then possible to do 'comparative law by numbers'.[142] The holders of capital have created spatial hierarchies through 'cross-country comparisons including rankings of the attractiveness of different legal systems for doing business'.[143]

137 Crampton (n 136) 17, quoting Daniel Wood, *The Power of Maps* (The Guildford Press 1992).
138 See the 'Climate Change Performance Index' (CCPI) <www.climate-change-performance-index.org>. MSCI Climate Change Index <;www.msci.com/climate-change-indexes>; the Common Sense Climate Index <https://data.giss.nasa.gov/csci/> accessed 27 September 2024.
139 See Matteo Nicolini, *Legal Geography. Comparative Law and the Production of Space* (Springer 2022) Ch 4.
140 See, for example, MM Siems, 'Varieties of Legal Systems: Towards a New Global Taxonomy' (2016) 12 Journal of Institutional Economics 579, who divides 156 countries into four clusters (European legal culture, mixed legal systems, rule by law, weak law in transition) based on density and by applying 15 socio-legal variables.
141 La Porta et al. 2008 (n 35) 286.
142 Michaels (n 24) 768. Vivian Grosswald Curran, 'Comparative Law and the Legal Origins Thesis: "[N]on scholae sed vitae discimus"' (2009) 57 Am J Comp L 863.
143 Michaels (n 24) 766.

10 Societal Contexts in a World of Indicators

'Comparative law cannot remain purely descriptive. Comparative lawyers must criticise'.[144] This poignant predicament by Frederick Henry Lawson grasps the point of our study on the Fabric of the Law. Immersed, as we are, in a 'World of Indicators', we comparative lawyers are compelled to engage in a conversation with the state-investors intercourse. The law manufactured from the outside is not merely a question of how constants become part of publicly made legislation; nor is this question confined to how private orderings (and privately made law) are able to infiltrate the public sphere. It is also a matter of grasping the world in general and the World of Indicators, in particular. And our methodology fulfils this function. We, comparative lawyers, are called to de-construct the presuppositions and explain the politico-normative agendas lying beneath the numerical surface of global legal indicators. In the realm of the law, our critical approach unveils long-term trends that go beyond the social environment in which they originated.

There is one more thing that deserves to be considered, namely, the absolute reliance on quantitative methods. It is not our intention to deny its relevance in triggering the correlation that indicators attempt to demonstrate; our purpose is limited and complements the study of the Fabric with a more contextual approach to the manufacturing of the law from the outside. Our point is this: If comparative law endorses a critical approach to legal studies, quantification in law also deserves to be assessed. Particularly when the *inductive* and *empirical* approach of quantification by numbers – as McCloskey puts it – becomes functional to demonstrating the *deductive* and *theoretical* 'why'. It is what, with Petersen and Chatziathanasiou, we have termed the lawyers' *deterministic understanding of causality.*

In numerical comparative law, the approach becomes unfettered from contexts. Simply take 'a technique' from hard sciences – McCloskey suggests maths, whereas Farlow physics – and demonstrate the hunch which is the desired statistical regression: What we shall have is 'a random sample . . . from a definitely existing universe of events to determine the probability characteristics governing future random samples' that 'must necessarily nest into each other'. We agree with Andrew Farlow that this is 'methodologically unsound', because 'in the world of social and economic relationships . . . apparent correlations' can be quantitatively processed, but in most cases, these 'are based on configurations of economic forces and players, the possible persistence of which requires some economic, and indeed historical, judgment'.[145]

What the Fabric takes too lightly is the context where indicators exercise their soft, albeit mighty, power – that is, the context as the recipient of the law from the outside. Here, we found the most critical voices as regards the World

144 FH Lawson, 'Comparative Law as an Instrument of Legal Culture' in *The Comparison, Selected Essays*, Vol II (North-Holland Publishing Company 1977) 78.
145 Farlow (n 93) 224.

of Indicators. It can be argued that being postmodernists certainly means constructing a reality by focusing on data collection; yet quantitative methods usually disallow the participation of the general public in the evaluation of their own society. All indicators should therefore follow in the footsteps of, say, the 'Ibrahim Index of African Governance' (IIAG), that is, a managerial tool taking the form of a policy indicator that measures and monitors governance performance in African countries. We shall see in Chapter 3 how indicators impact on constitutional arrangements and the rule of law. Suffice it here to remember that the Ibrahim Index also takes into account societal and cultural contexts within which the law is applied with the aim of grasping the context and avoiding indicators' 'erasure of narratives': persons, places, communities, and territories are often considered striations and discrepancies to be removed from indexes.[146]

We have indeed seen that the Fabric peruses generalisations to seek a connection with the public sphere, tending to influence and shape its decision-making processes. Evidently, the connection with the public sphere is functional to promote interests that lie at the heart of commercial communities. Concerned, as they are, about their own transnational economic interests, they suggest the political community adopt legal devices through which their practical affairs might be organised. To this extent, transnational legal derivatives are the outputs of further processes of legal generalisations functional to the protection and enforcement of their own interests. There is nothing universalistic in the use of indicators, just the need to create contextual responses to constants surpassing state borders (such as mobilisation of goods, services, and capital to maximise investors' profits). To a certain degree, the Fabric has to do with communities (especially that of the holders of capital) whose activities transcend borders and state-related law-making. And the idea of privately made law as a 'transnational legal ordering' resonates with the aforementioned processes of generalisations.

Again, the risk is to ignore the contexts within which the constants are applied. Firstly, these replace former local, that is, territorial, legislation with new legal devices that possess universal substance because of their conveying the generalised values of economic sectionalities. Secondly, the law manufactured from the outside is servient to investors' financial interests, denying the relevance of those of several other discrete sectionalities that lie beneath domestic legislation. Functional, as it is, to interests intruding from the outside, it leaves out of the picture the striations that may disturb the application of transnational derivatives, wherever economic interests deem it fit to do so. As a result, the interests of economic sectionalities are turned into *the* organising theme of political communities and count as the interests of the whole.

Here, I argue, lies a further flaw in the Fabric of the Law as regards societal contexts. Indicators usually promote the generalisation of Western derivatives.

146 See 'Ibrahim Index of African Governance' <https://iiag.online/about.html> accessed 29 September 2024.

As seen, quantification in law has indeed its roots in the West, and the (global) standards and benchmarks suggested to developing countries are usually drafted after the legal toolkit of the Global North. Siddharth Peter de Souza explains that this is a 'reproduction [of] legal indicators . . . with a focus on values from the North'. Again, reproducing their frameworks in the context of the Global South means 'using them to understand local contexts' from the outside, 'organizations regardless of their contextual relevance'.[147] In comparative legal terms, this denies 'sustainable diversity in law', which is at the heart of comparative legal studies.[148] From the perspective of the Fabric, the legal constant manufactured from the outside can be considered a disturbing replica of colonial approach. It is true that the state–investor intercourse is now referred to cross-border economic interests, that is, concerns that are shared by transnational communities; but beyond economic interests and the law from the outside, there are often communities located in the Global South. Unsurprisingly, this predicament is upheld by the same LLVS. In *The Economic Consequences of Legal Origins* (2008), the same Rafael La Porta argued that the values of the common law (i.e. 'the strategy of social control that seeks to support private market outcomes', its 'rules, but also human capital and legal ideologies') has been reproduced quite literally in the Global South by way of transplantation 'into much of the world through conquest and colonization'.[149]

Instead of activating processes of 'transformation' and 'co-production' – which would have meant 'greater participation, iteration and input from the community'[150] – indicators still share the biases of traditional legal cartography. As traditional legal mapping adopted projections and scales to accommodate the world to Europe's worldview, indicators nesting into each other are used 'to offer a more comprehensive picture of reality', and their 'connections . . . can also distort and misrepresent the reality in certain ways'.[151] Evidently, 'through numerical representation, one always loses some aspects of the reality'.[152] The ability of indicators to reconcile scientific objectivity and measurement with real-world tests is attained by leaving out of the picture the striations that may disturb the application of transnational derivatives wherever economic interests deem it fit to do so.[153] They thus deliberately omit data and variables, notwithstanding their relevance in real-world assessments. And such omissions may also trigger a strabismus in metrics, which unavoidably affects the

147 de Souza (n 57) 122.
148 HP Glenn, *Legal Traditions of the World: Sustainable Diversity in Law* (5th edn, OUP 2014).
149 La Porta et al. 2008 (n 35) 286.
150 See de Souza (n 57) 12: By 'transformation', she points to 'legal indicators . . . not merely accepted but . . . re-examined and reimagined in order to make them suitable for a local context', whereas the 'idea of co-production' gives voice to the people of the Global South, 'drawing from the context and the societal milieu to produce knowledge in a deliberative and reflexive manner'.
151 Arslan (n 3) 21. On the bias of legal cartography, see Nicolini (n 2022) Ch 4.
152 Rottenburg and Merry (n 16) 8.
153 Davies (n 31) 285.

reliability of their outlook. Odd as it may seem, this type of strabismus may prevent them from scratching the surface of the data and realising that there are concrete signs of danger, if not of a catastrophe. Indicators indeed point to dangers, which we may either ignore or take seriously. The strabismus of indicators occurred, for instance, just before the 2007 financial crisis, when 'all the standard financial indicators declared that the financial system was safe'. It could have been sufficient to scratch the surface and realise that the real economy exhibited signs of danger, and yet there was a 'collective declaration of safety being issued by the financial market indicators'.[154]

11 Indicators and Complexity

Why did indicators not realise that there were signs of danger in 2007? Why were they not able to understand that the system was vulnerable? Perhaps most striking of all is that the answer to this question lies in the very soft power of indicators; more precisely, it lies in this soft power being a powerful act of simplification achieved through numbers and metrics. Complexity – and for what concerns us here, legal complexity – is indeed the main concern for the Fabric, that is, a concern that it tries to manage through indicators. Within the Fabric, complexity is supposed to undermine the whole process of incorporation of the constants into domestic legislation. Andrew Farlow explains why. Besides economic and financial reasons,[155] complexity might make it 'easier to hide risk and poor quality, not just from regulators, but also from management'. In addition, it may be argued that complexity makes it 'difficult to model, and to verify, default risks' – yet as Farlow suggests, it was precisely 'modelling default possibilities' that, 'naturally enough, made the crash worse' in 2007.[156]

We may say that, in both cases, not only did simplification by numbers point to danger, but it was also unable to tackle risks. To this extent, it is true that comparative law presupposes variety, whereas the efficiency rule promoted by the Fabric requires more homogeneous politico-legal features throughout the world: Only shared legal devices are able to ensure that the deterministic correlation between legal and improved economic performance is part of our constructed reality. Yet the correlation does not necessarily extend to the *scientific state of mind* in the sense that it promotes homogeneity, which, in an economic-oriented environment, aims to manage (i.e. simplify) legal complexity. In our opinion, the scientific state of mind is also a cultural competence, a faculty of mind, a capacity for comprehension, synthesis, and creativity.[157] There is no doubt that, as comparative legal scholars, it is of utmost

154 Farlow (n 93) 221–22. The predicament was also valid for the DBRs: see Davis (n 8) 32.

155 From the financial perspective, in 2007 'complexity aided and abetted misselling'. Likewise, 'complex financial structures facilitated tax avoidance, and, in turn, tax avoidance encouraged complexity'. Farlow (n 93) 244.

156 Farlow (n 93) 242–43.

157 James Boyd White, *The Legal Imagination* (The University of Chicago Press 1973) xiii.

importance to us, as it helps them recognise the legally significant patterns of quantification and to respond to risks in ways that fit the legal system within which the constants outside the law will operate. Instead of erasing it, we assume that the scientific state of mind is also made of 'narrating numbers', that sustain us in accepting and understanding complexity without reducing it. It is indeed difficult to draw inferences about our deterministic correlation without understanding how the law performs in our complex World of Indicators.[158] Or – which is the same thing – 'simplification also inevitably results in loss of information, giving rise to error'.[159]

We therefore agree with Mathias Siems, according to whom 'a numerical comparative law approach may only be a starting point for further research, which intends to look at the social, cultural and economic circumstances that underlie specific legal rules. Therefore, comparative law remains complex despite using statistical evidence in law'.[160] Even in a World of Indicators. As comparative legal scholars, we should warn against the application of a purely deterministic leximetrics approach to the 'Fabric of the Law'.

158 Espeland (n 28) 56.
159 Davis (n 2) 41.
160 Siems (n 32) 540.

3 Legal Indicators and Constitutional Governance

1 The State and the New Fabric of the Law

In the previous chapters, the huge transformations affecting the law were located within the 'Factory of Global Legal Indicators', allowing us to examine how the law itself has become an 'output' now 'manufactured' from the outside.

Managing the law from the outside signposts a new methodological trend in comparative law research. We have been reflecting on the 'soft power' of indicators, that is, on the cooperative intercourse that lies at the heart of the Factory. This takes place among private actors, investors, organisations, and states; through it, national public spheres are encouraged to code (that is, generalise) their uncodified economic and financial interests through the law. In so doing, non-legal instances become legal constants which are turned into *the* interests of the whole community. The intercourse assumes the relevance of privately made law, whose transformative potential is useful for manufacturing 'better' legislation through a comparative process – and therefore for providing lawmakers with the practical knowledge (*external* to domestic legal systems) to frame new laws. This is precisely what indicators do, and their 'soft power' is a metaphor grasping the 'superiority' of the legislative solutions they endorse.

So far, we have approached their 'soft power' from a theoretical standpoint. Chapter 1 has explained how indicators favour a connection between capital and the public sphere, which is functional to incorporating investors' interests into states' legal systems. This is made possible because of the normative character of indicators, which combine scientific objectivity and real data useful for fabricating legislation from the outside. Chapter 2 has supplied a further theoretical explanation for their proliferation and use, which lies in the recursivity of the state–investor intercourse. All members of the transnational community are fascinated by indicators and exhibit a fideistic attitude towards them. This type of knowledge production reflects a new way of conceiving, understanding, and manufacturing the law nurtured by the law–economic growth correlation.

It is now time to focus on how such changes impact on the law. This is precisely what we shall be doing in the three last chapters, which are devoted

DOI: 10.4324/9781003304333-4

to assessing how the scientific state of mind, the 'Factory', and the 'soft power' of indicators affect constitutional law, international financial regulation, and the global standards adopted in international insolvency law. These chapters reappraise how, as drivers for change, indicators cause a shift from the old to the new world economic order.

This chapter locates indicators within constitutional legal studies, by focusing on how their normative force affects nation states in terms of law-making, human rights protection, the rule of law, and liberal democracy. What is at stake here is the endurance of constitutionalism; by putting bridles on power and limiting it, constitutionalism has traditionally been setting the legal, political, and cultural background of the Western legal tradition – also leaving long-lasting marks on globalisation.[1] This entails challenging two deeply rooted theories of law in Western political thought, namely, legal positivism and legal liberalism.[2] We have upheld elsewhere that the Western legal tradition, in general, and the common law, in particular, constitute the backbone of global law.[3] Consequently, common-law paradigms are now applied globally for processing things as wealth and turning them into capital; no wonder, therefore, that the legal constants outside the law still refer to 'stocks, shares, bonds and the like . . . crossing oceans at the touch of a key-pad in the search for a fiscal utopia'.[4]

This does not entail the end of publicly made law, though. Managed from the outside, it still matters as a means to increase wealth, as well as a 'powerful social ordering technology' used by private groups to control 'the levers for the distribution of wealth in society'.[5] The law has become even more business-friendly; it boosts economic growth, reduces risks, and makes financial ventures predictable. Its 'alleged private-law bias is hardly surprising'.[6] The fact that states incorporate privately made law into their publicly made law to attract foreign investors has clear-cut consequences in terms of constitutional law and governance. Take for example the sovereign debt crisis we

1 *Cf.* Robert Schütze, 'Constitutionalism(s)' in R Masterman and R Schütze (eds), *The Cambridge Companion to Comparative Constitutional Law* (Cambridge UP 2019).

2 Alicia Pastor y Camarasa, *Transnational Constitution Making. External Actors, Expertise, and Democratic Transition* (Routledge 2024) 49 and 174, respectively.

3 See Matteo Nicolini, '"Inequality of Goods and Lands" in Mortgaged Democracies: Paradigms and Effects of Global Comparative Law' (2021) 41 Liverpool L Rev 27, 33. See also Katharina Pistor, *The Code of Capital. How the Law Creates Wealth and Inequality* (Princeton UP 2019) 176, 158. The same US common law, which is supposed to be the hegemonic legal system, owes its features to English law. On the English origins of (global) US law, see WE Nelson, *Americanization of the Common Law: The Impact of Legal Change on Massachusetts Society, 1760–1830* (Harvard UP 1975).

4 Bernard Rudden, 'Things as Thing and Things as Wealth' (1994) 14 Oxford J Legal Studies 81, 82.

5 Pistor (n 3) 17 and 19.

6 Peer Zumbansen, 'Transnational Law: Theories & Applications' in Peer Zumbansen (ed), *The Oxford Handbook of Transnational Law* (OUP 2021) 6.

referred to in Chapter 1. To tackle it, the 'Treaty on Stability, Coordination and Governance in the economic and monetary union' (TSCG), signed in Brussels on 2 February 2010, set (and still sets) several constraints on EU member states' (more precisely, on its signatories') budgetary policies, which must be balanced or in surplus. More on this in due course. Suffice it here to point to this as a way of depriving EU member states of their constitutional *Kompetenz-Kompetenz*; the TSCG, indeed, 'requires . . . constitutional changes in each of the signatory states but also raises significant questions about . . . the extent of the discretion left to member states to make fundamental decisions about taxation and spending'.[7] The several credit lines set up in 2020–2021 during the pandemic (such as the Pandemic Crisis Support of the European Stability Mechanism and the 'Next Generation EU' funds) might have had analogous effects on member states' public finance. These unavoidably create constraints, limit states' discretion as regards taxation and spending policies, and change the way constitutions should be interpreted, and human rights and state policies should be implemented to secure financial stability.[8]

The pre-eminence of economic universals results in a noticeable process whereby the public–private divide is often blurred by blending finance and banking legal instruments with constitutional systems. In an output-oriented approach, countries must provide a comfort zone for foreign investments if they wish to survive in a globalised economy. The state–investor cooperative intercourse is therefore still pivotal to code, that is, generalise, the financial interests of the latter through the law, mainly because it avoids the – political, legal, and accountability-related – risks that are connected to traditional comparative law. Likewise, states are also crucial when assessing legal constants manufactured from the outside, the underperformativity of which would cause a non-reception of the constants and flaws in the Fabric if its legal solutions were deemed to be unable to reach the desired goals of the state–investors intercourse.

This chapter illustrates how the Factory makes use of the cooperative intercourse to fabricate publicly made law suitable for private investors' economic interests. Firstly, the Factory suggests a common language be framed to facilitate such intercourse. In terms of constitutional law, this has several implications. The audit culture is extended to constitutional arrangements and implies attracting investors' confidence politically and financially. Secondly, this means demonstrating that each state is legally fit *also* in terms of constitutional law. To this extent, we shall see that indicators have twisted the rule of law into a measurable value-neutral legal concept that secures predictability on

7 Steve Peers, 'The Stability Treaty: Permanent Austerity or Gesture Politics?' (2012) 8 Eur Const L Rev 404. See also Alberto Saravalle, *Introduction to the Law of Economic and Monetary Union* (Edward Elgar 2021) 49 et seq.

8 Caroline de la Porte and Elke Heins, 'Introduction: EU Constraints and Opportunities in the COVID-19 Pandemic – the Politics of NGEU' (2022) 20 Comp Eur Polit 135. See also David Bokhorst and MG Schoeller, 'Managing Constraint: Frugal Opposition to European Fiscal Solidarity' (2024) 31 J Eur Publ Policy 3275.

investment returns. Thirdly, the Fabric requires a frame of government rooted in liberal democracy, which encourages countries to arrange their own constitutional frameworks around a legal architecture managed from the outside to promote institutional efficiency. As the rule of law has become the driver promoting good governance, we are witnessing a shift towards economic democracy, according to which states are held accountable *vis-à-vis* financial markets and international investors.

2 Beyond the Public–Private Divide: The State as a 'Development Enterprise'

As we stated in the Introduction, we are experiencing remarkable changes in the realm of the law. It is a true epistemological paradigm shift, which affects both the meaning and function of the law.

The shift is particularly apparent as far as constitutional arrangements are concerned. In her *Transnational Constitution Making* (2024), Alicia Pastor y Camarasa provides us with several insights that might help us unpack this paradigm shift, as well as to understand which role the soft power of indicators plays within constitutional legal studies. There, she refers to the so-called 'development enterprise'. Characterised by 'external actors' involvement in constitution-making',[9] this enterprise has two basic features, legal liberalism and the role of experts within the constitutional settlement. Leaving this latter feature aside,[10] this section assesses legal liberalism as a paradigm to interpret the Factory.

The expression under scrutiny 'refers to a particular set of beliefs about how [the] law can impact economic and political change'. Nothing new under the sun as far as the Factory is concerned. Legal liberalism upholds our way of conceiving and understanding the law, that is, the law as an 'output' often 'manufactured' from the outside. According to legal liberalism, 'legal . . . reforms are treated as a catalyst to reach liberal democracy . . . through importing rational modern law'. And nothing, we add, is more 'rational' than a piece of 'better' legislation manufactured from the outside, providing that it is able to maximise investors' profits. A predicament like this also endorses the legal-deterministic correlation between legal fitness and economic growth (Chapter 2): If states adopt the legal constants proposed by indicators, economic growth will necessarily follow. This type of predictability is undoubtedly a consequence of legal liberalism, inasmuch as 'the rationality of the law leads to a predictable process, where political and economic development can be accelerated'. Thirdly, the law embeds rationality also because the Factory has triggered a change in the law-making process; looking beyond 'traditional hard law norms to discover the process of creating laws', it has indeed paved

9 Pastor y Camarasa (n 2) 56 (and Ch 3 for the role of the expert).
10 For more on this, see Bengt Jacobsson, 'Standardization and Expert Knowledge' in Nils Brunsson et al. (eds), *A World of Standards* (Oxford UP 2000).

the way to the cooperative intercourse. This leads us to the cornerstone of our theorisation, that is, the 'soft power' of indicators as a form of law-making and cooperative practice.[11]

As said earlier, this shift is a real challenge to domestic law-making, with clear-cut consequences in terms of constitutional law. No wonder that, within our quantitative-oriented world, '[n]ational sovereignty is at stake', because it is 'limited, superintended and redirected by indicators'.[12] Every feature of states' constitutions may be assessed through them. The examples are manifold and range from the rigidity/flexibility of a given constitution to the performativity of political branches,[13] from the 'performance quantification' of constitutional policies to the 'creditworthiness of sovereign states',[14] from human rights protection to the rule of law, sustainability, and climate change–related policies.[15] We have already encountered some of these indicators in Chapter 2: Most of them are pre-indicators (e.g. the Index of Economic Freedom, the Global Health Security Index, the Human Development Index, and the Global Multidimensional Poverty Index). Others measure constitutional legal contexts (e.g. the Corruption Perception Index, the Rule of Law Index, the Press Freedom Index, the Global Democracy Index) in relation to the rule of law (e.g. the WB's World Governance Indicators Project, the Heritage Foundation, Freedom House, and the World Justice Project). Several other indicators (such as the WB's 'Prosperity Data360') gather data dealing with inclusive and sustainable growth, often allowing users to compare countries across similar benchmarks.[16]

11 Pastor y Camarasa (n 2) 56, 60, and 63, respectively. In her opinion, a last feature helps us unpack legal liberalism, that is, 'rationalisation is a unique feature of the West' – and the West is 'the ultimate stage of development' (64).

12 John Harrington, 'Indicators, Security and Sovereignty During COVID-19 in the Global South' (2021) 17 Int'l J L in Context 249. See also DV Malito, Gaby Umbach, and Nehal Bhuta (eds), *The Palgrave Handbook of Indicators in Global Governance* (Palgrave Macmillan 2018); SP de Souza, *Designing Indicators for a Plural Legal World* (CUP 2022) 20.

13 See, respectively, Nuno Garoupa and Catarina Santos Botelho, 'Measuring Procedural and Substantial Amendment Rules: An Empirical Exploration' (2021) 22 German LJ 216; PG Monateri and Mauro Balestrieri, *Quantitative Methods in Comparative Law* (Edward Elgar 2023) 122 et seq.

14 See Marta Infantino and Mauro Bussani, 'Rule by Metrics. Performance, Quantification, and the Law' (2023) 11 European J Comp L Governance 187, 196.

15 See, for example, UN OHCHR, 'Universal Human Rights Index (UHRI)' <https://uhri.ohchr.org/en/search-human-rights-recommendations> accessed 26 December 2024. Mila Versteeg and Tom Ginsburg, 'Measuring the Rule of Law: A Comparison of Indicators' (2017) 42 Law Socl Inquiry 100; Adam Chilton and Mila Versteeg, *How Constitutional Rights Matter* (OUP 2020) Ch 5. See also AnnJanette Rosga and ML Satterthwaite, 'Measuring Human Rights: UN Indicators in Critical Perspective' in Davis Kevin et al. (eds), *Governance by Indicators: Global Power Through Quantification and Rankings* (Oxford UP 2012); Maria Green, 'What We Talk About When We Talk about Indicators: Current Approaches to Human Rights Measurement' (2001) 23 Human Rights Quarterly 1062.

16 See the Prosperity Data 360 <https://prosperitydata360.worldbank.org/en/home> accessed 23 December 2024.

In terms of constitutional law, a further feature characterises the state–investor intercourse. Not only are the holders of global capital the major force of the whole process of change, but the process itself also extends over several jurisdictions, turning transnational investors' privately made law into domestic publicly made legislation.[17] There is, we argue, a real pre-eminence of economic universals with a further noticeable outcome: The public–private divide is often blurred by blending finance and banking legal instruments with constitutional legal systems.[18] The private–public divide has strategically been 'maintained or crossed according to the interest involved', with the aim of allowing transnational 'private authority and lawmaking', 'private or non-state legalities', and 'hybrid public–private law-makers' to make a constant, albeit imperceptible, 'shadow contribution' to domestic decision-making processes.[19] The divide has been blurred so that transnational actors (which are and remain external to domestic systems) can manage legal – and for what concerns us here, constitutional – change from the 'outside'. Again, this is the outcome of the law-making process in an evidently post-Westphalian regulatory environment.[20]

The way the divide is strategically blurred is part of the development enterprise. Take the legal correlation with its deterministic relationship between democracy and economic performance.[21] We shall see that liberal democracy is the form of government that is supposed to boost economic growth. Yet the predicament is decisively simplistic. We all know that even a superficial comparative survey of the world's constitutions confirms that what we label as liberal democracy has been inflected in a variety of ways, both linguistically and legally. Democracies thus vary from one constitutional context to another: They reflect different theoretical types of democracy in which both social and political values and the role of the leadership change. There are indeed 'many varieties of liberal democracy', which are periodically assessed by the several indices that make up the Variety of Democracy – V-Index.[22] The correlation is concerned

17 Jaakko Husa, *Advanced Introduction to Law and Globalisation* (Edward Elgar 2018) 48, labels these processes and subjects 'globalising legalities'.

18 '[L]et us . . . be practical and realistic. Although the state could refuse to honor privately made law, it does not': DV Snyder, 'Private Lawmaking' (2003) 64 Ohio St LJ 371, 413.

19 Horatia Muir Watt, 'Private International Law's Shadow Contribution to the Question of Informal Transnational Authority' (2018) 25 Indiana J Glob Leg Studies 37, 37–39.

20 See William Twining, 'Review: A Post-Westphalian Conception of Law' (2003) 37 L Soc Rev 199.

21 See, among the others, Adam Przeworski and Fernando Limongi, 'Political Regimes and Economic Growth' (1993) 7 J Ec Perspectives 51; John Helliwell, 'Empirical Linkages Between Democracy and Economic Growth' (1994) 24 British J Pol Sc 225; Adam Przeworski and others, 'Political Regimes and Economic Growth' in Adam Przeworski and others (eds), *Democracy and Development: Political Institutions and Well-Being in the World, 1950–1990* (CUP 2000); Daron Acemoglu and others, 'Democracy Does Cause Growth' (2019) 127 J Pol Ec 47; Mariana Mota Prado and MJ Trebilcock, *Advanced Introduction to Law and Development* (2nd edn, Edward Elgar 2021) 71 et seq.

22 DK Joshi, 'The Protective and Developmental Varieties of Liberal Democracy: A Difference in Kind or Degree?' (2013) 20 Democratization 187, 190. See also Jonas Wolff, 'From

not with the variety and heterogeneity of constitutional arrangements but with the idea that there is something more important and worth being spread, that is, that 'a global legal language' is being conveyed through such variety, and that this 'global legal language [is necessarily] based on economic models' (and correlations), as well as being embedded in the soft power of indicators.[23]

This type of cooperative intercourse discloses an intriguing way of fabricating the law from the outside: Publicly made law is reimagined in a way that best suits private investors' economic interests and privately made law. It is no longer possible to refute its legal relevance; nor can we deny its legal character. Through indicators, our cooperative intercourse infuses constitutional environments with 'mechanisms associated with neoliberal restructuring of the global political economy'. It does this by respecting constitutional variety and diversity. Indicators exert influence on states as to the result to be achieved but leave to the national authorities the choice of form and methods to protect investors' interests.

This reflects the shift towards the creation of a global common regulation of international financial relations and markets. The public–private divide is thus blurred because of the universalising legal code of financial assets. ***Durability***, ***priority***, and ***convertibility*** are assisted by ***universality***, which extends the scope and applicability of financial instruments. Universality undermines the relation between state and capital and, at the same time, upholds the superiority of privately, that is, sectionally, coded assets and their new contractual devices.[24] To this extent, Katharina Pistor is undoubtedly right when she points to legal 'vindication of private coding efforts by a court of law'.[25] In seeking legal vindication, financial operators mitigate uncertainty and prevent volatility of liquidity (Chapter 1). Blurring the divide means allowing privately made law to use the publicly made law to avoid the – political, legal, and accountability-related – risks connected to state business and finance law.

3 Semantic Shifts: Manufacturing Constitutional Changes From the Outside

Embedded, as it is, in the development enterprise, our cooperative intercourse resorts to a vast array of strategies when it comes to managing legal – and

the Varieties of Democracy to the Defense of Liberal Democracy: V-Dem and the Reconstitution of Liberal Hegemony Under Threat?' (2022) 29 Contemporary Politics 161. See V-Dem Institute, 'Varieties of Democracy (V-Dem)' <https://v-dem.net/> accessed 29 December 2024. On the possibility of having hugely differentiated declensions of constitutional democracy within the context of Western constitutionalism, see, for example, Matteo Nicolini, 'The Constitutional Implications of Democracy in Governing Complex Societies' (2017) 21 Revista General de Derecho Público Comparado 1.

23 Horatia Muir Watt, 'Further Terrains for Subversive Comparison: The Field of Global Governance and the Public/Private Divide' in PG Monateri (ed), *Methods of Comparative Law* (Edward Elgar 2012) 272.

24 Pistor (n 3) 21.

25 Pistor (n 3) 21, 43.

for what concerns us here, constitutional – changes from the 'outside'. To a certain extent, its way of impacting on state constitutions is more subtle than one might expect.

In the previous section, we maintained that the intercourse usually respects constitutional variety and diversity. Far from requiring formal convergence, what really matters is the result, that is, reimagining publicly made law to make it suit private investors' economic interests and privately made law. In several cases, this can be achieved without resorting to formal constitutional (or legal) amendments. There are thus ways that are slyer than formal changes for establishing the connection with the public sphere to foster, protect, and secure investors' financial interests. If the cooperative intercourse aims to turn their interests into interests of state communities, then the Factory has to promote a change that is both legal and cultural – and the cultural is more relevant than the legal. Nothing bears more fruit than a fertile and financially friendly environment, where business culture, better legislation manufactured from the outside, and attractiveness to foreign investors represent the new 'morally eligible foundation on which' communities might 'organise their practical affairs'.[26]

If we understand it correctly, this new eligible foundation is to be understood as a reform agenda. Formulated as it is by transnational economic actors, it suggests adopting economic policies along the lines of what Friedrich von Hayek proposed in his *The Constitution of Liberty*.[27] Accepted as early as the 1980s in the USA and the UK, this agenda was re-proposed as part of the economic austerity 'recipe' to get out of the sovereign debt crisis. The neoliberal agenda is economic, political, and legal. Economically, it supports the freedom and autonomy of the market, the centrality of property rights, such as the 'freedom of contract and alienability of property'.[28] From a political standpoint, it promotes minimal state intervention in the market, demanding the privatisation of public goods and the formation of 'unrestrained markets'.[29] At the legal level, it advocates the incorporation of privately made law into publicly made law to create the 'law that is wanted' by global economic actors.[30] To put it differently, state intervention is functional to the market, which in turn serves the sectional interests of the holders of global capital. Through a

26 R Mullender, 'Context, Contingency and the Law of Negligence (or from Islands to Islands of Time' (1997) 29 Bracton L J 23, 25.

27 Friedrich Von Hayek, *The Constitution of Liberty* (Chicago UP 1960). See also L von Mises, *The Free and Prosperous Commonwealth: An Exposition of the Ideas of Classical Liberalism* (Van Nostrand 1962); NR Van Nostrand, *Anarchy, State and Utopia* (Basic Books 1974). The agenda is summarised in the formula where 'economic value [is] measured only by price, what [has] no price [has] no value': Guy Standing, *Plunder of the Commons. A Manifesto for Sharing Public Wealth* (Pelican 2019) viii. See also Ugo Mattei and Laura Nader, *Plunder: When the Rule of Law Is Illegal* (Blackwell 2008) Ch 2.

28 Husa (n 17) 79.

29 Husa (n 17) 53, 79.

30 Alan Watson, *Failures of the Legal Imagination* (University of Pennsylvania Press 1988) 87.

strategic blurring of the public–private divide, it allows the global Factory to maximise profits.

What is at stake here is the perception of which interests, within state societies, shall be given priority. It is also a change in the broader mentality of state communities; changing their perception entails persuading them that, in so doing, the connection is indispensable to finance. The organising theme is the promotion of efficient institutional legal paradigms, which are ranked as superior to all other societal paradigms and interests. By arranging the public sphere around the interests pursued by privately made law, the laws of the market have also started percolating through the political system; and the new foundation of the political obligation allows communities to reconcile the variety of conflicting economic interests giving primacy to private actors' legal constants.

The most prominent example of how financial global dominance causes a shift from the political to the economic sphere is related to sovereign debt rating. This is indeed a true cultural change in how a country's creditworthiness is now assessed both at the national level and within the transnational community. Fitch Ratings, Moody's Investors Service, and Standard & Poor's – that is, the three major and *de facto* oligopolistic rating agencies – measure the overall economic conditions of a given country, from investments to capital market transparency, also taking into account foreign currency reserves. We all know that credit ratings have to do with predictability, particularly in terms of solvency, and that solvency depends on states' ability to meet their obligations when it comes to repaying bonds and other debt instruments. On the one hand, states do this by boosting their economic growth. Indicators supply legal solutions manufactured from the outside to attract investors: The adoption of the proposed legal constants (factor *X*) will lead to an increase in commerce and profits (occurrence of factor *Y*). No wonder, therefore, that ratings connected to the 'health conditions' of national ability to repay the debt also rely on policy pre-indicators to assess these conditions. Restrepo Amariles provides us with an example: Standard and Poor's sovereign ratings (S&P) is 'in principle . . . alien to the measurement of legal performance'; in assessing sovereign performances in five areas (political, economic, external, fiscal, and monetary), it 'uses nonetheless the scores of', say, the 'WGI Rule of Law Indicator . . . to calculate the primary factor of political' – and legal, we add – 'performance of states'.[31] It is something that has to do with risk: The healthier the situation, the less dangerous the political, legal, and accountability-related risks, particularly if these are connected to positive (i.e. state) business and finance law.[32] Indeed, when Moody's, Fitch, or Standard &

31 David Restrepo Amariles, 'Supping with the Devil? Indicators and the Rise of Managerial Rationality in Law' (2017) 13 Int J L Context 465, 478.

32 For more on this, see Daniele D'Alvia, *International Insolvency and Finance Law: Legal Constants in Times of Crises* (Routledge 2022) Ch 3.

Poor's downgrades 'a country's sovereign credit rating . . . purchasers of bonds and securities know that they will need to absorb greater risk'.[33]

On the other hand, attracting investors also means sharing their aims (i.e. maximising profits), allowing their 'entrepreneurial activity to flourish' and only 'accidentally also promoting the wellbeing of the [domestic] society at large'.[34] This entails nesting in a common direction by adopting their desired legal toolkits without overtaxing and overburdening them with tax reforms or spending plans. As we said in Chapter 1, if such policies are perceived as unsustainable (as in the case of the UK's mini-budget in 2022), it can lead to a loss of confidence, higher borrowing costs (through higher bond yields), and challenges in raising funds. If their interests count as the interests of the whole community, the state–investor cooperative intercourse will undoubtedly change the meaning of the sustainability of fiscal policies.[35] A less-interventionist state means changing budgetary and fiscal policies. If the sovereign debt outlook is negative, 'even the least responsible rulers of the downgraded countries' have to intervene by cutting expenditures. This is detrimental to their communities but, at the same time, attracts more and more investors. Likewise, ratings such as Standard & Poor's also assess 'whether policy-making and legal reforms may "weaken support for sustainable public finances and balances economic growth"', – for example, levying new taxes to finance social policies, thus affecting the interests of the investors.[36]

Accepting that outside-the-law constants constrain our rights is a burden all citizens bear 'largely because' – they are usually told – 'this is in their personal self-interest; their political futures and the incomes of their countries are affected'.[37] In this regard, the shift is cultural because it endorses the transformation of the legal and economic premises of national policymaking. International financial actors suggest the adoption of policies that may sustain their capitalist socioeconomic model. The model might be detrimental to social welfare policies[38] because it is a way of reducing the discretionary powers of

33 RI Rotberg, 'Strengthening Governance: Ranking Countries Would Help' (2004) 28 The Washington Quarterly 71, 73.

34 Marta Infantino, 'Quantitative Legal Comparisons: Narratives, Self-Representations and Sunset Boulevards' (2019) 6 J Int'l Comp L 287, 302, and 304.

35 Paul Burger, 'Sustainability, Sustainability Assessment, and the Place of Fiscal Sustainability' in Nehal Bhuta, Debora Valentina Malito, and Gaby Umbach (eds), *The Palgrave Handbook of Indicators in Global Governance* (Palgrave Macmillan 2018).

36 Restrepo Amariles (n 31) 479, quoting Standard & Poor's, 'Sovereign Government Rating: Methodology and Assumptions' (2011) 12 <www.concertedaction.com/wp-content/uploads/2012/05/Standard-Poors-Sovereign-Government-Rating-And-Methodology.pdf> accessed 3 January 2025.

37 Rotberg (n 33) 73.

38 If not to the very idea of the social market economy (or *Soziale Marktwirtschaft*). On the negation of the *Soziale Marktwirtschaft* model in Germany, the country where the model was invented, see Mathias Ruffert, 'Public Law and the Economy: A Comparative View from the German Perspective' (2013) 11 Int J Const Law 925. On the risk of weaking the welfare

political branches when levying taxes and appropriating funds. It rests on a new form of 'confidence' between the political power and the sovereign financial market, where 'distressed sovereign debt can be sold on private equity markets and the debtor [is] subjected to the harsh economics of private law'.[39]

This is a remarkable change in how the public sphere is organised; and the change is even more remarkable inasmuch as it does not require any amendment to the black-letter constitution. What has occurred is a semantic shift in how constitutional arrangements are conceived, understood, or – which is the same thing – interpreted. Not only do investors seek a connection with the public sphere, but they also promote a change in how constitutional law must regulate the interests of their communities. The shift is caused by some intrinsic features of the legal language; 'characterised by neutrality and generality', it avoids 'subjective and personal attitudes'.[40] And yet these features often conceal 'anonymous authority and power'.[41] The Factory may challenge the meaning of the legal lexicon related to the constitutional foundations on national communities, therefore imposing a new sense (the language of economics) on existing lexical items.

The whole process is facilitated by the law. As an open texture, every single provision may visualise and convey different legal meanings and contents, which may thus be pragmatically enriched by new factors. A new sense is thus assigned to existing lexemes without the necessity of formally altering the law, because the new sense acts as an additional meaning that complements the former one. This gives expression to the view that, as the morally eligible foundation of a given community changes over time, so too should their interpretation. Likewise, the Factory purposely resorts to the semantic shift to complement the way the law is made from the outside: Through this deliberate re-engineering practice, a new organising theme is distilled from the process of constitutional interpretation.

The shift from the 'legal' to the 'economic' is patent in budgetary policies, whose stringent application requires that countries ensure efficiency. Take for example Article 140 of the Treaty on the Functioning of the EU (TFEU), originally laid forth in Articles 121(1), 122(2), second clause, and 123(5) of the 1992 Treaty on the European Community. As regards economic and monetary policies, what concerns us here is that member states' 'high degree of sustainable convergence' is assessed by taking into account 'the sustainability of the government financial position', that is, the achievement of a 'government budgetary position without a deficit that is excessive'. It is a patent

state, see Mark Verdussen, 'The Constitutional Stakes of the Golden Rule' in Elena-Simina Tănăsescu and Eric Oliva (eds), *Constitutional Law and the EU Balanced Budget Principle* (Routledge 2021).

39 Muir Watt (n 23) 286.

40 Matti Rissanen, 'Standardisation and the Language of Early Statutes' in Laura Wright (ed), *The Development of Standard English 1300–1800: Theories Descriptions Conflicts* (CUP 2000) 120.

41 Matti Rissanen (n 40) 121.

'use of performance-based governance' which now percolates 'many other policy areas including employment, social protection, education, youth and vocational training', thus constraining the constitutional policies a government should implement to match its citizens' needs.[42]

The shift is even more significant when the substitution of meaning is complemented by the substitution of the word, that is, when economic lexemes replace legal jargon. This shift occurs when formal constitutional amendments are enacted to match the development enterprise. The case of the TSCG is illuminating. In the course of the sovereign debt crisis, as said, several EU member states amended their constitutions to introduce the principle of balanced budgets.[43] Thus, limitations on financial powers were (and remain) the outcome of the entrenchment of economic budgetary policies. As Mark Verdussen correctly states, the risk is again of 'weakening' the 'viability of the welfare state', also in light of the decision of the European Council of 25 March 2011. By amending Article 136 TFEU, it incorporated the stability mechanism for those member states whose currency is the euro. This European constitutional reform ensures that the budgetary position of member states is balanced or in surplus according to Article 136 TFEU and the TSCG.[44]

The shift thus entails a change in the nexus between democracy, accountability, and financial responsibilities, as well as the deletion of several constructs purporting one of the main core values upon which constitutionalism was erected, that is, the idea of the supremacy of those same constitutions. Last but not the least, these reforms secure the legal fitness of EU member states.

4 Symptoms and Effects of the Semantic Shift

4.1 The 'Golden' Budgetary Rule

There are noticeable symptoms of this cultural and semantic change – and these have visible effects in terms of constitutional law. Take for example the relationship between the scientific state of mind and legal quantitative measurement, which is expressed to its fullest extent through the constitutionalisation

42 Restrepo Amariles (n 31) 479.

43 This occurred in nearly all EU federal and regional countries, such as Austria, Germany, Spain, and Italy. For Austria, see Art. 13.2 B-VG, as inserted by the 2008 constitutional reform (BGBl. I 1/1008). For Germany, see Arts. 109 and 110 GG, as amended by the 2009 (and 2025) constitutional reforms. For Spain, see Art. 135 of the Constitution, amended in 2011. For Italy, see Arts. 81 and 119.1 of the Constitution, as amended by Constitutional (Amendment) Act No. 1/2012. See Elena-Simina Tănăsescu and Eric Oliva, 'Constitutional Law and the EU Balanced Budget Principle' in Elena-Simina Tănăsescu and Eric Oliva (eds), *Constitutional Law and the EU Balanced Budget Principle* (Routledge 2021).

44 Sandrino Smeets, 'The European Stability Mechanism and the Fiscal Compact in European Integration' in *Oxford Research Encyclopedia of Politics* (OUP 2020) <https://oxfordre.com/politics/view/10.1093/acrefore/9780190228637.001.0001/acrefore-9780190228637-e-1069> accessed 10 January 2025.

of the 'golden rule' of liberal (and neoliberal) economic thought: the principle of balanced budgets.[45]

Such constitutionalisation is a symptom of the quantitative change. It is, we argue, a symptom inasmuch as it fits into the Factory: As the politico-cum-fiscal agenda of its actors is now enshrined in national constitutions, the maximisation of their interests counts as the interests of national communities. To this extent, the process is part of the broader semantic transformation of the constitutional lexicon in terms of both form and substance: The incorporation of the golden rule alters the contents traditionally entrusted to constitutional texts. A further effect complements this semantic change. The constitutionalisation of balanced budgets turns the golden rule from one of the principles of economic liberalism into an econometric criterion to oversee public authorities and limit their spending. Willy-nilly, the constitution incorporates the economic lexicon to the extent of conveying its prescriptive rules through mathematical signs, models, and fractions. Percentages and economic formulas have never been part of constitutionalism, yet they now saturate the 'Fabric' of the constitutions manufactured from the outside. The infusion of items borrowed from financial maths is so pervasive that even the TSCG rewrites welfare state policies in mathematical terms: According to Article 3.1.b, the golden rule is respected provided that

> the annual structural balance of the general government is at its country-specific medium-rowth Pact, with a lower limit of a structural deficit of 0.5% of the gross domestic product at market prices.

The impact is so massive that constitutions now exhibit an econometric approach to 'balance the income and expenditure in . . . budget, taking into account adverse and favourable phases of the economic cycle', also requiring 'a forecast of the evolution of the main macroeconomic indicators that have an influence on the Budget'.[46] Likewise, Article 135 of the Spanish

45 See Maurice Adams, Federico Fabbrini, and Pierre Larouche (eds), *The Constitutionalization of European Budgetary Constraints* (Hart 2014); Michel Bouvier 'La règle d'or: Un concept à construire' (2011) 113 Revue Française de Finances Publiques v. For a critical approach, see Michel Bouvier, 'Balanced Budgets – the Vanity of a Principle' in Elena-Simina Tănăsescu and Eric Oliva (eds), *Constitutional Law and the EU Balanced Budget Principle* (Routledge 2021). See also Clemens Kaupa, 'Has (Downturn-)Austerity Really Been "Constitutionalized" in Europe? On the Ideological Dimension of Such a Claim' (2017) 44 Journal of Law and Society 32.

46 Article 81 of the Italian Constitution and Article 105.4 of the Portuguese Constitution, respectively. France avoided constitutionalising the principle because, already in 2008, Article 34 was amended to incorporate the 'objective of balancing the accounts of public administrations'. For the 'mathematical' part, see the Organic Law of 17 December 2012 on public finances and the Law of 22 October 2012, which authorised the ratification of the TSCG. Ireland, in turn, added subsection 10 to Article 29.4 of the Constitution, thus enshrining the TSCG.

Constitution expressly refers to 'structural deficit', 'gross domestic product', thereby endorsing expressions that we find in the TSCG. But the most complex and econometric approach is in the Basic Law for the Federal Republic of Germany. It is the so-called German Brake (*Schuldenbremse*) to indebtment.[47] Amended in 2009, it was partly changed in 2025 to allow, *inter alia*, the deduction of military expenses, too loosen its grip on the total amount of the debt cap, and to favour infrastructural investments (see Article 143). In its current form, Article 109(3) still states that '[t]he budgets of the Federation and the *Länder* shall, in principle, be balanced without revenue from credits'. The goal is achieved if 'the borrowing of funds does not exceed 0.35 per cent in relation to the nominal gross domestic product'; evidently, 'debits exceeding the threshold of 1.5 per cent in relation to the nominal gross domestic product are to be reduced in accordance with the economic cycle', with the exception now represented by defence expenditures (Article 115(2)).

4.2 *Citizens' Rights*

The legal-cum-cultural change is patent in the field of individual rights. We all have traditionally been taught that constitutionalism protects citizens' rights and freedoms by setting limitations on political-economic power. If budgetary policies are supposed to contain and reduce expenditures, what is at stake is the scope of the welfare state, which means restricting and limiting the same rights.

With this, we are not saying that the Fabric points to restrict and limit constitutional rights. It is evident, however, that sovereign financial markets consider states' financial sustainability and stability as a security appended to the sovereign debt. And this requires a careful use of fiscal policies, as well as sober welfare policies. Coupled with the soft power of indicators, the maximisation of their interests runs counter to the idea of overtaxing the interests of transnational actors. As Minkler and Prakash argue, it is true that the 'effects of economic and social rights on poverty' are 'conditional on many other factors'. Among these factors, they number the credit market and the rule of law (in the sense of whether and how 'agents have confidence in and abide by the rules of society, and in particular the quality of contract enforcement' and 'property rights'), which constrain 'policymakers to enact, fund, monitor, and enforce poverty reducing policies'. In other terms, the coupled effect of the soft power of indicators and of the semantic shift are the 'constitutional

47 See Giacomo Delledonne, 'A Legalization of Financial Constitutions in the EU? Reflections on the German Spanish Italian and French Experiences' in Maurice Adams, Federico Fabbrini, and Pierre Larouche (eds), *The Constitutionalization of European Budgetary Constraints* (Hart 2014) 187; RP Schenke, 'The German Debt Brake' in Elena-Simina Tănăsescu and Eric Oliva (eds), *Constitutional Law and the EU Balanced Budget Principle* (Routledge 2021).

meta-rules, which we measure with our country specific constitutional economic and social right (ESR) provision variables'.[48] The impact is remarkable because, as said, the law is an open texture. Every single provision may visualise and convey different legal meanings and contents: Constitutional rights are often framed as 'directive principles', thus leaving political power to determine its effective scope and goal. ESRs are usually 'framed as directive principles in order to reflect their aspirational nature', as well as 'to indicate that the rights should be progressively realized over time as resources and capabilities grow'. If, by embedding a constant manufactured from the outside, the morally eligible foundation of a given community changes, so, too, should its scope, meaning, and implementation.[49]

Minkler and Prakash add that if ESRs 'are framed as enforceable law . . . constitutional provisions are negatively associated with poverty'.[50] From a legal standpoint, this predicament is erroneous. On the one hand, it should be argued that the semantic change has minor transactional costs than the formal replacement of legal provisions. In other terms, it is easier to trigger the paradigm shift without formally altering them. Who would indeed dare ask a political community to change the form, the pith, and the substance of their constitutional guarantees? Do we really think that they would be so keen on adopting investors' interests and, at the same time, giving up theirs? Do we think that they would throw the baby out with the bathwater? On the other hand, the meaning of constitutional provisions usually changes over time irrespective of their character (directive principles or enforceable law). To this extent, the constitutionalisation of fiscal/financial principles formally respects constitutional variety and diversity as regards rights and freedoms. Indicators and ratings will subsequently exert influence on states as to the result to be achieved, leaving to the national authorities the choice of form and methods to protect investors' interests, even if this unconsciously means shielding 'dominant economic forces . . . from democratic rule and popular accountability'.[51]

Whether constitutional provisions are directive principles or enforceable law, the results are the same. 'Balanced budgets' means correspondence between revenues and expenditures that influences the enjoyment of rights during good economic times. In other words, it allows the welfare state to work (1) during favourable economic cycles (i.e. revenues exceed or correspond to expenditures; benefits are sustainable); (2) if expansionary cycles are lacking, expenditures are possible, provided that, during favourable economic phases, the state has accumulated the necessary funds ('rainy day'

48 Lanse Minkler and Nishit Prakash, 'The Role of Constitutions on Poverty: A Cross-National Investigation' (2017) 45 Journal of Comparative Economics 563, 567.

49 Minkler and Prakash (n 48) 567.

50 Minkler and Prakash (n 48) 567.

51 Stephen Gill, 'New Constitutionalism, Democratisation and Global Political Economy' (1998) 10 Global Change, Peace and Security 23.

funds) to finance the fiscal deficit during 'bad economic times'.[52] The 'legal' applicability of the 'economic' principle of balanced budgets thus depends on whether it is enshrined in federal and regional constitutions, such as in Switzerland. The budget must be balanced both at the federal level (Article 126 of the Constitution) and at the cantonal level. For instance, the cantonal constitutions of St Gall, Solothurn, Grison, and Appenzell Outer-Rhodes prescribe that governments 'accumulate savings in order to equalize revenue fluctuations over the business cycle [and] to build up reserves in good times and to eliminate structural deficits'.[53] Likewise, in the United States of America, state constitutions require that expenditures match revenues: The 'golden' budgetary rule imposes that a surplus of revenues be accumulated as 'rainy day' funds 'that can cover what would otherwise be fiscal deficits in bad economic times'.[54] The pre-eminence of economic universals entails the superiority of finance and banking legal instruments on constitutional systems. In Latin America, for example, several constitutions, such as the Brazilian Constitution, have incorporated the so-called neoliberal orthodoxy (foreign investors protection, limitations to social policies and expenditures).[55]

4.3 *Public and Territorial Authorities*

The aforementioned process of semantic change has resulted in the thorough application of public finance budgetary principles to the whole public sector. To this extent, the constitutionalisation of the balanced budgets principle has re-organisational effects on public authorities – and, for what concerns us here, its territorial articulation – which must now comply with the golden rule. As a further outcome of the Factory, these changes affect fiscal (and financial) relations and are offshoots of economic-oriented representations of the law, which is now manufactured from the outside and promotes the global economic legal language 'spoken' by international financial actors.

As far as public debt is concerned, its sustainability and profitability depend on consolidated financial statements, whereby the state, like a holding company, displays all its activities to financial investors – a bit of a collateral, we said, for its 'distressed sovereign debt'. Again, this is a subtle way of impacting on state constitutions when it comes to managing legal – and

52 Mark Tushnet, *The Constitution of the United States of America: A Contextual Analysis* (2nd edn, Hart Publishing 2009) 161.

53 Gebhard Kirchgässner, 'Swiss Confederation' in Anwar Shah and John Kincaid (eds), *The Practice of Fiscal Federalism: Comparative Perspectives* (McGill-Queen's University Press 2007) 328.

54 Henning Bohn and RP Inman, 'Balanced-Budget Rules and Public Deficits: Evidence from the U.S. States' (1996) 45 Carnegie-Rochester Conference Series on Public Policy 13.

55 HA Alviar García, 'Neoliberalism as a Form of Authoritarian Constitutionalism' in HA Alviar García and Gunther Frankenberg (eds), *Authoritarian Constitutionalism: Comparative Analysis and Critique* (Edward Elgar 2019).

for what concerns us here, constitutional – changes from the 'outside'. Or – which is the same thing – this is a further way of crossing the public–private divide – with the pendulum swinging only towards the 'harsh economics of private law'.[56]

Unavoidably, this has determined what we comparatists label as an 'informal modification' of the constitutional order – that is, a change in how constitutions work without adopting any formal amendment to it. Owing to this semantic change, the public sector is an asset provided that it is performative – and it is performative 'only (if) it knows how to be efficient'.[57]

The change has a heavy impact on territorial governance. Indeed, the re-organisational effects of the balanced budgets principle appear to have taken on a completely new 'meaning of territorial autonomy . . . from a budgetary value to a flexible instrument' of public governance, which is now instrumental 'to the interests of the national framework in which it is inscribed and to the objectives that this framework establishes from time to time'.[58] Perhaps, territorial administration has become a tool for managing economic interests from the outside. The semantic change helps us explain the extent to which territorial autonomies have been undergoing a tremendous restructuring process in the last few decades. The process re-interprets the open texture of constitutional provisions in an unceasing search for administrative efficiency and economic attractiveness of state public authorities.

A further change impacts on the performance of territorial autonomy with the aim of boosting an efficient local administration. The constitutionalisation of the balanced budgets principle has the ability to modify the distribution of financial resources among levels of government. In federal constitutional contexts, for example, financial relations between national, subnational, and local levels are arranged in terms of revenues and expenditures, and these are usually complemented by solidarity (or equalisation) mechanisms providing additional funds aimed at increasing local fiscal capacity.[59] Hence, revenues, expenditures, and equalisation mechanisms allow the different levels of governments to fully finance and carry out their constitutional responsibilities. A *correspondence* is therefore established between revenues, expenditures, and competences, thus enabling subnational and local units to discharge such responsibilities without any interference from the central level of government – that is, according to what we may term the principle of *separation*. Separation enhances both fiscal

56 Muir Watt (n 23) 286.

57 See Fulvio Cortese, 'L'autonomia regionale? in Francesco Palermo and Sara Parolari' (eds), *Riforma costituzionale e Regioni. Riflessioni a prima lettura sul nuovo Titolo V della Costituzione* (EURAC 2015) 34. This change has several antecedents, among which is the so-called regulatory competition: Johanna Stark, *Law for Sale: A Philosophical Critique of Regulatory Competition* (Oxford UP 2016).

58 Cortese (n 57) 33.

59 That is, constituent units' ability to generate revenue. See, for example, HH Landreth, 'The Measurement of Local Fiscal Capacity' (1961) 16 J Finance 105.

responsibility and accountability of constituent units; at the same time, it preserves their constitutional autonomy.[60]

Both principles have undergone a remarkable shift with tremendous consequences on the constitutional regime and meaning of financial relations (i.e. the nexus between taxing, spending, and discharging responsibilities). The semantic shift is not related to the linguistic variety through which *correspondence* and *separation* display their function but, instead, impacts the lexical semantics of the legal language, that is, the function of the correspondence rule itself. This has also caused a shift from the 'legal' principles of *correspondence* and *separation* to the 'economic' principle of fiscal equivalence, whose application requires that funds and proceeds be definitively allocated at the central/national level of government, which is the only actor deemed capable of ensuring such efficiency.[61]

The linguistic change is apparent when it comes to the expression 'financial relations' (or its equivalents: 'distribution of finance', 'fiscal relations', 'financial (or fiscal) arrangements', 'fiscal federalism', 'fiscal' or 'financial constitution'), whose meaning depends on whether financial relations are examined through the lenses of economics or from a legal perspective. Again, the linguistic change has experienced the use (or perhaps abuse) of the expression 'fiscal federalism'. Although it is very common among political scientists and lawyers, we find its use very contentious, inasmuch as it pertains to public finance studies, and therefore denotes 'which functions and instruments are best centralized and which are best placed in the sphere of decentralized levels of governments'.[62]

Fiscal economists consider 'state and local finance as a field of research'[63] for the allocation of revenue and expenditure powers and address the following questions: '[W]hich taxes are best suited for use at the different levels of government?' '[P]laced in a context of a federalist government, should distribution be a national or a local responsibility?'[64] Questions like these denote

60 For more on these principles, see Matteo Nicolini, 'The Principles of Separation and Correspondence, the Comparative Method, and the Problem of Semantic Change' in Francesco Palermo and Alice Valdesalici (eds), *Comparing Fiscal Federalism* (Brill-Nijhoff 2018) 100.

61 In economic terms, centralisation is decisively apparent when it comes to the allocation of revenue powers (the so-called 'tax-assignment problem'): see RA Musgrave, 'Who Should Tax, Where and What?' in CE McLure (ed), *Tax Assignment in Federal Countries* (ANU Press 1983). For a critical approach to the tax-assignment problem, see also CE McLure, 'The Tax Assignment Problem: Ends, Means, and Constraints' (1998) 9 Public Budgeting and Financial Management 652; R Bird, 'Tax Assignment Revisited' in JG Head and RE Krever (eds), *The 21st Century: A Volume in Memory of Richard Musgrave* (Kluwer Law International 2009).

62 WE Oates, 'An Essay on Fiscal Federalism' (1999) 37 J Ec Lit 1120. The expression was firstly used in RA Musgrave, *The Theory of Public Finance* (McGraw-Hill 1959), and then in subsequent studies. See, for example, RA Musgrave, 'Economics of Fiscal Federalism' (1971) 10 Nebraska J Economics and Business 3; WE Oates, Fiscal Federalism (Harcourt Brace Jovanovich 1972).

63 Musgrave (n 62) 3.

64 Oates (n 62) 1125; RA Musgrave, 'Devolution, Grants, and Fiscal Competition' (1997) 11 J Ec Perspectives 65, 67.

fields of research that are very different from those characterising comparative federal studies. Public finance has a normative approach, and 'fiscal federalism' conveys a non-legal definition of financial relations; with its 'need for every collective good with a unique boundary', it establishes 'a match between those who receive the benefits of a collective good and those who pay for it'. 'This match we define as "fiscal equivalence"'.[65]

The expression does not consider legal features – in particular, the constitutional ones – related to the allocation of financial powers. Fiscal federal studies are aimed at maximising the efficiency of public policies and services by establishing an appropriate distribution of revenue powers. The expression denotes an approach that is different from financial relations and 'legal' fiscal federalism, which analyses the constitutional foundations of financial powers and the principles of correspondence and separation, that is, the mechanisms through which national and subnational levels appropriate funds to finance their constitutional responsibilities.

In this regard, 'fiscal federalism' is related to the principle of fiscal equivalence, surmising that legal financial relations must be governed by budgetary policies and economic theories. Public finance in general, and fiscal equivalence in particular, conveys the 'efficiency rule', that is, the optimisation of the allocation of proceeds, the strengthening of fiscal responsibility, as well as the promotion of an equilibrium between the estimates of revenues and expenditures. Evidently, the efficiency rule does not match 'legal' fiscal federalism, which upholds the idea that the budgetary position of federal and regional states should be balanced or in surplus.

The normative approach of public finance is not the result of the economic reflexes of the legal correspondence rule: As for the revenue side, *de facto* imbalances, social federalism, and democratic accountability are not considered necessary presuppositions that allow the allocative efficiency model to work. If we turn to the expenditure side, the public finance model is challenged by the lack of legal limitation in the exercise of spending powers. To sum up, both taxing and spending powers are in the hands of the political branches, and the effective amount of money to be raised by taxation and collected under the authority of law depends on the economic situation.

Consequently, economic 'fiscal federalism' changes the role attributed to the different tiers of government in the distribution of finance from the outside. The 'economic' approach to the correspondence rule focuses on the 'efficiency rule' for the best allocation of functions between the central and the decentralised levels of governments. This, however, does not legally define *which* are the decentralised levels of government concerned. It merely 'lays

65 Quotations are from Mancur Olson Jr, 'The Principle of "Fiscal Equivalence": The Division of Responsibilities Among Different Levels of Government' (1969) 59 Papers and Proceedings of the Eighty-First Annual Meeting of the American Economic Association 479, 482, 483, and 485, respectively.

out a general normative framework for the assignment of functions to different levels of governments and the appropriate fiscal instruments for carrying out these functions'.[66]

This change in the meaning of financial relations in general, and in the applicability of the principle of correspondence in particular, is threefold. Firstly, the shift is towards centralisation, which reflects the creation of a global legal language and common regulation of financial relations also in decentralised countries and markets. Secondly, there is a remarkable shift towards the efficiency rule, whose application requires that funds and proceeds be allocated at the central level of government. Thirdly, this is financially responsible *vis-à-vis* financial markets and international investors.

With its economic-oriented meaning, the change from the outside crosses the public/private divide again and is subsequently enforced under private law mechanisms. In this respect, these centralising trends must now cope with two new necessities. On the one hand, the 'correspondence rule' requires the application of the efficiency rule to the revenue–responsibilities equation and to the necessity of ensuring the homogeneity of economic and social conditions. On the other hand, this rule interweaves with the new 'legal' budgetary policy (i.e. budgetary positions must be balanced or in surplus) that percolates through the whole constitutional design.

This entails a reconfiguration of financial relations. The principle of correspondence now rests on the sustainability of what we may call 'financial equivalence' – that is, an asset that can be traded in global equity markets. Further, this imposes an extreme connection between the powers of levying taxes, imposing fees, and equalisation mechanisms to allow constituent units to fully discharge their constitutionally assigned responsibilities under the budgetary guardianship of an ever more pervasive central level of government.

5 The Remarkable Shift: The Rule of Law as Good Governance

5.1 *'Semantic Complexity': From Government to Governance*

The shift from the legal to the economic is more and more remarkable as far as the rule of law is concerned. As we shall see in this section, this legal concept is now applied when it comes to assessing efficient institutional changes.[67] In other terms, the rule of law has undergone a remarkable shift, that is, from *government* (as limitation of power) to *governance*. The latter refers to 'the performance of agents' (the states) that carry out 'the wishes of principals' (i.e. the actors of the Fabric maximising profits and applying laws manufactured

66 Oates (n 62) 1120–21.

67 See Mariana Mota Prado and MJ Trebilcock, *Advanced Introduction to Law and Development* (2nd edn, Edward Elgar 2021) 37, 48–50, and 52–66.

from the outside).[68] Within global contexts, the rule of law has become the driver promoting good governance, also acting as a 'guiding light', ensuring elevated economic performance.

From a legal perspective, however, the rule of law is neither the by-product of global international law nor a politico-economic driver. Before it became the shibboleth of global governance, it had a different legal meaning: It traditionally set constraints on political power in order to protect the rights and freedoms of the individuals. Although we shall concentrate on its meaning within the Anglo-British legal tradition, the expression has variants in other legal environments: Although they 'make reference to partially different concepts and principles', its German and French counterparts (the *Rechtsstaat* and the *État de droit*) purport the same goal the rule of law purports, that is, 'the overcoming of absolutism, due to the affirmation of citizens' rights of liberty and equality'.[69] Its historical lineage stretches back through the centuries, even before A. V. Dicey epitomised it in his seminal *Introduction to the Study of the Law of the Constitution*.[70] In the Middle Ages, for instance, Henry de Bracton considered that the king was limited by the law of the land.[71] Fortescue did the same in *De laudibus legum Angliae* (1471): When referring to fifteenth-century England, he wrote that the English king 'rules his people politically, because he himself is not able to change the laws without the assent of his subjects nor to burden an unwilling people with [a] strange imposition'; ruled, as they are, 'by laws that they themselves desire, they freely enjoy their goods, and are despoiled neither by their own king nor any other'.[72]

Royal power is clearly delimited, and the Anointed English Monarch is subject to the law of the land. No wonder, therefore, that, within the Anglosphere, the rule of law is 'considered as one of [the] most cherished political ideals – to protect people's property from these sorts of regulative incursions'.[73] This is not just a matter of jurisprudence, as one could easily infer from *Prohibitions del Roy*, *Petition of Rights*, and *Entick v Carrington*.[74] Rooted in the tradition

68 Francis Fukuyama, 'What Is Governance?' CGD Working Paper 314. Washington, DC: Center for Global Development, at 4 <www.cgdev.org/content/publications/detail/1426906 accessed 15 January 2025. See also Monateri and Balestrieri (n 13) 75–76.

69 Paolo Alvazzi Del Frate and Alberto Torini, 'Rule of Law Between the Seventeenth and Nineteenth Centuries' in Giuliano Amato et al. (eds), *Rule of Law vs Majoritarian Democracy* (Hart 2021) 12.

70 AV Dicey, *An Introduction to the Study of the Law of the Constitution* (8th edn, Macmillan 1915) 110.

71 'Ipse autem rex, non debet esse sub homine, sed sub Deo et sub lege, quia lex facit regem'. Henry de Bracton, *De Legibus Et Consuetudinibus Angliæ. Libri Quinque in Varios Tractatus Distincti* (Travers Twiss ed, CUP 2012) I, 8 at 38.

72 Sir John Fortescue, *De laudibus legum Angliae – In Praise of the Laws of England* (Shelly Lockwood tr, CUP 1997) Ch IX.

73 Jeremy Waldron, *The Rule of Law and the Measure of Property* (CUP 2012) 5.

74 See *Prohibitions del Roy* 12 Co Rep 63, 64–65; *Petition of Rights* 1628; *Entick v Carrington* (1765), 19 St Tr 1029; (1795) 95 ER 807.

of the common-law constitution, the principle can also be found in literary texts. James Harrington and Algernon Sidney, for example, confirmed that 'kings [are] within the power of the law, and the law [is] a guide to kings' and 'equally provide[s] for the good of king and people'.[75] Even John Bunyan relied heavily on the laws of England during his persecution and imprisonment: 'The old laws, which are the Magna Charta, the sole basis of the government of a kingdom, may not be cast away for the pet that is taken by every little gentleman against them'.[76] And the Leveller John Lilburne praised the common-law constitution at his trial for treason in 1649.[77]

To the best of our knowledge, the 'semantic complexity' of the rule of law became particularly apparent with the fall of the Berlin Wall and the end of the Cold War.[78] Indeed, 'after the seminal changes of the year 1989, it seemed as if democracy and the rule of law had established themselves as a universal model for the organisation and legitimation of public authority'.[79] As Versteeg and Ginsburg uphold in *Measuring the Rule of Law: A Comparison of Indicators* (2017), there was then a truly '[g]lobal effort to build the RoL'.[80] It is striking, however, how they explain how this shift occurred: 'The rule of law', they write, 'is an age-old political ideal that celebrates the limitation of arbitrary power, *but* it is also increasingly a transnational industry worth multiple billions of dollars'. What these authors do is commend the cause of such remarkable semantic change to an adversative 'but' (which we deliberately wrote in Italics) without any other consideration of the background (or even the factors) triggering the change.

What we know for certain is that the shift is historical and cultural: Within the Fabric of indicators, it is not the state that aims to protect its citizens' rights; what we have instead are '[b]ilateral aid donors, international financial institutions, and privately funded nongovernmental organizations' that 'dedicate substantial resources to building' the rule of law. It is an 'enterprise' (the development enterprise, we argue) that pursues 'various important goals and values, such as promoting justice, improving economic development, building democracy, and increasing international cooperation'.[81] The takeaway

75 James Harrington, *A Commonwealth of Oceana* (CUP 1992) 35. The quotation is from Algernon Sidney, *Discourses Concerning Government* [1698] (London: J. Darby 1704) 219.

76 John Bunyan, 'Israel's Hope Encouraged: Or, What Hope Is, And How Distinguished from Faith' in *The Works of the Eminent Servant of Christ, Mr John Bunyan, Minister of the Gospel, and Formerly a Pastor of a Congregation at Bedford*, vol 3 (4th edn, Edinburgh: David Ogilvy 1766) 380.

77 Diane Parkin Speer, 'John Lilburne: A Revolutionary Interprets Statutes and Common Law Due Process' (1983) 1 Law and History Review 276.

78 Luigi Lacchè, 'Rule of Law Metamorphoses in the Twentieth Century' in Giuliano Amato et al. (eds), *Rule of Law vs Majoritarian Democracy* (Hart 2021) 25.

79 Dieter Grimm, 'Rule of Law and Democracy' in Giuliano Amato et al. (eds), *Rule of Law vs Majoritarian Democracy* (Hart 2021) 61.

80 Versteeg and Ginsburg (n 15) 101.

81 All the quotations are from Versteeg and Ginsburg (n 15) 100.

message is that 'one of the striking features' of this development enterprise 'is the explicit embrace of law as an engine of development', as well as a malleable tool for national governance from the outside.[82]

5.2 *Predictability: The Rule of Law as an Indicator*

That the rule of law could (and still can) be functional to the development enterprise, as well as to fulfilling the purposes of the Fabric, is evident as regards globalisation. Particularly in the aftermath of the Cold War and the collapse of the Soviet Union in the late 1980s. Time was ripe to trigger the transition of several countries in Europe, Asia, and Africa towards an open society, which should conform with the rule of law.[83] Various economic and international actors started pointing to the possibilities that the inception of this democratisation waves might have had in terms of the economic enterprise. We have got used to localising trade and civilisation within globalised markets. Our Western minds describe them in accordance with a narrative of *superiority* and *progress*: The world was 'moving towards a global consensus, based on an integrated global economy, free markets, deregulation, privatisation, a minimal state subordinate to multilateral organisations, and international property rights for foreign investors'.[84] To this extent, the Fabric could provide its actors with several instruments that could possess a liberating force facilitating the harmonisation of laws, stimulating economic development, and promising an 'impending radiant future' to humanity.[85] The post–Cold War era thus offered new perspectives. It does not come as a surprise that global markets benefitted from the reopening of former communist countries (and their renovated legal spaces) to favour the smooth flows of goods, capital, and services across frontiers and national legal systems.

The reopening of territories did not mean rubbing borders out of maps. It solely required (and still requires) new legal geographies to enforce the *governance* endorsed by globalisation, that is, the outcome of spatial production stimulated by transnational actors. Henri Lefebvre highlighted that, as it is produced by socio (and legal) practices, even space is not immune from

82 Tor Krever, 'Quantifying Law: Legal Indicator Projects and the Reproduction of Neoliberal Common Sense' (2013) 34 Third World Quarterly 131.

83 On the rule of in Eastern Europe, see Anna Piekarska, 'Challenging the Rule of Law Universalism: Why Marxist Legal Thought Still Matters' (2023) 34 Law & Critique 269, 275; Smoki Musaraj, 'Indicators, Global Expertise, and a Local Political Drama: Producing and Deploying Corruption Perception Data in Post-Socialist Albania' in SE Merry, KE Davis, and Benedict Kingsbury (eds), *The Quiet Power of Indicators: Measuring Governance, Corruption, and Rule of Law* (CUP 2015); Mihaela Serban, 'Rule of Law Indicators as a Technology of Power in Romania' in SE Merry, KE Davis, and Benedict Kingsbury (eds), *The Quiet Power of Indicators: Measuring Governance, Corruption, and Rule of Law* (CUP 2015).

84 Krever (n 82) 133 terms this consensus 'the neoliberal consensus'.

85 Mikhaïl Xifaras, 'The Global Turn in Legal Theory' (2016) 29 Canadian Journal of Law & Jurisprudence 215, 216.

the exercise of the hegemony of the holders of global capital. They make 'use of it . . . on the basis of an underlying logic and with the help of the knowledge and technical expertise, of a "system"'.[86] To reach their goals, financial actors created this system with its admixture of cross-border regulatory systems matching their 'private ordering in the name of party autonomy'.[87] They also need to generalise their interests by promoting changes in national spaces.

The change was found in the very concept of predictability, that is, a core value that the rule of law would have probably secured. Citizens – Jeremy Waldron explains – 'need predictability in the conduct of their lives and businesses'. Evidently, what matters here is the conduct of businesses. In the reopening of territories and in the extension of capitalist markets to former socialist countries, predictability offered a mechanism that could make economic and financial 'freedom . . . possible', inasmuch as it allowed investors to 'know in advance how the law will operate, and how they must act to avoid its having a detrimental impact on their affairs'.[88] It became part of the broader *governance* (and law-making) process activated from the outside, because it could make the maximisation of profits less risky through the assessment of states' functioning against the interests pursued by privately made law. In other terms, the rule of law became a 'basic requirement . . . for a modern state',[89] because the good governance it promotes is made up of 'those legal institutions which provide predictability for private commerce and market-based business activity'.[90]

Not only does predictability mean economic growth and maximisation of profits, but it also has to do with the 'law matters' correlation underpinning both the discontinued *Doing Business Reports* and the 'law and finance' movement. The rule of law makes a given country attractive for foreign investors; through it, it is possible to evaluate the economic performance of legal systems by applying quantitative methodologies and numerical indicators. Among these, the most renowned is the WJP Rule of Law Index, that is, an indicator that evaluates 142 countries applying a variety of factors.[91] Likewise, the Worldwide Governance Indicators (WGI) gathers data from several sources to

86 Henri Lefebvre, *The Production of Space* (D Nicholson-Smith tr, Blackwell 1991) 11.

87 Horatia Muir Watt, 'The Relevance of Private International Law to the Global Governance Debate' in Horatia Muir Watt (ed), *Private International Law and Global Governance* (CUP 2014) 9.

88 Jeremy Waldron, *Thoughtfulness and the Rule of Law* (Harvard UP 2023) 37.

89 IFI Shihata, *The World Bank in a Changing World: Selected Essays* (Martinus Nijhoff 1991) 85.

90 Krever (n 82) 143.

91 World Justice Project, 'WJP Rule of Law Index', comprises eight factors (constraints on government powers, absence of corruption, open government, fundamental rights, order and security, regulatory enforcement, civil justice, criminal justice) <https://worldjusticeproject.org/rule-of-law-index/> accessed 15 January 2025. See Rene Urueña, 'Indicators and the Law: A Case Study of the Rule of Law Index' in SE Merry, KE Davis, and Benedict Kingsbury (eds), *The Quiet Power of Indicators: Measuring Governance, Corruption, and Rule of Law* (CUP 2015).

describe how the quality of governance is perceived across countries and over time.[92] There is also the Heritage Foundation's Index of Economic Freedom. Being created by a conservative US think tank, it has constructed its index with a 'conservative stance', which 'views the [Rule of Law] as one of the four core economic freedoms, together with limited government, regulatory efficiency, and open markets'.[93] There is then the Freedom House, a US NGO 'dedicated to the expansion of freedom around the world', whose rule of law 'is heavily focused on human rights'.[94]

In Chapter 2 we mentioned a further set of indicators, namely, the 'Ibrahim Index of African Governance' (IIAG). This is a managerial tool taking the form of a policy indicator that measures and monitors governance performance in African countries. In impacting on constitutional arrangements and the rule of law, the Ibrahim Index processes societal and cultural contexts within which the law is applied. This biennial index contains 81 indicators gathered around four categories of the IIAG (safety and rule of law; participation, rights, and inclusion; sustainable economic opportunity; and human development). Participation, rights, and inclusion, in turn, contain sub-categories (participation, rights, inclusion and equality, and women's equality), with the aim of grasping the context and avoiding the 'erasure of narratives' by indicators: Persons, places, communities, and territories are often considered striations and discrepancies to be removed from indexes.[95]

All these indicators are pre-indicators that mathematise the 'state of the art' across jurisdictions in terms of policy design and action, but they also aim to put pressure on countries to improve their legal environmental fitness, which will be visible in its next iteration and in reputational terms.

What we are saying is that, through the soft power of its indicators, the Fabric has twisted the rule of law into a measurable value-neutral legal concept that secures predictability on investment returns. The World Bank upholds that liberal democracy perfectly fits the new universals of global economic and financial dominance. The use of quantification allows us to measure, inter alia, 'global-transnational influences on constitutional human rights',[96] thus

92 World Bank Group, 'Worldwide Governance Indicators' (WGI). Data are drawn from a variety of sources (e.g. think tanks, international and nongovernmental organisations, and private actors) and then combined into aggregate indicators of six dimensions of governance for over 200 economies (voice and accountability, political stability and absence of violence/terrorism, government effectiveness, regulatory quality, rule of law, control of corruption) <www.worldbank.org/en/publication/worldwide-governance-indicators> accessed 15 January 2025.

93 Versteeg and Ginsburg (n 15) 107. See Heritage Foundation, 'Index of Economic Freedom' <www.heritage.org/index/> accessed 16 January 2025.

94 Versteeg and Ginsburg (n 15) 107. See 'Freedom House' <https://freedomhouse.org/report/freedom-world#Data> accessed 16 January 2025.

95 See 'Ibrahim Index of African Governance' <https://iiag.online/about.html> accessed 29 September 2024.

96 CJ Beck and others, 'Constitutions in World Society: A New Measure of Human Rights' in Gregory Shaffer, Tom Ginsburg and TC Halliday (eds), *Constitution-Making and Transnational Legal Order. Comparative Constitutional Law and Policy* (CUP 2019) 95.

assessing the 'quality' of the legal systems and ranking them, say, on how they actually implement human rights global indexes. Since they have built the current global system, only Western liberal democracies are 'compatible with economic success and [the] rapidly integrating information-intensive world economy'.[97]

In sum, linguistic and legal change are a projection of global financial dominance, and the rule of law expresses a performance measure which evaluates the efficiency of the legal systems and their attractiveness towards international investments: The more efficient the system, the more likely the investment, and the higher the economic return.[98]

6 Politics Manufactured From the Outside?

In *Quantifying Law: legal indicator projects and the reproduction of neoliberal common sense* (2013), Tor Krever thoughtfully reflects on the twists and turns of the rule of law within the fabric of global legal indicators. His is probably a harsh judgement, yet we think that some of his arguments resonate with the semantic shift that the rule of law has undergone in the last few decades.

As we saw in the previous section, the idea of measuring the legal environment (as well as its related fiscal policies) is servient to the predictability of financial investments, which undoubtedly depends upon the political (i.e. democratic) and legal performance of states. It is a way of reducing the risk that is inherent to every speculative venture. At the same time, it represents a shift 'from the political, the site of deliberation and choice, to the domain of technical expertise'. Indicators turn what we consider 'political questions about justice, equity and distribution' into 'technical questions about measurement and methodology'.[99]

Likewise, the presence of several 'rule of law' indicators has been functional to generalising the correlation between law and economic growth, thus establishing a solid cooperative intercourse between states and transnational economic actors. States are therefore more prone to accepting indicators in the area of the rule of law, because all of them operate *in the same direction*. The constellation of indicators precisely fulfils this function, reinforcing the idea that the rule of law is beneficial to economic attractiveness, as well as an output manageable from the outside. The 'rule of law' indicators indeed nest within each other in the same direction. In Chapter 2 we said that this is decisively patent in its four indicators (the WB's World Governance Indicators project (WGI), the Heritage Foundation, Freedom House, and the World

97 Miljia Kurki, 'Democracy and Conceptual Contestability: Reconsidering Conceptions of Democracy in Democracy Promotion' (2010) 12 International Studies Review 366; Tom Ginsburg, 'Authoritarian International Law?' (2020) 114 AJIL 221.

98 Daniel Oto-Peralía and Diego Romero-Ávila, *Legal Traditions, Legal Reforms and Economic Performance. Theory and Evidence* (Springer 2017) 85–119 and 121–35.

99 Krever (n 82) 144.

Justice Project), which 'are remarkably similar to each other' – and probably capture its essence.[100] They are similar – we repeat here – because, by nesting within each other *in the same direction*, they fit into the 'Factory' and reach its desired ends.

Which leads us to consider a further predicament that Krever outlines in *Quantifying Law*. The Factory aims to reach the legal environmental uniformity required by its actors and their constants. This is true to the extent that, nesting within each other, indicators give us a fairly unambiguous idea of what 'the neoliberal rule of law' is: It is an admixture of legal toolkits reflecting 'the ideal of the standard'; as such, they 'are treated as the technical necessities of any modern and developed legal system'. Equality, democracy, judicial independence, and lack of corruption (to name just a few) become 'naturalised and reified, no longer understood as socially produced but rather as fixed and immutable'.[101]

There is a visible reduction in political discretion. Not only do all these pre-indicators nest within each other, but they also show all countries the direction they need to take in economic, financial, and fiscal policies. Also, in environmental terms. When tackling climate change, indicators advocate for the convergence towards common universal standards of sustainable development, measuring, inter alia, the impact of climate change mitigation policies. Coupled with the scientific state of mind, state–investor cooperative intercourse allows us also to assess the 'environmental quality' of legal systems and rank them, say, on how they actually implement global policies indexes, such as the 'Climate Change Performance Index' (CCPI), the MSCI 'Climate Change Index', and the 'Common Sense Climate Index'.[102] But the measurement of the rule of law may also benefit from the 'Good Country' Index, which assesses each country's contribution 'to the common good of humanity, and what it takes away, relative to its size'.[103]

As we infer from the aforementioned indices, the fairly unambiguous idea of the neoliberal rule of law is Western-related. In assuming that state policies and strategies are generalised throughout the world, these indicators require a common standard that is roughly the same, say, in the Global North and in the

100 Versteeg and Ginsburg (n 15) 100.

101 Krever (n 82) 144. The rule of law is thus instrumental to the development enterprise: Pastor y Camarasa (n 2) 59–61.

102 See the 'Climate Change Performance Index' (CCPI) <www.climate-change-performance-index.org> accessed 17 January 2025; 'MSCI Climate Change Index' <www.msci.com/climate-change-indexes> accessed 17 January 2025; 'The Common Sense Climate Index' <https://data.giss.nasa.gov/csci> accessed 17 January 2025.

103 Anholt & Co., 'Good Country' Index <https://goodcountry.org/index/about-the-index/> accessed 16 January 2025. The index assesses contributions by perusing 35 category ranks in the following areas: contributions to science and technology, contributions to culture, contributions to international peace and security, contributions to world order, contributions to planet and climate, contributions to prosperity and equality, contributions to health and well-being.

Global South. The rule of law thus becomes a set of legal toolkits manufactured from the outside that can perfectly be coupled with our legal-deterministic correlation. If we bear in mind Petersen and Chatziathanasiou's predicament examined in Chapter 2, the rule of law is an ideal standard that is in a close relationship (and correlation) with democracy and economic performance. In our legal (i.e. deterministic) understanding of causality, we assume that the rule of law complements liberal democracy as the form of government that does boost economic growth and development. No wonder that the 'rule of law' toolkit is set down in the so-called Copenhagen criteria (now enshrined in Article 2 of the EU Treaty), establishing the legal requirements for the admission of new states into the EU, which are also constitutional constraints.[104]

The principles set forth therein (stability of institutions guaranteeing democracy; the rule of law; human rights; respect for, and protection of, minorities; the existence of a functioning market economy; and the capacity to cope with competitive pressure and market force within the Union) indeed refer to the prototypical Western conception of democracy, that is, 'the *liberal democratic model* of democracy':[105] '[T]he classical nineteenth-century balance of power system' is 'dominated by constitutional democracies, notably the United States and member states of the European Union, which requires democracy as a condition of accession'.[106]

However multifaceted the society may appear, and however tremendous the innovations may be in order to cope with complexity, the rule of law seems to propose changes that are not only consistent but also coherent with the original conception of democracy that it is being incorporated into the indices. In fact, constitutional systems are democratic not only because they are implemented through manifold forms of democracy but also because these forms are coherent with the theoretical foundations promoting institutional change, revealing the democratic character as inherent to the same constitutional system.

When, through the soft power of indicators, the Factory promotes a paradigm for innovation, the proposed paradigm coincides with that of liberal democracy: '[T]he one thing that has been almost completely absent from the 50 or so cases of attempted democratization since 1974 is experimentation beyond the basic institutions of liberal democracy'.[107] Rule of law, political accountability, efficient governmental action, protection of fundamental rights, and a market economy are both presuppositions and reflections of

104 See European Council, Presidency Conclusions European Council, 21–22 June 1993. Copenhagen, Denmark <http://europa.eu/rapid/press-release_DOC-93-3_en.htm?locale=en> accessed 9 May 2017.

105 Kurki (n 97) 365.

106 RO Keohane, 'Nominal Democracy? Prospects for Democratic Global Governance' (2015) 13 Int'l J Const L 343, 344.

107 PC Schmitter, 'More Liberal, Preliberal, or Postliberal'? (1995) 6 Journal of Democracy 15, 16.

liberal democracy. Our state–investor cooperative intercourse is thus legally limited in its powers, and its authority or legitimacy depends on its observing these limitations, which also constrain its ability to promote legal and institutional change.

In sum, liberal democracies and constitutions perfectly fit the development enterprise: 'Western liberal democracies have acted together to construct the current system that enables the global economy to operate'[108] and are thus 'the only viable societal model left, for only they are compatible with economic success and [the] rapidly integrating information-intensive world economy'.[109]

7 The Risks of Economic Democracy

The idea that, like the law, democracy can be manufactured from the outside raises several objections.

The first one is related to the flaw in the Fabric we examined in Chapter 2. Indicators, we clarified there, usually promote the generalisation of Western derivatives. Setting a (global) ideal standard of the rule of law (and a legal constant manufactured from the outside) is nothing else than a disturbing replica of the colonial approach. No wonder, therefore, that this has triggered the 'Global South critique', which is often used to protect the 'Global South version' of human rights and its own rule of law.[110]

Again, what the Fabric takes too lightly is the context where indicators exercise their soft, albeit mighty, power – that is, the context as the recipient of the (rule of) law manufactured from the outside. If public finance budgetary policies are now economic reflections of constitutional economic democracy, constraints and limitations are set by external actors, which also establish new procedural and substantive limitations on democratic environments. Indeed, if 'constitutional (economic) democracy' merely designates a system of governance according to which political decisions are taken in terms of the constitution, economic democracy prescribes the terms and the conditions under which these decisions may be made. This is what is also called 'nominal democracy', that is, a regime that 'meets democratic standards on the surface and embodies the rhetoric of democracy but lacks the content. Transnational and trans-governmental elite networks can play valuable roles in world politics, but they do not constitute democracy in the classic sense'.[111] By contrast, communities require an effective rule of law with protection of individual rights; the existence of a vibrant civil society whose discussions are heard throughout

108 James Bohman, *Democracy across Borders. From Dêmos to Dêmoi* (The MIT Press 2010) 28.

109 Kurki (n 97) 366.

110 Ran Hirschl, *Comparative Matters. The Renaissance of Comparative Constitutional Law* (OUP 2014) 207. For some example of the Global South critique, see Matteo Nicolini, 'Methodologies of Comparative Law: Universalistic Approach' in *Max Planck Encyclopaedia of Comparative Constitutional Law* (2nd edn, OUP 2023) at 55.

111 Keohane (n 106) 344.

the polity; substantial governmental transparency and procedures to ensure that leaders defend their policies in public, along with some opportunities for confidential discussions to promote compromise.[112]

The same holds valid for climate change, which is 'an environmental problem that is characterized by extreme heterogeneity'.[113] Even when perused to create contextual responses, indicators-related mitigation strategies tackle climate change in a similar way only superficially. Like rule-of-law indicators, climate change indicators resonate with universalism, inasmuch as they reconcile scientific objectivity and measurement with real-world tests. Likewise, climate change indicators might also deliberately omit data and variables, notwithstanding their relevance in real-world assessments. And such omissions may also trigger a strabismus in metrics, which unavoidably affects the reliability of their outlook. Again, this type of strabismus may prevent them from scratching the surface of the data and realising that there are concrete signs of dangers, if not of an irremediable ecological catastrophe.

112 Keohane (n 106) 344.

113 Cinnamon Carlarne and Daniel Farber, 'Law Beyond Borders: Transnational Responses to Global Environmental Issues' (2012) 1 Transnat Env L 13, 19.

4 The International Financial Architecture

Financial History and Evolution

1 The Onset of the International Financial Architecture

In the Introduction we saw how the secularisation of the state, together with the separation of moral principles from legal arguments, is at the core of the old world. For what concerns us here, it is the world of Kelsen where codifications (and, more broadly, the coding of assets through the law) mattered. Likewise, Pistor's world is one where private and public interests are made legal and vindicated by virtue of coding. Today, as this chapter assumes, the new architecture of contemporary financial markets – or, better, financial systems – is explicitly based on sustainability; decisions are taken at the 'periphery' (the constellation of private orderings, which is transnational law) rather than at the apex of a decadent Westphalian state. This is due to the absence of a central planner or supreme architect of the financial system.[1]

The international financial architecture and international financial law emerged as a response to global economic challenges and the need for a coordinated approach to financial stability, economic development, and the regulation of international financial markets. More specifically, the Latin American debt crisis of the 1980s, the Asian Financial Crisis of 1997, and its spillover effect in Eastern Europe in 1998 exposed the vulnerabilities existing in the international financial system, including weak regulatory frameworks, lack of transparency in financial markets, and inadequate risk management by financial institutions. The response to these crises led to the development of international financial standards or soft law standards and the recognition of the need for a global regulatory framework. Indeed, international financial law evolved as a framework of norms, standards, and practices aimed at ensuring financial stability, market integrity, and the protection of global financial systems. Key developments include the emergence of soft law, as it has been explained in our book and will be addressed further here and in Chapter 5 with an examination of international insolvency law. Unlike traditional international law, in fact, international financial law relies heavily on soft law instruments

1 See Ch 2 and 5.

DOI: 10.4324/9781003304333-5

that influence state behaviour and financial regulation. And soft law is often created through legal indicators, as we shall see as far as the development of cross-border interests is concerned.[2]

Therefore, this chapter represents an introductory analysis of how the international financial regulation was born, the issues it sought to address, the role of standard-setting institutions, and why they matter. To achieve this goal, we need to start from the birth of the Bretton Woods system and outline the peculiar historical background that has led to its final adoption.

2 The Bretton Woods System at the Root of the International Financial Architecture

After World War II, the Allied powers met at the United Nations Monetary and Financial Conference, held in Bretton Woods, New Hampshire, in July 1944, and negotiated different agreements in order to redesign the global economic order.

The main objectives were to prevent future crises after the Great Depression of 1929 and, particularly, to design a sustainable economic system capable of avoiding wars.[3] To this end, the Bretton Woods agreements[4] created two international organisations, namely, the International Monetary Fund (IMF, or Fund) and the International Bank of Reconstruction and Development (World Bank Group), with the aim of addressing the fluctuating exchange rates and the currency devaluations that had taken place in the 1920s and the 1930s, respectively.

With the following words, Henry Morgenthau addressed the delegates at the opening of the 1944 Bretton Woods conference. And his remarks still resonate today:

> Prosperity has no fixed limits. It is not a finite substance to be diminished by division. On the contrary the more of it that other nations enjoy, the

2 See Ch 5.

3 Ross P Buckley, *International Financial System: Policy and Regulation* (Kluwer Law International 2008) 3–14. Specifically, the author highlights that, from 1873 until World War I, the economic conditions were favourable due to increasing trade agreements between states, but the decade after World War I was determined by 'isolationism between countries and declining trade and capital flows, and this led to the Great Depression of 1929. The Depression in many ways persisted until the advent of World War II. So, it was to the forefront of the minds of those who designed the post-was system'.

4 Buckley (n 3) 3. In particular, the Bretton Woods negotiations were based on proposals inspired by two important economists of the time: Keynes and White. They were intellectuals that belonged to the most influential Allied powers of that time, namely, the United Kingdom and the United States. In the end, the proposal that largely inspired the Bretton Woods negotiation process was modelled on White's approach that was mainly centred on the establishment of a fund to regulate exchange rate stability and a global bank for reconstruction and development. The choice of following White's proposal was based on the fact that the United States was the dominant partner in the wartime alliance and strongest economic power.

> more each nation will have for itself. . . . Prosperity like peace is indivisible. We cannot afford to have it scattered here or there among the fortunate or to enjoy it at the expense of others. Poverty, where it exists, is menacing to us all and undermines the well-being of each of us. It can no more be localised than war.[5]

The main instrument to achieve exchange stability was a system of fixed exchange rate parity enshrined in Article IV of the IMF Articles of Agreement. The parties that were members of the Fund would undertake to maintain official par values for their currencies, expressed in gold or US dollars. The par value could be changed only in case of 'fundamental disequilibrium' in a country's balance of payments,[6] and any divergence in excess of 10% from initial parity would require IMF approval. The members of the IMF furthermore consented under Article VIII to the implementation of a system of conversion for their currencies. As a result, the final removal of controls over currency transactions, combined with a predictable system of exchange rates, was intended to promote international trade. Rather than the World Bank Group, which was designed as an international actor whose main aim was to alleviate global poverty, the IMF became by far the most important institution for the functioning of the international financial system. The main objectives of the IMF, as agreed at Bretton Woods, are now enshrined in Article 1 of the Articles of Agreement:

> A) To promote international monetary cooperation through a permanent institution, which provides the machinery for consultation and collaboration on international monetary problems.
> B) To facilitate the expansion and balanced growth of international trade, and to contribute thereby to the promotion and maintenance of high levels of employment and real income and to the

5 Address by Henry Morgenthau Jr (US Treasury Secretary and Permanent Secretary of the Conference) at the Inaugural Plenary Session, 1 July 1944, *United Nations Monetary and Financial Conference, Bretton Woods, New Hampshire, July 1 to July 22, 1944: Final Act and Related Documents* (US Government Printing Office 1944).

6 The *balance of payments* is an accounting record of all economic transactions between residents of a country and the rest of the world over a specific period, typically a year or a quarter. A balance of payments deficit occurs when the total payments made to other countries (outflows) exceed the total receipts from other countries (inflows) across these accounts. Components of the balance of payments are the current account, the capital account, and the financial account. The *current account* comprises records of trade in goods and services, income flows (e.g. dividends, interest), and unilateral transfers (e.g. foreign aid, remittances). The *capital account* relates to records of capital transfers, such as debt forgiveness and the transfer of ownership of fixed assets. The *financial account* comprises records of cross-border investments, including foreign direct investment, portfolio investments (stocks and bonds), and changes in foreign reserves. A balance of payments deficit means that a country spends more on foreign transactions than it earns. This can result in an accumulation of liabilities to foreign entities or a drawdown of the country's foreign currency reserves to finance the deficit.

development of the productive resources of all members as primary objectives of economic policy.

C) To promote exchange stability, to maintain orderly exchange arrangements among members, and to avoid competitive exchange depreciation.

D) To assist in the establishment of a multilateral system of payments in respect of current transactions between members and in the elimination of foreign exchange restrictions which hamper the growth of world trade.

E) To give confidence to members by making the general resources of the Fund temporarily available to them under adequate safeguards, thus providing them with opportunities to correct maladjustments in their balance of payments without resorting to measures destructive of national or international prosperity.

F) In accordance with the above, to shorten the duration and lessen the degree of disequilibrium in the international balances of payments of members.[7]

These objectives were far too ambitious and/or difficult to apply in practice. The possibility of modifying the par value system was limited, and the system itself was rigid, especially considering that most countries were reluctant to devalue their currencies as a response to external imbalances. This is because the devaluation process was seen as an indirect admission of economic failure that could expose those countries to currency speculation and lead to capital flight.[8] Therefore, the initial objectives of Bretton Woods in terms of promoting international trade were not fulfilled due to the formal rigidity of a system which led countries to adopt or maintain capital controls in order to manage foreign exchange risk.

For these reasons, although this first implementation of Bretton Woods partially prevented volatility in currency markets,[9] in the early 1970s, US President Nixon eliminated the Bretton Woods fixed exchange rate parity with

7 International Monetary Fund, 'Articles of Agreement of the International Monetary Fund' <www.imf.org/external/pubs/ft/aa/index.htm> accessed 27 January 2025.

8 Buckley (n 3) 7, according to whom the limit of a rigid exchange rate parity was more evident with the growth of capital mobility as well as following two important political events: the Cold War, which created limitations to the level of economic cooperation that could be achieved, and decolonization in the 1950s and 1960s, which resulted in the creation of new nations, such as Asia and Africa. These latter were highly interested in benefiting from the World Bank funds, but they could not apply for those funds without firstly being official members of the IMF. This resulted in an evident limitation.

9 Alexander Kern, Dhumale Rahul, and Eatwell John, *Global Governance of Financial Systems: The International Regulation of Systemic Risk* (OUP 2006) 21. According to the authors, 'the Bretton Woods framework sought to avoid the economic disaster of the interwar period when microeconomic instability spread like contagion through the financial sector and destabilized the macro economy. Those lessons were now embodied in appropriate policies and institutions. Important among these institutions were powerful regulatory structures and interventionist central banks dedicated to the reduction of systemic risk'.

gold, and the Bretton Woods system as it had been first designed was overturned. This was the start of a process of privatisation of foreign exchange risk.[10]

Specifically, under the original Bretton Woods legal framework, each member of the IMF was obliged to pay the Fund at least 25% of the quota in gold or US dollars and the remainder in the member's own currency. This compelled the national banks of non-reserve countries to peg their currency to the dollar and to keep sufficient dollar reserves in order to intervene in their currencies by buying or selling dollars to maintain fixed exchange rates. Hence, in the aftermath of the 1970s, banks started to implement hedging strategies to diversify their investment portfolios.[11] Consequently, governments began to deregulate their financial markets, with the main objective of allowing banks to diversify their investments as well as manage financial risks more efficiently.

However, privatising financial risks contributed in the long term to a process of its socialisation: risks were socialised first as bail-out procedures first and then as bail-in resolution, which made international financial markets more permeable to systemic risk.[12] The clearest example of this privatisation can be identified in the conflict of interest of rating agencies that occurred during the 2007–2010 global financial crisis. Before this, it was believed that market forces could effectively provide discipline for rating agencies,[13] but one of the main causes of the 2007 credit bubble of mortgage-backed securities was in fact created by 'private' ratings assigned to 'private' clients.[14]

Finally, in this changing environment, the role of the IMF was also subverted. Now the IMF is

> no longer a stabilisation fund but has instead become a broader international financial institution focused on debtor nation crisis management, surveillance, conditional financial support and technical assistance.[15]

10 Kern and others (n 9) 20.

11 Kern and others (n 9) 22.

12 Peter Nunnenkamp, 'Liberalisation and Regulation of International Capital Flows: Where the Opposite Meet' in Reiner Grote and Thilo Marauhn (eds), *The Regulation of International Financial Markets: Prospective and Reform* (CUP 2006) 262.

13 Joel Trachtman, *International Law and Politics (The Library of Essays in International Relations)* (Routledge 2008).

14 Committee of European Securities Regulators Press Release, 'CESR Advises the European Commission to Take Steps and Offers Its Proposals to Enhance the Integrity and Quality of the Rating Process' (19 May 2008) <www.esma.europa.eu/document/press-release-cesr-advises-european-commission-take-steps-and-offers-its-proposal-enhance> accessed 27 January 2025.

15 Buckley (n 3) 10.

This is because, at the global level, the financial system lacks a common and uniform bankruptcy or insolvency regime, which is universally applicable; nor does it have a single financial regulator or a lender of last resort capable of exercising the same functions of national competent authorities or national central banks.

To sum up, the process can be described as the beginning of globalisation and internationalisation of financial markets in modern economies by the implementation of liberal policies; this phenomenon can be understood as a new paradigm entailing the definition of a new phenomenology of contemporary financial markets which can be represented as a complex system.[16]

3 Market Failure and Systemic Risk

The most important feature of financial markets today is their integration and globalisation, made possible by rapid technological improvements. As Buckley suggests, the globalisation era finds

> its fullest expression in global capital flows and capital markets. The level of financial integration within, and across, the international economy is high and increasing because capital is perfectly suited to a global market – it moves around the world at the touch of a keyboard, and in response to information that comes in, principally, on a computer screen.[17]

The integration of markets contributes to their intimate connection and interdependence, and their global nature makes them international. Capital flows are no longer restricted to national borders, and financial risk is diversified through cross-border investments. In other words, in global financial markets today, space and time are irrelevant, and this revolution has been achieved mainly by liberal policies and deregulation and the reformation of the initial Bretton Woods system.

As noted, there is no proof that the lack of domestic capital controls in terms of inflows and outflows can make one country more prosperous than another.[18] The most contentious question today, especially in the aftermath of the financial crisis of 2007–2010, is whether regulation or deregulation can still be considered as one of the main triggers for a financial crisis. In fact,

16 To this end, financial markets are complex systems, as outlined by Daniele D'Alvia in *The Speculator of Financial Markets. How Financial: How Financial Innovation and Supervision Made the Modern World* (Palgrave Macmillan 2023); 'Risk, Uncertainty, and the Market: A Re-Thinking of Islamic and Western Finance' (2020) 16 Int'l J L Context 339; *Mergers, Acquisitions and International Financial Regulation: Analysing Special Purpose Acquisition Companies* (Routledge 2021); 'Law and the Market: Private Actors and Self-Regulation "Towards a New Role of Public International Law"' (2018) 29 Eur Business L R 929.

17 Buckley (n 3) 16.

18 Nunnenkamp (n 12) 262.

today's regulatory paradigm seems to have shifted once again towards deregulation, especially following Trump's election win in November 2024.

For these reasons, if the nature of today's financial markets is global, the nature of a financial crisis is global too, and it can potentially affect every single sector of the financial markets. Consequently, the classic and rhetorical question is whether markets can achieve efficiency by themselves or regulation is needed in order to guarantee, or at least promote, a national economic order.

It has already been said that the global financial crisis of 2007–2010 is connected to the internationalisation of financial markets, as well as to the privatisation of financial risk and the emergence of systemic risk. Indeed, in global financial markets, issuers may be interested in raising funds outside their local or domestic capital market due to the process of globalisation and internationalisation of markets.[19]

There are different justifications for raising funds outside the local market (i.e. from an investment diversification perspective to a cost funding advantage). However, it is important to bear in mind that the motivations for raising funds generally follow the classification of 'completely segmented' or 'completely integrated' capital markets that represents what Modigliani and Fabozzi[20] termed 'world capital market' as their ideal representation. As opposed to the 'world capital market', the 'real capital market' can face hurdles or specifications, such as diversity in regulatory provisions, tax regimes, foreign exchange rates, and many other variables that can effectively hinder and frustrate the possibility of raising new funds abroad in certain primary markets. They might also lead to an identification of the 'real capital market' as 'mildly segmented' or 'mildly integrated'.

The pragmatic concerns that exist in 'reality' can change the perception of how issuers approach primary capital markets for funding. This is why in global financial markets, speculation can be seen potentially as the rational choice of the investor rather than as a form of exploitation of resources for the self-interested achievement of profit. In other words, today an under-regulated market can be perceived as a suitable environment for a firm to reduce costs, so that states under globalisation should protect themselves against 'imported fraud', and this can lead to regulatory competition concerns. This phenomenon has also been defined as a 'race to the bottom' or regulatory arbitrage, where companies tend to transfer their investments to states that offer favourable economic conditions in order to reduce wage costs.[21]

19 Indeed, the internationalisation of capital markets started with the petrodollar recycling in the 1970s but reached its peak in the 1990s, after the economic reforms of Thatcher in England and Reagan in the United States. See Ravi Tennekoon, *The Law and Regulation of International Finance* (LexisNexis 1991).

20 Frank Fabozzi and Franco Modigliani, *Capital Markets: Institutions and Instruments* (2nd edn, Prentice Hall 1996) 125–57.

21 Karl-Heinz Ladeur, 'Globalization and the Conversion of Democracy to Polycentriy Networks: Can Democracy Survive the End of the Nation State?' in Karl-Heinz Ladeur (ed), *Public Governance in the Age of Globalization* (Ashgate 2004) 89.

The global nature of capital markets gives rise to two further consequences. Firstly, the openness of financial markets today to going beyond national borders makes financial risk systemic, and secondly, the information asymmetry that dominates the market can constitute, at least potentially, a theoretical justification for an effective need of regulatory responses.[22]

Although there is no agreed definition of systemic risk,[23] the main feature that our book aims to highlight is to understand systemic risk as the product of the mispricing of financial risk, through which private actors who create financial risks do not internalise its cost but spread it onto society. In sum, this new connotation of financial risk is seen as a form of negative externality similar to pollution.[24] In addition, in the attempt to reduce financial risk in complex financial systems, banks and corporations have started to use financial innovations to diversify risks and have engaged in cross-border activities offering a wide range of financial services that normally incorporate insurance and securities activities as well as traditional banking facilities. These are defined as financial conglomerates,[25] which call for supervision due to the contagion risk and the cascades-failure effect that might arise in case of their collapse.[26]

For this reason, overexposure to financial risk, its privatisation, and the 'socialisation' of its cost make global markets endemically destined to fail or collapse. This is a central argument for regulation, and at the same time, it outlines the need for an uncertainty-aversion paradigm, although the latter assumption fully reveals the paradox of modern economies that still reject uncertainty and try to govern it, though its full negation or mitigation can translate into a significant reduction in, or even elimination of, profit as well as a reduction in the creativity of market participants in relation to financial innovations.

The endemic failure of markets shows a need for regulation and supervision. To this end, it is essential to outline what financial regulation is in modern economies and how the paternalistic role of the state has been irreversibly modified towards a new global governance paradigm in financial markets.

If internal capital controls are reduced or eliminated, then domestic firms gain more room for taking financial risks. This theoretically is not an issue as long as there is perfect competition and information in the market. However,

22 JE Stiglitz, 'Government Failure vs. Market Failure: Principles of Regulation' in EJ Balleisen and DA Moss (eds), *Government and Markets Toward a New Theory of Regulation* (CUP 2010) 16.

23 Kern et al. (n 9) 24–33.

24 Kern et al. (n 9) 24.

25 International Organisation of Securities Commissions, *Principles for the Supervision of Financial Conglomerates* (Cmd 1992) para 2. According to the report, 'there are three different kinds of financial conglomerate where this might be the case: i) groups where securities business is the predominant activity; ii) groups where securities business is not predominant activity, although the predominant business is financial (e.g. banking or insurance); iii groups where the predominant activity is commercial or industrial'.

26 The Joint Forum, *Principles for the Supervision of Financial Conglomerates* (Cmd 2012) para 2.

markets always register a lack of the latter, so that 'financial markets will . . . be affected to some degree of adverse selection, moral hazard, principal-agent problems, and herding behaviour'.[27] Furthermore, the lack of theoretical grounds for the justification that self-regulated markets can achieve market equilibrium alone has always supported the argument for top-down government interventions. To this end, the theory of Smith that markets can be efficiently self-governed by an 'invisible hand'[28] has always been contrasted to the Westphalian system,[29] that is, a model based on a paternalistic view of the state, in which regulation is imposed from the top as an expression of traditional state sovereignty. According to this paternalistic view, the state is also capable of influencing the expansion of domestic markets by legal impositions and internal capital controls.

Nonetheless, one of the most relevant features of financial markets today is that markets are not exclusively based on state regulation, but especially on private actors' decisions and inter-agency forums that give rise to hybrid forms of regulation. In other words, the current dynamics of market governance are global rather than international. Additionally, this trend has given rise, *inter alia*, to democratic, discriminatory, and participatory concerns,[30] as well as to the establishment of an ambiguous legal status for such private organisations or non-state actors.[31]

Apart from the political issues that hybrid regulation gives rise to, which are the result of privatisation of financial risk, the hybrid feature of the system

27 Barry Eichengreen, Michael Mussa, et al., 'Capital Account Liberalization: Theoretical and Practical Aspects' (1998) IMF Occasional Paper n. 172.

28 In particular, the idea of an 'invisible hand' has been borrowed by Smith from Shakespeare, Daniel Defoe, and others. It is a thinking that reminds us how human beings as well as animals are governed by instincts. These natural instincts spur us to create order and progress in communities. Specifically, the progress becomes the natural outcome of a general instinct that is not determined by conscious motives. In *The Wealth of Nations*, Smith illustrates whether legal restrains on trade would harmonise private interests with public ones. Smith concludes that no restrain is desirable because business traders prefer to keep their capital at work in their domestic country. This because in Smith's view merchants know domestic laws, and also they trust more people of their national system. This means that more capitals will stay with Britain, therefore, favouring the economic growth of the country and generating a greater number of jobs and security. In Smith's words, '[b]y preferring the support of domestic to that of foreign industry [the merchant] intends only his own security; and by directing that industry in such a manner as its produce may be of the greatest value, he intends only his own gain, and he is in this, as in many other cases, led by an invisible hand to promote an end which was no part of his intention': Adam Smith, *The Wealth of Nations* (Harriman House 2009) 293.

29 Nunnenkamp (n 12), who mentions private actors, such as the IOSCO, which is a private organisation; the International Association of Insurance Supervisors; or the Basle Committee, which is hosted by the Bank for International Settlements. These actors have reframed the classic public–private divide.

30 Nunnenkamp (n 12).

31 Chris Brummer, 'Why Soft Law Dominates International Finance – and Not Trade' in JH Jackson, Thomas Cottier and RM Lastra (eds), *International Law in Financial Regulation and Monetary Affairs* (OUP 2012) 95.

makes the involvement of private actors a fundamental instance of regulatory responses, as opposed to governments or governmental agencies, which are part of the public sphere. Indeed, it has been noted that the Westphalian model of regulation, in its traditional guise, has failed from several angles in a post-regulatory world:[32] in its inability to design effective legal rules for addressing complex social problems (instrument failure), its incapacity to implement rules (implementation failure), and its inability to persuade regulated entities and individuals to comply with those rules (motivational failure). In other words, nowadays it is not possible to rely exclusively on states' intervention in governing complex financial markets or systems, where it can be said that the final outcome of the regulation processes derives from a mixture of sources, especially self-regulatory responses developed by the private industry.

In light of this, the role of government is overturned from the classical conception that it acts externally and outside of the markets, although the financial crisis of 2007–2010 has provided evidence for opposite conclusions,[33] and one could say there is a counter-trend with the re-emergence of a new Westphalian system that aims to reframe and disempower the traditional role of independent agencies in financial regulation. Indeed, according to other scholars,[34] although a new role for the government as an entity external to the market can be identified, there are also clear instances where governments exercise a foundational role, which is internal to markets.

For this reason, it can be misleading to illustrate the global governance of financial markets as a public–private divide *tout court*, as if governments and markets were relegated, respectively, to the public and the private spheres with society internal to the market's logics. This is only a preliminary and simplistic view of the financial system because there are instances where governments act in a 'market actor role', using private means to public ends, and in so doing, they act as private actors in markets.[35]

Despite this,[36] however, one must bear in mind that governments always pursue public ends, at least to re-distribute justice and establish or influence

32 Julia Black, 'Decentring Regulation: Understanding the Role of Regulation and Self-Regulation in a "Post-Regulatory" World' (2001) 54 Current Legal Problems 106.

33 Stavros Gadinis, 'From Independence to Politics in Financial Regulation' (2013) 101 California L R 322. To this end, in the aftermath of the financial crisis of 2008–2009, it has been noted as the role and paradigm of independent agencies have been restructured. Indeed, governments have started to be again in charge of banking supervision and be empowered in order to impose veto rights in relation to the liquidation of financial institutions as well as restructuring plans or insolvency declarations of banks. This trend is against the traditional role of independent agencies that have always been in charge, especially in financial regulation, of overseeing delegated powers.

34 RC Hockett and ST Omarova, '"Private" Means to "Public" Ends: Government as Market Actors' (2014) 1016 Cornell Law Faculty Publications 54, 55.

35 Hockett and Omarova (n 34) 56.

36 Hockett and Omarova (n 34) 56. The authors firstly mention the existence of private laws that exercise a foundational role of the markets, such as laws establishing proprietary interests

prices. These activities are not pertinent to private actors. This is because, in some instances, private actors lack financial resources or trust in the market, and this can also prevent them from implementing government-like strategies because of competition concerns (for instance, a private market participant will never be allowed to influence or impose prices, because such behaviours are clearly against competition concerns, which aim to avoid the creation of market abuses or dominant positions). For this reason, if it is true that, on the one hand, markets are destined to experience systemic failures due to their internationalisation and privatisation, on the other hand it is not possible for private actors to rectify or even counterbalance such collapses. Furthermore, private actors operate within a 'recursive collective action problem'[37] that prevents them from achieving public ends. By contrast, they do pursue egoistic objectives based on the achievement of profit. For these reasons, private actors can be responsible for systemic failures, although markets themselves are destined to collapse.

The dynamics of financial markets are therefore very unstable, and one can say that if there is a recursive collective action problem on the side of private actors, governments are not totally exempted from what can be termed a 'recursive agent problem'. In this case, governments are market actors in the sense that they are collective agents playing a market-moving role.[38] Yet they can be as unstable as their private counterparts, influencing speculative spirals (for instance, the decision by a central bank to employ quantitative

in market exchange, or contract law in the case of future performance in market exchange. Furthermore, they identify, for expository purposes, four different forms of the 'market actor role' of governments, namely, 'market-making', 'market-moving', 'market-levering', and 'market-preserving'. Governments in 'market-making' roles bear risks that private actors are 'unable or unwilling to bear', such as the risk that some products will not be sold on the market, and they agree to act as a 'buyer of last resort' through a private means, that is, underwriting. Governments in 'market-moving' roles are affecting prices on certain markets instead of allowing private actors to do this, for instance, when central banks open market operations, such as the purchasing or selling of treasury securities or the 'short-selling [of] commodities whose quantitative easing-inflated prices disproportionately harm the poor'. Governments in 'market-levering' form can improve existing private markets' outcomes, such as in the case of public pensions, whose investments can influence the practices of other firms, and finally, when they act in 'market-preserving' roles, possible collapses of the market are prevented in order to avoid negative externalities; in other words, it is the role of the government to act as a collective agent.

37 RC Hockett, 'Recursive Collective Actions Problems: The Structure of Procyclicality in Financial and Monetary Markets, Macro Economies and Formally Similar Contexts' (2015) 3 J Financial Perspectives 36. See also RC Hockett, 'A Fixer-Upper for Finance' (2010) 87 Washington University Law Review 1213. With the idea of recursive collection action problem, Hockett would like to highlight how decisions that are taken rationally by multiple individuals can generate and result in self-defeating outcomes. The problem is recursive, because the negative movement in one direction is destined to move further in the same direction, ending in unsatisfactory equilibrium. For instance, the case of mortgage-backed securities in 2007 leading to the credit crunch is an evident sign of recursive collective action problem.

38 Hockett and Omarova (n 34).

easing policies can influence the money supply by maintaining low interest rates, and this, in turn, can translate into speculative activities). For this reason, the phenomenology of contemporary financial markets looks complex, and one can say that one possible way to understand it better is to make reference to network theories and the study of complex systems in markets.

4 The Role of Law in Systemic Failure and Self-Regulation

Financial markets as complex financial systems are dominated by risk and uncertainty,[39] and therefore, the role of derivatives has been to allow private actors to diversify risks and hedge against them.

Nonetheless, derivatives are complex financial products that can hardly be defined in law because of the uncertainty of their purposes. A derivative product can be seen as a contract whose value is based on the value of underlying assets, which in turn can be a commodity or a financial product, such as interest or exchange rates. The determination of the value of the derivative can be contested because of the impossibility of determining the actual financial and real value of those instruments.[40] This can translate, in turn, into speculation and 'betting behaviours' that are responsible for the creation of pure risks in subjective terms. Although derivatives can be criticised *per se* for their functioning and their value assessment, it has been noted that one of the real causes of the financial crisis (2007–2010) was not the inability of the system to keep up with financial innovations but the possibility, guaranteed under the law, of trading derivatives on non-regulated and private venues.[41] To this end, it is worth noting that a 'law' consented to the trading of derivatives on a non-regulated venue, namely, the over-the-counter (OTC) market. This created the assumption that a lack of regulation can be responsible for an increase in opportunistic behaviours and inefficient market dynamics. In particular, the lack of regulation in those venues led to a rise in financial speculation, and in addition, the emergence of a credit default swaps market was critical in the determination of negative outcomes, such as the subprime mortgage and securitisation schemes.

However, regulation itself can be seen and is often perceived as a limit to a free-market economy, where the symbol of the 'invisible hand' is preferred to restrictions and controls. Despite the instincts of human society towards

39 Daniele D'Alvia, *The Speculator of Financial Markets: How Financial: How Financial Innovation and Supervision Made the Modern World* (Palgrave Macmillan 2023).

40 Donatella Alessandrini, 'Regulating Financial Derivatives? Risks, Contested Values and Uncertainty Features' (2011) Social & Legal Studies 1, 2.

41 LA Stout, 'Derivatives and the Legal Origin of the 2008 Credit Crisis' (2011) 1 Harvard Business Law Review 1, 3. The author outlines how the law passed by Congress in 2000 called the Commodities Futures Modernization Act was mainly responsible for the financial crisis (2007–2010) because it allowed the trading of derivatives on OTC venues. Therefore, according to this view, changes in the law have been responsible for the collapse of the system, rather than the absence of regulatory guidelines.

progress and wealth, we have also previously outlined that the absence of perfect competition and perfect information leads to a 'need' for regulatory responses.[42] Among those regulatory instances, the Westphalian model of regulation seems to be gaining ground today due to a trend for reinforcement of regulatory controls by public centralised authorities or institutions. Llewellyn has pointed out several of the downsides or negative outcomes to which regulation can lead.[43] Although his critique can be perceived as a statement against regulation itself and the possible negative effects of over-regulation, it should be considered as a pure critique of an 'external' approach to regulation, namely, top-down models or Westphalian approaches. Indeed, in contrast to top-down approaches of regulation, one can find bottom-up instances that are market-oriented and directly represent the output of market operators and the financial industry.

This is identified as self-regulation, and it constitutes one of the most important elements of the modern global governance of financial systems that are today governed by a mixture of self-regulation and paternalistic approaches. Thus, the role of the law is modified towards hybrid models of regulation.

Indeed, as Coase argues,[44] the efficiency of free markets is reliant on considerable internal infrastructure and self-regulation with minimal transaction costs. Although parties can enter into private agreements in order to set interests, the sanctioning of those agreements or their practical enforcement must always be carried out by public laws, such as contract law and commercial law. Therefore, looking at free markets through Coase seems to reduce the role of private actors, who, in the end, must rely on the state, or rather on laws enacted by the state, to enforce their private rules and agreements.

The absence of a serious approach to self-regulation in the modern international financial architecture is justified, according to Omarova, by the unpopularity of the concept, due to casino capitalism and the negative image of financial markets and Wall Street. However, a new paradigm of self-regulation might take the form of 'embedded self-regulation'.[45] It has been seen that state

42 Charles Goodhart, Philipp Hartmann, et al., *Financial Regulation: Why, How and Where Now?* (Routledge 1998) 2. Indeed, famous economists are supporters of free banking, such as Dowd, Benston, and Kaufman, who theorise how regulation plays a negative role in financial crisis. Before them, one can think of Adam Smith's invisible hand that represents a symbol of free markets.

43 DT Llewellyn, 'Re-Engineering the Regulator' (1996) 1 The Financial Regulator 21, 23–24. According to the author, highly prescriptive regimes of regulation can lead, *inter alia*, to the following downsides: (1) The industry can perceive such regime as excessive and redundant; (2) risks are usually so complex they cannot be covered by mere rules; (3) they prevent financial innovation; (4) they can cause rules escalation, by which new provisions are added into the system but the old norms are not withdrawn; (5) information is lost; and (6) over-regulation is not responsive to market conditions.

44 RH Coase, *The Firm, the Market and the Law* (University of Chicago Press 1988).

45 ST Omarova, 'Wall Street as Community of Fate: Toward Financial Industry Self-Regulation' (2011) 159 University of Pennsylvania Law Review 412.

regulation can be evaded by financial arbitrage.[46] Therefore, it seems crucial to consider the opinions of private actors in regulatory processes, and sometimes even to allow private actors to become rule makers. According to Omarova, self-regulation is vital for achieving two main objectives: 'timely access to market information, on the one hand, and the need to monitor and manage risk across jurisdictional borders, on the other'.[47] Self-regulation must take into account public ends, especially financial stability and social values (this is the 'embedded' conception of self-regulation), but through private enforcement. This new role of self-regulation is, therefore, delicate and requires the imposition of collective self-restraint in order to avoid or limit the unscrupulous, profit-oriented activities of private members. This is what Omarova terms 'community of fate', community belief in achieving a common future through self-restriction.

Nonetheless, a macroeconomic approach is more popular today, where no space is left for self-regulation in the financial industry, which, in contrast to other industries, is permeated by systemic risk and public safety nets or crisis management mechanisms as official responses. Take for example the lender of last resort, resolution tools, and deposits insurance schemes, which prevent private and public actors from being seriously interested in the implementation or enforcement of self-regulation approaches within their industry. Nonetheless, Omarova's term of ***embedded self-regulation*** is in vogue again. Essentially, private actors today seem to aim towards public objectives, such as consumer protection and financial stability, through private enforcement and virtuous mechanisms of compliance and soft law governance codes.

5 The Birth of Sovereign Debt Restructuring and Sovereign Bonds

The Brady Plan of the 1980s was the turning point for sovereign debt litigation;[48] today's investors in sovereign debt markets differ from a handful of major syndicated commercial banks prior to the Brady Plan. The growth of secondary sovereign bond markets and transferability of bonds has opened up access to a wide range of new investors, including professional sovereign debt litigants. These are distressed debt funds that have taken advantage of a business opportunity presented by the secondary market in the absence of a sovereign bankruptcy regime to operate a business model based on sovereign litigation. They have been labelled 'vulture funds' as they acquire defaulted (or nearly defaulted) sovereign debt at a significant discount from their issue

46 Victor Fleisher, 'Regulatory Arbitrage' (2010) University of Colorado Law Legal Studies Research Paper No. 10–11, 1–67.

47 Omarova (n 45) 418.

48 The Brady Plan involved exchanging outstanding commercial bank loans for bonds in order to relieve the emerging market debt crisis of the late 1980s and early 1990s.

price on the secondary market, with a premeditated view to hold out[49] from a restructuring and to litigate for the debt's full face value with interest and delay penalties and subsequently pursuing the debtor country's assets to realise the full value of the claim.[50] They sue sovereigns in multiple jurisdictions in order to seize sovereign assets to satisfy their court judgements. Under the threat of potential litigation, states try to pay the majority of debt the majority of the time in the hope that this can more easily enable them to access further financing through capital markets and official sector intervention. On the other hand, the litigation risk has exponentially escalated due to the fact that sovereigns frequently issue debt to foreign investors. The latter bring arbitration proceedings against the state once it defaults on its external debt.

This dynamic evolution of regulatory regimes has contributed to the exponential growth of hybrid models of regulation.[51] This serves as a clear illustration of how the law plays a pivotal role in shaping the future, while also indirectly granting private organisations the discretion to dictate market practices. As Pistor argues, this creates a form of centralised authority capable of wielding its influence to shape the legal framework. Such a central authority may be a public organisation, like the International Capital Markets Association (ICMA), which in 2014 introduced a revised standard for the *pari passu* clause (the so-called collective action clauses, or CACs) to be incorporated into the terms of sovereign debt instruments, along with an updated version of aggregated collective action clauses for sovereign bond agreements.[52]

Specifically, a *CAC* is a provision included in the terms of sovereign bonds that allows a supermajority of bondholders (typically 75% or more) to agree to changes in the bond's terms, such as restructuring the debt or reducing the repayment amounts, which then become binding on all bondholders, including dissenters. The purpose of CACs is to facilitate orderly debt restructuring, reduce the risk of holdout creditors, and prevent litigation that could obstruct a country's financial recovery. Aggregated CACs extend this

49 Holdout litigation has proliferated since courts have explicitly upheld the vulture funds' business model of the late 1990s. In *Elliot Associates v Republic of Peru* (1998) the US Court of Appeals dismissed Peru's champerty defence on the grounds that Elliot's principal intent was to be paid in full, and that Elliot's litigation was incidental and contingent on Peru's non-performance of obligations under the contract. Champerty prohibited the purchase of debt with the intent, and for the purpose, of bringing a lawsuit. The court rejected the champerty defence even though it was clear that, at the time of buying Peru's debt, Elliot, a vulture fund, would have known that Peru would not be able to pay in full. Vulture funds then lobbied in NY legislature in 2004 to amend NY Judiciary Law 489 so as to prevent the defence of champerty from arising for any debt purchases above $500,000.

50 Julian Schumacher et al., 'Sovereign Defaults in Court' (2018) ECB Working Paper 2135, 17.

51 See Ch 5.

52 International Capital Markets Association, 'Standard Collective Action and Pari Passu Clauses for the Terms and Conditions of Sovereign Notes' (2014) <www.icmagroup.org/Regulatory-Policy-and-Market-Practice/Primary-Markets/primary-market-topics/collective-action-clauses/> accessed 4 January 2025.

principle to bonds issued under multiple jurisdictions or in different series. These clauses enable bondholders from various bond issuance to collectively agree on restructuring terms, minimising the ability of dissenters to block a comprehensive debt deal. A good example is Ecuador's debt restructuring in 2020 when a severe economic crisis was exacerbated by the Covid-19 pandemic, leading to an unsustainable debt burden. The restructuring involved $17.4 billion of bonds issued with aggregated CACs, allowing Ecuador to re-negotiate terms across multiple series. Eventually, Ecuador secured the support of over 98% of bondholders, demonstrating the efficiency of CACs in achieving consensus.

To this end, Ecuador successfully deferred payments, reduced debt service costs, and gained financial breathing room without prolonged disputes. As can be seen, CACs prevent holdout creditors from blocking restructuring agreements, enabling countries to achieve a comprehensive settlement. By defining the thresholds for bondholder approval, CACs reduce also litigation risks and enhance predictability in sovereign debt markets by simplifying restructuring processes. At the same time, indirectly the inclusion of CACs in sovereign bonds encourages lenders to assess sovereign creditworthiness more rigorously. Aggregated CACs became the market standard, as embodied in the model promulgated in 2014 by the ICMA, and earlier-generation CACs, based on series-by-series voting, essentially only strengthened the hand of potential holdout creditors. These are standard contractual terms to ensure the legal enforcement of financial obligations, but at the same time, such 'soft law' incorporated in contractual terms of sovereign debt bonds is creating a 'global hierarchy of finance' where transactions can take different forms, depending on parties and their importance in the financial ecosystem. This is a direct example of what Pistor defines as the 'code of capital', where she argues that 'law is code'. Hence, for every legal enforcement of obligations, we might find ways to 'escape' those obligations, such as in the case of CACs. Furthermore, states are in greater proximity to the apex, and the enforceability of sovereign debt contracts is elastic.

In addition to CACs, states' assets cannot be seized and liquidated, and only assets located overseas can be frozen (if ever). States cannot be subject to liquidation, as happens in the case of private distressed companies that might be liquidated – as we shall see in Chapter 5 – if they do not find a viable alternative to restructure their finances. Sovereign governments that owe debt to many foreign creditors can choose which to favour when making payments by implementing a *de facto* seniority structure of sovereign debt.[53] Essentially, the state can 'escape' legal obligation by changing the law or altering the order of priority of payments.

53 Matthias Schlegl, Christoph Trebesch, and MLJ Wright, 'The Seniority Structure of Sovereign Debt' (May 2019) Research Division Federal Reserve bank of Minneapolis – Working Paper 759, 1.

By contrast, this book focuses on a new role of comparative law in financial crises, as we have claimed manifold times. Since Covid-19 in 2020, the nature of law and the role of comparative law have dramatically changed. The law is no longer the 'input' but rather the 'output'.

6 The 2020 Covid-19 Crisis

The recession caused by the Covid-19 pandemic is one of the worst global recessions in modern times. Back in March 2020, the IMF warned that in light of Covid-19, the expectations of a deep global recession were almost certain.[54]

As a result of the crisis, businesses needed to restructure both operationally and financially. Because of Covid-19, some businesses had to be liquidated. The crisis quickly moved from the corporate sector, especially small and medium enterprises (with losses of output, redundancies, and some closures) to public finances, where pressure became enormous. This is true especially in developing countries that had already been highly indebted. Also, the internal situation of businesses in those countries had often been compromised. Their insolvency law frameworks do not always recognise new development trends in insolvency practices that, today, are based on business rescue, out-of-court arrangements (private workouts), and preventive restructuring (see Chapter 5). To this end, out-of-court reorganisation agreements could be an efficient alternative to formal insolvency proceedings. As the World Bank Group has argued,[55] in times of Covid-19, informal reorganisation agreements, due to their flexibility, will contribute in a less time-consuming way towards rescuing viable companies.

Likewise, the growing indebtedness of developing countries led the World Bank, the IMF, and the UN to launch various initiatives to relieve the public debt burden in this unusual situation triggered by Covid-19. A first step was taken when the G20 countries agreed to grant a moratorium on official bilateral debt of the world's 76 poorest economies (the Debt Service Suspension Initiative – DDSI – to cover the official debts of poor countries). Since it took effect on 1 May 2020, the initiative has delivered more than $5 billion in relief to more than 40 eligible countries.[56] The suspension period, originally set to end on 31 December 2020, was extended through to December 2021.

54 Kristalina Georgieva, 'Transcript of Press Briefing by Kristalina Georgieva Following a Conference Call on the International Monetary and Financial Committee' (27 March 2020) IMF <www.imf.org/en/News/Articles/2020/03/27/tr032720-transcript-press-briefing-kristalina-georgieva-following-imfc-conference-call> accessed 5 January 2025.

55 World Bank Group, 'Covid-19 Outbreak: Implications on Corporate and Individual Insolvency' (13 April 2020) <https://pubdocs.worldbank.org/en/912121588018942884/COVID-19-Outbreak-Implications-on-Corporate-and-Individual-Insolvency.pdf> accessed 5 January 2025.

56 World Bank, 'Covid-19: Debt Service Suspension Initiative' (18 June 2021) Brief <www.worldbank.org/en/topic/debt/brief/covid-19-debt-service-suspension-initiative> accessed 5 January 2025.

Borrowers under the DSSI scheme commit to using freed-up resources to increase health, social, or economic spending in response to the pandemic crisis. Specifically, the approach of G20 to the pandemic follows the six principles of the Paris Club.[57] These include solidarity, consensus, and information sharing among the Club members, as well as participation on a voluntary basis by private and multilateral creditors. These are also the foundations of the DSSI. Furthermore, due to its initial limited operability, in November 2020, the G20 announced an agreed 'Common Framework for Debt Treatments beyond the Debt Service Suspension Initiative'. This framework includes the G20 and the Paris Club and requires domestic approval by all the participants; it aims to address the problem of unsustainable debt based on an IMF and World Bank debt sustainability analysis. The framework requires countries to seek similar treatment from private creditors in nominal, net-present-value, and duration terms.

Those historical reforms tested the international financial architecture. 'Sustainability' became a term that is now ubiquitous in global finance and investment. Indeed, the principles embodied in the UN Sustainable Development Goals are devoted to building a better world. These principles are deeply relevant when it comes to the sovereign debt of struggling developing countries. For example, in February 2020, before the Covid-19 crisis became acute, the IMF concluded that Argentina's public debt was 'unsustainable'.[58] Indeed, debt sustainability had been increasingly at risk even before the Covid-19 crisis: Out of 69 countries applying the Low-Income Countries Debt Sustainability Analysis in 2019, half had already been either in debt distress or at high risk of debt distress, compared to 23% in 2013.[59]

As a result, debt sustainability for low-income economies and debt relief became the most attractive ways to combat the pandemic. Furthermore, climate change and falling biodiversity have become a new trigger to justify reforms in sovereign debt crisis. In light of this, the example of Barbados is self-explanatory. Back in 2018–2019, during its debt restructuring, Barbados exchanged old debt with natural disaster clauses. Under these clauses, when an international organisation such as the World Health Organisation declares a natural disaster, the debt service is immediately suspended for two years. At first glance, natural disaster clauses can provide an immediate instrument to secure debt relief in the event of a natural disaster, including a pandemic. However, as has been authoritatively outlined, it is controversial which developing countries can be allowed to use a natural disaster clause and which

57 Paris Club, 'The Six Principles' <https://clubdeparis.org/en/communications/page/the-six-principles> accessed 5 January 2025.

58 IMF, 'IMF Staff Statement on Argentina' (19 February 2020) <www.imf.org/en/News/Articles/2020/02/19/pr2057-argentina-imf-staff-statement-on-argentina> accessed 5 January 2025.

59 International Monetary Fund, 'The Evolution of Public Debt Vulnerabilities in Lower Income Economies' (February 2020) IMF Policy Paper.

cannot.[60] One size does not fit all, especially if we consider larger developing economies.

Climate change and sustainability are a new challenge for the financial ecosystem that is possibly preparing the ground to broaden the mandates of central banks too. For instance, within the central bank monetary policy mandate, the importance of implementing a green quantitative easing, or within micro-prudential supervision by following ESG criteria to sanction unsustainable activities (such as lending linked to deforestation), and finally in terms of macro-prudential supervision, the application of macro-prudential tools to carbon markets. It is difficult to assess whether this move is a useful addition to curtail environmental challenges and help sustainable businesses soar. The world is too interconnected and complex today to express a final judgement on this new trend, but surely, it is a remarkable transformation where non-legal words such as *sustainability* are even affecting financial tools in monetary and supervision policies, and in so doing, they are becoming legal constant(s).

In the absence of an international convention to deal with sovereign debt issues, soft law fills the vacuum. For example, the same concept of 'responsible financing' has also become a new outside-the-law meaning to inform the establishment of new legal constant(s). Essentially, responsible financing has posed the question on how we can embed in international soft law ways in which sovereign debt should be contracted and negotiated between debtors and creditors, including the 2012 UNCTAD Principles on Responsible Sovereign Lending and Borrowing.[61] On 10 September 2015, the UN General Assembly adopted Resolution 69/319, declaring that sovereign debt restructuring processes should be guided by nine basic principles, including the right to sovereign debt restructuring, good faith, transparency, equitable treatment, sovereign immunity, legitimacy, sustainability, and majority restructuring. Such a soft law framework has also been supplemented by the G20 Operational Guidelines for Sustainable Financing of 2017.

Because of its oversight and financing roles enshrined in its Articles of Agreement, the IMF is often central to the debt restructuring process with regard to financing. In fact, the IMF provides balance of payments financing 'under adequate safeguards' (e.g. conditionality) to a member country implementing an economic adjustment program. Whether a country requires debt restructuring will depend on a debt sustainability analysis (DSA). The IMF's DSA also effectively identifies the 'envelope' (financing/restructuring envelope) of resources available for debt service payments to official and private creditors. Furthermore, the IMF encourages its members to engage in a

60 Rodrigo Olivares-Caminal and Paola Subacchi, 'Letter: Barbados Debt Relief Model Is Hard to Extend to All Poor States' *Financial Times* (8 July 2021) <www.ft.com/content/ef2f6603-66bb-47fe-83ba-fcbe5a61a5a1> accessed 5 January 2025.

61 UN Trade and Development, Principles on Promoting Responsible Sovereign Lending and Borrowing' <https://unctad.org/publication/principles-promoting-responsible-sovereign-lending-and-borrowing> accessed 6 January 2025.

collaborative process with their creditors when seeking a restructuring without intervening on issues of inter-creditor equity.

Notwithstanding the efforts that we have so far outlined, it is self-evident that there is no coherent international law framework to deal with sovereign debt crises. In the absence of such a system, we rely on arbitration, national law and national courts of justice, *ad hoc* solutions and negotiations, and international soft law. But national law and national courts of justice are neither equipped nor designed to deal with broader public policy considerations (poverty alleviation, sustainability, human rights) that are at stake in sovereign debt crises. To this end, in financing state sovereignty, a concept anchored in constitutional law meets finance and financial markets (i.e. bonds). With the restrictive theory of sovereign immunity, it is financial markets rather than sovereigns that provide the framework. At stake there is the interaction between public interest of sovereign governments (as well as broader policy considerations) and private interests of financial market participants. To this end, the contractual approaches we have outlined before are, in terms of CACs, limited to contractual issues and thus are not suitable to deal with policy issues.

From the aforementioned examples, we argue that the Covid-19 crisis has dramatically contributed to a rapid reshaping of the outlook of international financial architecture, in its search for less-cumbersome debt restructuring procedures, debt suspensions, and moratoriums, and its orientation towards flexible paradigms of the law that necessarily sit far beyond the purposes of a codification of the law as an 'input', as Pistor contends. Similarly, debt restructuring in private businesses is taking the form of out-of-court reorganisation agreements between debtors and their creditors, as the next chapter will further explain.

5 The Benchmarks of International Insolvency Law

1 International Insolvency Law

This chapter describes instances of soft law that are compelling illustrations of constants outside of the law created by global legal indicators. Soft law instruments are increasingly widespread as far as corporate restructuring and insolvency law is concerned. In the area of international insolvency law, there is no global framework, and regional frameworks are limited.[1] The alternatives are soft law instruments, which are of non-binding nature. This is sometimes explicitly stated in the instrument itself,[2] but this does not imply it has no impact.[3] In fact, this chapter deals with the distinctive ways in which non-binding and non-enforceable soft law instruments impact the field of corporate restructuring and insolvency.

Furthermore, we will focus, *inter alia*, on the legal frameworks and international benchmarks of the EBRD Core Principles of Insolvency (Core Principles), the World Bank Principles for Effective Insolvency and Creditor/Debtor Regimes (Principles), and the UNCITRAL Legislative Guide to Insolvency Law and the UNCITRAL Model Law on Cross-Border Insolvency (the 'Model Law'), thus unpacking their being legal constants in times of crisis. Also, the World Bank and the UNCITRAL, in consultation with the IMF, designed the Insolvency Creditor Rights Standard (ICR Standard), which represents the international consensus on best practices for evaluating and strengthening

1 For instance, in Latin America, see the Montevideo Treaty on International Commercial Law (1889); Havana Convention on Private International Law (1928); Montevideo Treaty on International Commercial Terrestrial Law (1940); Montevideo Treaty on International Procedural Law (1940). For Europe, see EIR 2015 (for EU member states, excluding Denmark), the Nordic Bankruptcy Convention 1933 (the latest revision of 1982) (for Denmark, Finland, Iceland, Norway, and Sweden), and for the 17 members of the *Organisation pour l'Harmonisation du Droit des Affaire* (OHADA) (or Organization for the Harmonization of the Business Law) in the central African region, the Uniform Act on Bankruptcy Proceedings (2015).

2 For instance, INSOL Europe IOH Principle 1.1.

3 For instance, see Dinah Shelton, 'Introduction: Law, Non-Law and the Problem of "Soft Law"' in Dinah Shelton (ed), *Commitment and Compliance: The Role of Non-Binding Norms in the International Legal System* (OUP 2000) 12.

DOI: 10.4324/9781003304333-6

national insolvency and creditor rights systems. The ICR Standard does this by combining the World Bank and the UNCITRAL Legislative Guide on Insolvency Law. Additionally, within the international financial architecture, the Financial Stability Board (FSB)[4] has recognised and designated the ICR Standard as one of the key standards for sound financial systems, deserving priority implementation depending on countries' circumstances.

Because of the soft nature of recommendations and guidelines, certain standard-setting organisations assist in reviewing and improving insolvency law frameworks based on soft law instruments. Think of the World Bank and UNCITRAL. The World Bank makes analysis of national laws by performing so-called 'Reports on the Observance of Standards and Codes', which are also implemented for insolvency regimes based on its Principles for Effective Insolvency and Creditor/Debtor Regimes (latest version of 2016). These assessments – as we claimed before – are also used in assisting countries in the reform of corporate insolvency regimes.[5] Also, the UNCITRAL provides assistance to those countries that are in the process of adopting legislation based on UNCITRAL instruments.[6] The Model Law has inspired legislation in some 50 jurisdictions. It has thus proven to be of significant use in countries with 'obsolete' international insolvency law legislation, such as Japan and Mexico, both of which are civil law (or non-common-law) legal systems. By contrast, a hard law instance such as the European Insolvency Regulation 2015 (EIR 2015)[7] does not deal with cross-border insolvency issues that extend beyond an EU member state (except for Denmark) into a non-member state. So far, several EU member states have adopted the Model Law, including the UK before Brexit.

As we said, international insolvency law is underpinned by international practices and soft law instruments that are always more focused on promoting and conceiving non-legal meanings. This chapter introduces the legal models,

4 The Financial Stability Board (FSB) is an international body that monitors and makes recommendations about the global financial system to promote stability. It was established in 2009 in response to the global financial crisis (2007–2010) in the United States, succeeding the Financial Stability Forum. The FSB is composed of members from the G20 countries, financial institutions, central banks, and international organizations, like the IMF and the World Bank. Key functions of the FSB include the identification of vulnerabilities in the global financial system, such as systemic risks or potential crises; setting standards with reference to the development of guidelines and standards for financial regulation, ensuring that financial institutions or financial intermediaries operate safely and transparently; and finally, assuring coordination and implementation with reference to national authorities, international organizations, and standard-setting bodies to foster global financial stability and to implement recommendations across jurisdictions.

5 The assessments are performed by the World Bank, in collaboration with the IMF and UNCITRAL. See for more information: <www.worldbank.org/en/programs/rosc> accessed 1 January 2025.

6 For the technical assistance offered by UNCITRAL, see: <https://uncitral.un.org/en/TA> accessed 1 January 2025.

7 Regulation (EU) 2015/848 of the European Parliament and of the Council of 20 May 2015 on Insolvency Proceedings (Recast), L 141/19.

or better, quasi-legal instruments, through which domestic legislations are subject to modifications. Those models also represent venues through which constant(s) outside the law access the legal sphere. They are examples of soft law and non-binding. However, those principles can be 'codified' within domestic binding legislations. These are the roles of global legal indicators and legal assessments, namely, to influence hard law-making processes through the identification of common commercial outside-the-law concepts that must find a 'legal space' for implementation. These are further instances of the 'uncodified codification' of the law, and this is how evidence is collected to support the claim that the law is the 'output' of any 'uncodified codification' process. To this end, a measurement of progress in legal reforms is to assess both the current laws 'on the books' (i.e. extensiveness) and how these laws work in practice (i.e. effectiveness). Reviewing the black letter of the law and analysing how these laws are applied reveal non-legal meanings that, in turn, generate further (legal) constant(s).

For these reasons, legislators or courts have recognised certain sets of soft law instruments in their policymaking. The UK, for instance, has in its UK Chancery Guide and in its legislative initiative on insolvency and governance referred to soft law instruments.[8] In light of this, and by taking into account cooperation and communication duties under the European Insolvency Regulation (EIR 2015), Dutch courts have opened a webpage where they elaborate on cooperation and communication but also refer to soft law instruments, such as the EU JudgeCo Principles.[9] References by these courts are welcomed in practice, but as such, they might alter the nature of such instruments as being legally non-binding. The next section will further analyse how court judgements and hard law instruments have been influenced by soft law recommendations in the past decades. The main research goal is to show how the interpretation activity of judges as well as the construction of policy objectives by policymakers can effectively modify the 'law in action' within corporate cross-border restructuring. In so doing, it also assesses how legal constant(s) outside of law are always more destined to play a remarkable role within the field of international law and the international financial regulation.

2 Between Soft Law and Hard Law in International Insolvency Law

Within the international financial architecture, soft law standards established by standard-setting organisations play a pivotal role in international insolvency

8 See, for example: UK Chancery Gide of 5 May 2017, par. 25.30 <www.gov.uk/government/publications/chancery-guide> accessed 1 January 2025; UK Government, Insolvency, and Corporate Governance, Government Response, 26 August 2018, par. 5.160 <www.gov.uk/government/consultations/insolvency-and-corporate-goveranance> accessed 1 January 2025.

9 See: <www.rechtspraak.nl/English/Pages/International-Insolvency.aspx> accessed 1 January 2025.

law, although their enforceability and implementation can constitute a challenge. This is because, while such standards provide a framework for global harmonisation, their adoption depends on national lawmakers and regulators, leading to variability in compliance and inconsistent application. In fact, soft law instruments give rise to questions concerning the true benefit that they can generate in comparison to instances of hard law, and how policymakers, lawmakers, and courts can take them into account in the field of restructuring and insolvency. Furthermore, different economic conditions and corporate insolvency frameworks (e.g. the G7 countries vs emerging market) face challenges in implementing soft law. For instance, emerging markets might struggle with resource constraints. For these reasons, cooperation and coordination among different countries – and specifically governments – at the international level are fundamental activities to set up a plain field where regulatory borders are established by soft law standards by anchoring them to specific benchmarks that constitute direct instances of macro-legislation, such as the European Restructuring Directive.[10]

Within international insolvency law and restructuring, one can find dedicated standard-setting organisations which establish soft law standards at international level in order to influence the enactment of new national acts or modification of national legislations. Think of the United Nations Commission on International Trade Law (UNCITRAL) Working Group V (Insolvency) and the World Bank Group in some of its recommendations, as well as insolvency practitioners' organisations, such as INSOL International[11] and INSOL Europe.[12] These are direct examples of standard-setting organisations which also frequently work in collaboration with multilateral development banks, such as the EBRD, to identify 'superior' benchmarks as model laws, elicit the establishment of shared practices that nation states should follow, and enact specific soft law standards inspired by shared benchmarks. To this end, for instance, the EBRD Legal

10 Directive (EU) 2019/1023 of the European Parliament and the Council of 20 June 2019 on preventive restructuring frameworks, on discharge of debt and disqualifications, and on measures to increase the efficiency of procedures concerning restructuring, insolvency and discharge of debt, and amending Directive (EU) 2017/1132 (Directive on Restructuring and Insolvency). See also Daniele D'Alvia, 'Law and the Market: private actors and self-regulation "towards a new role of public international law"' (2018) 29 (6) European Business Law Review, 929–48.

11 INSOL International is a global federation of national associations comprising accountants and lawyers who specialise in turnaround and insolvency. With over 44 member associations and more than 12,000 professionals worldwide, INSOL serves as a pivotal platform for professionals in the restructuring and insolvency sectors.

12 INSOL Europe is a leading European organisation for professionals specialising in insolvency, business reconstruction, and recovery. With over 1,300 members across 50 countries, including lawyers, accountants, judges, regulators, academics, and bankers, it serves as a pivotal platform for networking, knowledge exchange, and professional development in the field.

Transition team has the task to carry out periodic insolvency law assessment to evaluate the quality of selected elements of the insolvency framework in each of the countries of operation surveyed and provide an insight into the investment climate in EBRD countries of operations. The ultimate goal of the assessment is the facilitation of policy dialogue in insolvency and debt restructuring.

Conducting a periodic assessment of the insolvency framework and practice is important to identify weaknesses and areas for improvement that, by engaging in policy development and primary and secondary legislation reform, can contribute towards the enhancement of the law and facilitate the stakeholders' engagement with new tools/frameworks. The periodicity of these assessments is fundamental since needs and dynamics change over time. For instance, Croatia, Georgia, Kazakhstan, Latvia, Lithuania, Moldova, Poland, Romania, Serbia, Slovenia, Tunisia, and Ukraine are among EBRD countries of operations that have substantially reformed their insolvency laws in recent years.

A clear example of these changing dynamic can be drawn from the new elements introduced in the most recent European reforms, where we have witnessed a move towards new procedures that combine court intervention with private negotiations of the parties (the so-called 'hybrid mechanisms'), which represents an evolution towards pre-packaged reorganisation and expedited restructurings in general.

According to the EBRD, these reorganisations – not to say 'restructuring' – frameworks are very 'adaptable' to each country's financial and real sector-specific needs. As is evident, it is up to each country to 'develop its own restructuring tools and procedures suitable to address their needs and complement their current framework'. Sometimes, the EBRD argues, it is difficult 'to classify them in specific typologies', and sometimes the dividing line between the processes might not be so clear.[13]

Insolvency frameworks facilitate the extension of credit with several benefits for private sector development.[14] Countries might also want to adopt several (if not all) of these procedures, thus supplying stakeholders with a vast array of tools when it comes to addressing financial distress. As noted in 2017 by the World Bank,

> [e]conomy-specific research has shown that insolvency reforms that encourage debt restructuring and reorganization reduce both failure

13 EBRD, 'Insolvency Assessment on Reorganisation Procedures' (2022) 22 <https://ebrd-restructuring.com/storage/uploads/documents/Insolvency%20Assessment%20Database%20Report.pdf> accessed 29 January 2025. See also World Bank Group, 'Out-of-Court Debt Restructuring' (2012). Daniele D'Alvia acted as an external legal consultant to the assessment.

14 See, for example, the foreword to the 2015 World Bank, 'Principles for Effective Insolvency and Creditor/Debtor Regimes', published in 2016.

rates among small and medium-size enterprises and the liquidation of profitable businesses.[15]

Addressing the financial difficulties of a business at an early stage is critical for a successful turnaround. Early reorganisation can maximise the total value to creditors, employees, owners, and the economy as a whole. A number of countries in Western Europe, including Italy, Germany, the Netherlands, and Spain, have introduced new composition procedures for early reorganisation of corporate debtors that are not yet technically insolvent, a trend which has been followed in the EBRD region.

Nonetheless, such periodic insolvency law assessment will focus not only on the quality of the framework but also on the support around it, for example, the court's ability (that is, the intellectual capacity/training of judges dealing with insolvency matters and celerity/specificity of courts) and the insolvency practitioners (in a broad sense, including advisors, lawyers, accountants, etc.) and their suitability to deal with the issues at stake (capacity, training, professional qualification requirements, and so on).

The assessment provides the EBRD, its countries of operations, and investors with a comparative tool to

1. gauge the quality and effectiveness of a country's insolvency laws, benchmarked against international best practices in general, but with a particular focus on the expediency and facilitation of reorganisation options;
2. highlight major weaknesses that should be addressed by national legislators in order to improve the quality of the insolvency framework in respect to expedience and facilitation of reorganisation; and
3. enable the EBRD to promote the further development of insolvency legislation to encourage reorganisation in its countries of operations.

In order to assess the extensiveness and effectiveness of the relevant national insolvency laws, the method used by the EBRD are targeted questionnaires sent to identified persons at banks and law firms to obtain a comparable set of data; a review of the underlying legislation as part of the insolvency law assessment, including the assessment of data from the relevant government ministry or authority or the number of insolvency proceedings; and in particular, the number of pre-insolvency/reorganisation-type proceedings.[16]

As can be seen, soft law instruments are used in multiple ways. Insolvency protocols are another way to promote the application of recommendations and soft law standards especially when dealing with cross-border cooperation

15 See World Bank Doing Business Report 2017, the Resolving Insolvency Indicator: Why It Matters? <www.doingbusiness.org/data/exploretopics/resolving-insolvency/why-matters>.

16 This will help with the EBRD's analysis of the results of the questionnaire, since in some jurisdictions there may be little practical experience of these kinds of proceedings.

and communication. For example, important protocols have made reference to soft law instruments, such as the American Law Institute (ALI) Guidelines Applicable to Court-to-Court Communications in Cross-Border Cases (2001) (the 'ALI Guidelines'),[17] CoCo Guidelines (2007),[18] and the American Law Institute International Insolvency Institute (ALI-III) Global Guidelines for Court-to-Court Communications in International Insolvency Cases (the 'ALI-III Global Guidelines').[19]

Courts have explicitly referred to international soft law made by standard-setting organisations. While the ALI Guidelines are a non-binding soft law instrument, they have influenced judicial decisions and legal practices in several ways. For instance, courts in jurisdictions such as the United States, Canada, and the UK have occasionally referred to the ALI Guidelines in insolvency cases to establish communication protocols, particularly in proceedings involving the UNCITRAL Model Law or similar frameworks. In cross-border insolvency cases, judges have explicitly used these guidelines to justify conference calls or joint hearings between courts to align procedural steps.

Some jurisdictions have integrated concepts from the ALI Guidelines into national procedural rules or international agreements. Notably, protocols such as the JIN Guidelines (Judicial Insolvency Network Guidelines) (2016) share similarities with ALI's approach, suggesting an indirect influence. Such standards were developed by an international group of judges. The JIN Guidelines

17 The American Law Institute (ALI) Guidelines Applicable to Court-to-Court Communications in Cross-Border Cases (2001) provide a framework for facilitating cooperation and communication between courts in different jurisdictions during cross-border insolvency and other complex litigation cases. Developed as part of ALI's *Transnational Insolvency Project*, these guidelines aim to promote judicial efficiency, transparency, and comity by suggesting practical protocols for sharing information, coordinating case management, and ensuring fairness to all parties. They are a notable example of soft law designed to complement the UNCITRAL Model Law on Cross-Border Insolvency.

18 The CoCo Guidelines (2007), formally known as the European Communication and Cooperation Guidelines for Cross-Border Insolvency, are a set of principles aimed at fostering effective communication between insolvency practitioners and courts in cross-border insolvency cases. Developed by an expert group of European practitioners and academics, the guidelines were designed to complement the EU Insolvency Regulation (now the recast EU Insolvency Regulation, 2015/848), providing practical steps to ensure coordination in complex international insolvencies.

19 The ALI–III Global Guidelines were developed collaboratively by the American Law Institute (ALI) and the International Insolvency Institution (III) to provide a framework for cross-border restructuring and insolvency practices. These guidelines aim to harmonize legal approaches across jurisdictions, improving efficiency, consistency, and fairness in global restructuring cases. Among the key objectives of the recommendations, we find the encouragement of collaboration between courts, insolvency practitioners, and stakeholders in cross-border insolvency cases; the improvement of efficiency in terms of reducing costs and delays in cross-border restructurings by aligning legal practices and principles; the establishment of clear channels for communication between jurisdictions to resolve conflicts and ensure smooth proceedings; and the protection of rights of all creditors and stakeholders, ensuring that insolvency outcomes are just and equitable or fair.

provide a modern framework for court-to-court communication and cooperation in cross-border insolvency cases, and they have been adopted by courts in multiple jurisdictions, including the United States, UK, and Canada. The ALI Guidelines also inspired the drafting of the EU Cross-Border Insolvency Court-to-Court Cooperation Principles and Guidelines (JudgeCo Principles) (2015) that were developed to facilitate cooperation under the EU Insolvency Regulation. They draw upon foundational concepts established in the ALI Guidelines.

As stated before, the ALI-III Global Guidelines have been referenced to facilitate cross-border insolvency proceedings. In the United States, in the restructuring of the LATAM Airlines Group, the US Bankruptcy Court for the Southern District of New York approved a cross-border insolvency protocol that enabled direct court-to-court communication between courts in the United States, Chile, Colombia, and the Cayman Islands. The Chancery Division of the High Court of England and Wales has endorsed the use of guidelines for court-to-court communication in international insolvency cases. In May 2017, the Chancellor of the High Court approved an addition to the Chancery Guide, highlighting the desirability of adopting such guidelines, including the JIN Guidelines, which build upon the ALI Guidelines. Such approval is a formal recognition of the important influence of the ALI-III Global Principles, which have already been applied by the UK Supreme Court. For example, *Rubin & Anor v Eurofinance SA & Ors* and *New Cap Reinsurance Corp Ltd & Anor v Grant and others* [2012] UKSC 46 [2013] 1 AC 236 is rooted in

> the modern approach . . . which is that the jurisdiction with international competence is that of the country of the centre of main interests of the debtor (an expression not without its own difficulties) [and then referred to the Global Principles].

Another example is drawn from the United States Court of Appeals for the Third Circuit in *Re ABC Learning Centres* 728 F 3d 301 (3d Cir 2013), where reference is made to ALI-III Global Principle 1:

> [T]he overriding objective [is to enable] courts and insolvency administrators to operate effectively and efficiently in international insolvency cases with the goals of maximising the value of the debtor's global assets, preserving where appropriate the debtors' business, and furthering the just administration of the proceeding (305). . . . The emphasis must be on ensuring that the insolvency administrator, appointed in that proceeding, is accorded every possible assistance to take control of all assets of the debtor that are located in other jurisdictions.

Case law on the UNCITRAL Model Law on Cross-Border Insolvency also abounds. It endorses the use of soft law instruments, 'in particular for matters of cooperation and communication by courts and insolvency representatives'. In some cases, Boon and Wessels argue, 'legislators . . . refer to soft law instruments to extend hard law', as in recital 48 of the European Insolvency Regulation (EIR 2015), in force since June 2017:

> When cooperating, insolvency practitioners and courts should take into account best practices for cooperation in cross-border insolvency cases, as set out in principles and guidelines on communication and cooperation adopted by European and International organisations active in the area of insolvency law, and in particular the relevant guidelines prepared by the United Nations Commission on International Trade Law (UNCITRAL).[20]

Another example of how the Model Law has influenced the enactment of hard law can be found in Australia, which in 2008 adopted the Model Law in its Cross-Border Insolvency Act. As Wessels and Boon state, 'this has led to changes in the court rules in several states and territories. For instance, the Court Procedures Rules 2006 of the Australian Capital Territory introduced part 6.15A on proceedings under the Cross-Border Insolvency Act'. In 2017, court rules were amended to include explicit references to the Global Principles of ALI Guidelines and the ALI-III Global Guidelines. 'For instance, where a party applies for a form of cooperation (other than a coordination agreement), they are required to state what provisions of the Global Guidelines would apply'.[21]

Although the realm of soft law instruments has grown steadily, there is limited research on their relevance in the area of international restructuring and insolvency law. The use of soft law brings about various advantages and disadvantages. Soft law instruments are very well suited to developing ethical (and professional) standards, supporting coordinated action where hard law is lacking, and their use does not diminish a states' (or a court's) sovereignty. On the other hand, soft law instruments may be hard to find, and it can be particularly difficult to interpret their provisions. Furthermore, soft law instruments are non-binding; they do not usually provide for a revision procedure, and they may risk a lack of due process when, in the absence of a formal legislative process, the drafting and adoption of soft law instruments are not carefully performed. In addition, it may take considerable time before the impact of soft law instruments becomes visible.

20 See Gert-Jan Boon and Bob Wessels, 'Soft Law Instruments on Restructuring and Insolvency Law: Why They Matter (or Not)' *Oxford Business School Blog* (26 July 2019) <https://blogs.law.ox.ac.uk/business-law-blog/blog/2019/07/soft-law-instruments-restructuring-and-insolvency-law-why-they-matter> accessed 27 January 2025, from which we also drawn the judgements.

21 Bob Wessels and Gert-Jan Boon, 'Soft Law Instruments in Restructuring and Insolvency Law: Exploring Its Rise and Impact' (2019) 2 Tijdschrift voor vennootschapsrecht, rechtspersonenrecht en ondernemingsbestuur 53, 63.

Also, soft law instruments usually lack mechanisms for monitoring and resolving conflicts over the content of the instrument. Therefore, they may face the problem of 'incomplete contracts'. For example, soft law instruments may lack a mechanism for interpretation, which is present for hard law.[22] Furthermore, the dispute settlement may be more difficult with soft law instruments. Monitoring compliance with a soft law instrument is usually not present, just as there are no procedures for resolving conflicts. This is different from hard law which is embedded in a larger legal framework involving courts for resolving disputes.[23] These features of soft law instruments may lead to higher post-agreement costs for managing, monitoring, and enforcing the commitments.[24] Nonetheless, because soft law instruments are developed and used by legislators or, as we have shown, by courts, we must conclude they are relevant in the area of restructuring and insolvency. However, the role of soft law instruments could be improved. To this end, standard-setting organisations should focus on using clear language for ease of interpretation, which can further benefit from accompanying glossaries or explanatory guides.

3 The Role of Contract Law Versus Statute Law in Corporate Insolvency Law

In business, financial difficulties should be addressed at an early stage. This is critical for a successful turnaround; early restructuring can maximise the total value to creditors, employees, owners, and the economy as a whole. This new approach is informed by the so-called 'rescue culture', which is indirectly informed by a contractarian view of insolvency law focusing on finding the right balance with creditors' bargaining power. Rescue culture is becoming prominent in corporate insolvency practices that are always more focused on hybrid restructuring procedures, where the role of private law is maximised (see Section 5)

Contract law plays a vital role in corporate insolvency practices of business reorganisation. It is a driving force to create exceptions to established legal principles, such as *pari passu*. It is not by chance that this same principle is not defined in any legal instrument or legal provision. Law is not the input, although many times we might find a definition of the *pari passu* principle in private law, such as contractual arrangements and sovereign debt instruments (bond prospectus or the offering memorandum or circular). These same definitions are not legally binding to other debt instruments, and they are not of general application. This shows that the law is rarely the 'input' but often the

22 AT Guzman and Timothy Meyer, 'Soft Law' in Eugene Kontorovich and Francesco Parisi (eds), *Economic Analysis of International Law* (Elgar Publishing 2016) 123–24.

23 GC Shaffer and MA Pollack, 'Hard vs. Soft Law: Alternatives, Complements, and Antagonists in International Governance' (2010) 94 Minnesota Law Review 718.

24 KW Abbot and Duncan Snidal, 'Hard and Soft Law in International Governance' (2000) 54 International Organisation 434.

'output', especially in a post-pandemic world. Flexibility is key, and when dealing with financial innovations, we must find common meanings that can be subsequently codified as legal constants. Non-legal meanings are then many times recognised by soft law instruments, and therefore, non-binding instruments beyond a hard law conception of the law. The extent of the enforceability of these new legal constants will then depend on the level of cooperation and agreement to be found among international non-state actors (ICMA, ISDA, World Bank, IMF, etc.) and national governments. This is the new apex of contemporary financial markets, and it is here that the new role of the law is unfolding.

The emerging role of contract law in insolvency practices has a long history and can even be viewed as exceptional to established rules and law principles in insolvency law, especially regarding the principle of *pari passu*. Indeed, in corporate insolvency law, the common denominators to protect creditors' interests are the duty to provide the same treatment to creditors (*par condicio creditorum*), respect pre-insolvency entitlements, and observe the principle of *pari passu* according to which each creditor is paid equally and without preference in the distribution of any available debtor assets (or proceeds of sale from those assets) in proportion to debts due to each creditor.

The objectives of the *pari passu* principle are commonly considered to be fairness and the orderly distribution of assets as endorsed – for instance – by the Insolvency Act 1986 (UK).[25] This reflects the public policy that an insolvency regime should not be displaced by private arrangements (at least in theory). In other words, the application of the *pari passu* principle means that, under insolvency law, an insolvent company's estate must be distributed equally among creditors on a *pro rata* basis. Such a principle is mandatory in many jurisdictions. While commentators such as Goode have described the principle as 'fundamental' in theory, in reality it is subject to a large number of exceptions.[26]

The national level experiences an intricate web of exceptions to it, which vary across jurisdictions and aim to protect specific classes of creditors. In other words, to protect superior interests, the lawmaker in almost every legal system creates exceptions to the general principle of equality. For instance, statutory orders of priorities exist in insolvency proceedings that allow certain creditors to be paid before others in the event of a corporate liquidation (namely, insolvency expenses, salaries, or taxes must be paid before any other debt). The law aims to ensure that the legal procedure can be completed, and that liquidation

25 *Report of the Review Committee on Insolvency Law and Practice* (1982) Cmnd 8558, also known as the Cork Report in the UK, was an investigation and set of recommendations on modernisation and reform of UK Insolvency Law chaired by Kenneth Cork and commissioned by the Labour Government in 1977. The Cork Report was followed by a White Paper in 1984: *A Revised Framework for Insolvency Law* (1984) Cmnd 9175. And these led to Insolvency Act 1986 (UK).

26 Roy Goode, *Principles of Corporate Insolvency Law* (Sweet & Maxwell 1997).

does not cause excessive social harm to employees or diminish tax revenues on the side of the state. In such exceptions, it is possible to see the classic role of the law as 'input', where specific interests are codified by virtue of legal means. This is a direct example of the 'Code of Capital' for which Pistor has argued, the final question being, in her view, who decides and who has the discretionary powers to discriminate among creditors' interests. In short, the state sits at the apex of the system where, she argues, the necessary flexibility exists to adopt decisions that sometimes might even go against the protection of other interests, such as those of unsecured creditors in insolvency proceedings. The codification of capital is clear in these examples.

However, orders of priorities are not exclusively created by the law and, therefore, by the state. We could say that 'codification' of interests in insolvency law procedures is not necessarily based on the law in terms of hard law. Indeed, the principle of *pari passu* can also be – and in practice often is – altered through contract law and private autonomy of parties. A lender can ask for a security over a borrower's asset to grant a loan. Indeed, after a credit assessment of the borrower which measures its solvability risk, a creditor can ask for collateral in order to ensure that he will get paid. By using a security, the creditor moves up the waterfall of repayments since he will be paid in priority, provided that the debtor has enough assets to cover the losses until the corresponding rank is reached. Conversely, a creditor may want to be moved into a worse position through subordination in order to benefit from higher interest rates. Hence, the *pari passu* principle seems to be disregarded not only by the law itself but also in contractual arrangements. A creditor may want to have a lower ranking in the waterfall of payments because, although this desire is counter-intuitive, it can be justified by financial interests. The lower rank equates to higher interest rates because the probability of not getting paid is higher. The higher the risk, the higher the return: This is the main feature of debt and leverage finance. In creditors' ranking, after senior creditors come second liens, followed by mezzanine and high-yield debt. Creditors holding this last kind of loan are usually referred to as junior creditors. Hedge funds, for instance, are attracted by these loans because they tend to invest in high-risk assets.

In essence, using collaterals is the reverse of the *pari passu* principle. This is why it is sometimes said that the principle exists among unsecured or ordinary creditors. Secured creditors change the equal ranking among creditors. During a liquidation, a debtor's assets are sold through auction, and the overall amount is collected by the liquidator, who then distributes them among the creditors. Secured creditors have a collateral over a certain type of assets. For example, the collateral can be a mortgage for real estate or a pledge over shares. Creditors holding a security, also named senior creditors, are entitled to collect the amount obtained by selling the collateralised assets. Thus, they 'jump' the queue in comparison to other ordinary creditors, namely, those who do not hold any collateral. On the other hand, being placed higher in the hierarchy of repayments has a cost: Secured creditors have lower interest rates than creditors that do not hold any collateral. Sometimes, lenders that do not find an agreement on taking out a security ask for a covenant in the facility agreement called a negative pledge clause. Through this clause, the debtor undertakes to not provide any pledge on his assets to other lenders. This type of clause restores the equality of rank among creditors, which shows that contract law does not always alter it.

Finally, another contractual form reorganising the principle focuses on the function of inter-creditor agreements (ICAs). In modern transactions, particularly those related to leveraged buyout, numerous creditors will grant loans to one single debtor (the special-purpose vehicle, or SPV). The acquisition of a large company can be quantified in a deal worth millions, or sometimes billions; a single creditor alone cannot provide such a facility to the debtor, so a group of creditors comes together to finance the acquisition. Creditors will likely agree to enter into an ICA to settle their relations. This contract contains one main provision to modify the *pari passu* clause: the waterfall provision. This stipulates that creditors are ranked from senior to high yield. It also simplifies the relations between borrower and lenders as they nominate a creditor's agent and a security agent, who are generally senior creditors. Those agents mutualise the interests of all creditors by being the direct interlocutor with the borrower.

The main rationale of the ICA is to avoid the court's involvement in case of failure of repayment of the debtor. The relation between parties is already dictated by the ICA, and in theory, there is no need for the parties to go to court to settle the dispute, since the repayment order has already been established by the ICA. However, in practice, the negotiation process of an ICA is often distorted. Senior creditors tend to have a stronger position than juniors, so in practice, ICAs are more favourable to the former, and they tend to increase the enforceability of their collaterals. Indeed, once the borrower becomes insolvent, senior creditors are likely to force the sale of the collateralised assets while ensuring that junior creditors have no claims over them, in order to obtain the highest possible price at the auction. To do so, provisions called release clauses are inserted into ICAs, which authorise the security agent to get rid of all claims that junior lenders may have over secured assets during an auction process. Hence, according to Hooley, an additional layer of alteration is brought by contract law to the *pari passu* principle, as junior parties to ICA simply have no claim over secured assets and often find themselves 'out of the money'.[27]

There is evidence in American and English case law that ICAs can be enforced, further demonstrating how, at least in these common-law jurisdictions, private contracting can alter equal ranking. For instance, in a landmark English decision (*Re Maxwell Communications Corporation Plc* [1993]), it was argued that the *pari passu* distribution of assets among unsecured creditors was a general rule of insolvency law from which it was not possible to

27 Richard Hooley, 'Release Provisions in Inter-Creditor Agreements' (2012) 3 Journal of Business Law 213.

contract out, even to one's own disadvantage, particularly by analogy with cases on set-off in insolvency. The court held that this was not the law. There was no reason that a particular creditor should not waive his right to prove altogether or save to the extent of assets remaining after another creditor is satisfied, and that he could do this either in the insolvency or in advance of it. In other words, a secured creditor can lower his ranking if he has so agreed. Mokal argues that this decision makes it evident that the principle of *pari passu* is 'far from sacrosanct'.[28]

On the other hand, *Ion Media* was the first case in a series of bankruptcy court decisions since the global financial crisis (2007–2010) to rule on the enforceability of prepetition ICAs among lenders, and to a certain extent, it set the stage for decisions going forward. The ICA was enforceable where second lien and junior lenders challenged the validity of the first lien lenders' purported lien over debtor property, contested the priority scheme established, and objected to a reorganisation plan consistent with that scheme. It was held that by entering the ICA, the second lien lenders had contractually waived their standing to challenge the validity of the particular licenses, demonstrating that waivers of rights in the ICA would be enforced, putting first lien lenders in a strong position.

These cases show that, while common-law countries have an approach to contracting as *caveat emptor* – that is, the junior creditors should be aware of the agreement they entered into – civil law jurisdictions may favour protection of their interests to preserve fairness and apply the principle of good faith. However, even intuitively, it seems unfair to bring balance into the picture when parties have freely consented to enter the contract. Private autonomy matters, especially under French or Italian law, for instance. As long as there has not been fraud and misrepresentation on the part of contracting parties, their agreement should be honoured and fulfilled.

4 The UNCITRAL Legislative Guide on Insolvency Law

As we have noted in the EDBR's *Insolvency Assessment on Reorganisation Procedures* (2022), UNCITRAL is a subsidiary body of the General Assembly of the United Nations, which was established in 1966 with the general mandate to further the progressive harmonisation and unification of international trade law. UNCITRAL has prepared the 'Legislative Guide on Insolvency Law', with a broad and general description of objectives and key features that, UNICTRAL argues, should be a component of all insolvency regimes, and the criteria to be followed both in legal relations between debtors and creditors and in cases of out-of-court reorganisations of companies.[29]

28 Riz Mokal, 'Priority as Pathology: The Pari Passu Myth' (2001) 60 (3) Cambridge Law Journal 581.

29 EBRD (n 13) 32.

To meet its goals, the Guide presents several recommendations concerning the criteria and solutions to be followed by countries to contribute to an effective and efficient legal framework when debtors are in financial difficulties. At the same time, it embeds the more advanced developments as far as insolvency law is concerned. The Guide stresses that the proper development of an insolvency regime requires an adequate legal framework, an appropriate infrastructure, and resources to allow the process to develop efficiently. In light of this, the Guide orientates countries by proposing recommendations for the different problems that occur in most insolvency regimes and establishing common guidelines for solving them.

It is important to highlight that, among the main recommendations given by the 'Legislative Guide', special emphasis is placed on the treatment of secured creditors within insolvency proceedings, and therefore on the need for a legal framework to give this type of creditors protection. UNCITRAL also recommends that

> any insolvency law should include provisions governing both the reorganisation and the liquidation of a debtor, as well as establishing that where a security right is effective and enforceable under a rule outside the insolvency law, it must also be recognised in insolvency proceedings.[30]

No wonder, therefore, that any insolvency law

> should provide for a modern, harmonised and fair framework for effective settlement of cross-border insolvency cases. To this end, it is recommended that countries incorporate in their domestic law the UNCITRAL Model Law on Cross-Border Insolvency, in order to recognise claims and rights arising under national or foreign norms outside the insolvency law, subject to the limitations expressly foreseen in each case.[31]

For example, the importance of the Model Law on Cross-Border Insolvency can be appreciated in a recent decision rendered by a Brazilian court in late 2021 which recognised proceedings in Singapore for the restructuring of Prosafe SE and its Singaporean subsidiary, Prosafe Rigs Pts Ltd. The decision is the case of first impression because foreign insolvency proceedings were recognised for the first time since Brazil adopted the UNCITRAL Model Law on Cross-Border Insolvency. As economies and companies around the globe continue to face financial difficulties due to the Covid-19 pandemic, one might expect further instances of recognition of foreign insolvency proceedings in Brazil and elsewhere, although several countries in Europe have not yet adopted this framework, with the exception of, among others, Romania, Greece, Poland, UK, and Slovenia.

30 EBRD (n 13) 32.
31 EBRD (n 13) 32.

In Europe, the UNCITRAL Model Law may complement the EU Regulation on Insolvency Proceedings for cross-border insolvency procedures where the debtor has a centre of main interest in the European Union. This may be supplemented by the adoption of the UNCITRAL Model Law on Recognition and Enforcement of Insolvency-Related Judgements, which further assists the conduct of cross-border insolvency proceedings and increases the potential for successful reorganisation or liquidation.

These models are a guide, and states enacting legislation based upon a model law have the flexibility to depart from the text. Hence, each state's legislation should be considered in order to identify the exact nature of any possible deviation from the model in the adopted legislative text. This confirms our intuition on (legal) constants, according to which common or shared meanings might still be influenced by national law principles or rules. Once the common meaning has been identified as a sort of benchmark, then national provisions can still influence the interpretation of a legal transplant. According to the recommendations of the Legislative Guide on Insolvency Law, any insolvency legal system should have the following fundamental objectives:

1. Provisions of certainty in the market to promote economic stability and growth
2. Maximisation of value of assets
3. Striking a balance between liquidation and reorganisation
4. Ensuring equitable treatment of similarly situated creditors
5. Provision for timely, efficient, and impartial resolution of insolvency
6. Preservation of the insolvency estate to allow equitable distribution to creditors
7. Ensuring a transparent and predictable insolvency law that contains incentives for gathering and dispensing information
8. Recognition of existing creditor rights and the establishment of clear rules for the ranking of priority claims
9. Establishment of a framework for cross-border insolvency[32]

UNCITRAL proposes some basic features that any insolvency law must incorporate in order to be able to develop an effective and efficient framework. In particular, it has finalised the adoption of a Model Law on Micro-Small-Medium-Enterprise Insolvency in 2022.[33] The UNCITRAL Legislative Guide on Insolvency Law for Micro and Small Enterprises consists of the UNCITRAL Legislative Recommendations on Insolvency of Micro- and Small Enterprises, adopted by the United Nations Commission on International Trade Law at its 54th session in 2021, and the related commentary,

32 EBRD (n 13) 32.

33 See UNCITRAL, 'Legislative Guide on Insolvency Law for Micro – and Small Enterprises' <https://uncitral.un.org/sites/uncitral.un.org/files/media-documents/uncitral/en/msme_lg_insolvency_law_ebook.pdf> accessed 1 January 2025.

finalised by UNCITRAL Working Group V (Insolvency Law) at its 59th session in Vienna on 13 December 2021.

The main function of such a Legislative Guide is to provide a uniform set of principles and recommendations that countries can adopt to harmonise their insolvency laws for micro- and small enterprises (MSEs). In this function, one of the main aims of comparative law is fulfilled. Furthermore, the Guide offers flexibility to accommodate different legal traditions and economic conditions while addressing specific needs of MSEs. This is intended to support economic growth by enabling MSEs to resolve financial distress effectively, protecting jobs and businesses. Legal indicators, such as ease of doing business rankings, insolvency recovery rates, and access to credit metrics, are used to identify the gaps and inefficiencies in existing insolvency frameworks for MSEs. Empirical studies and data on MSE insolvencies orient the recommendations to ensure they are grounded in real-world challenges, and the establishment of best practices is focused on successful insolvency frameworks from different jurisdictions to create globally applicable standards. Usually, this is possible through feedback from practitioners, government agencies, and MSE representatives to ensure that the guide reflects practical needs and is sensitive to cultural and economic variations. Finally, legal indicators are also used within this context to evaluate the impact of reforms, providing benchmarks for countries to assess the success of their insolvency frameworks post-adoption. This embeds a classic function of monitoring.

5 The World Bank Principles for Effective Insolvency and Creditor/Debtor Regimes

The 'Principles for Effective Insolvency and Creditor Rights' by the World Bank Group are a synthesis of international best practices for insolvency systems and creditor rights. They have been designed as a broad-spectrum evaluation tool in order to assist countries in their efforts to assess and improve key aspects of their systems of commercial law, fundamental for a healthy investment climate, and to promote economic and commercial growth. The 'Principles' state that '[e]ffective, credible and transparent creditors' rights and insolvency systems are vitally important for achieving the redistribution of productive resources in the entrepreneurial sector, for investor confidence and long-term corporate reorganisation'.[34]

Corporate insolvency systems also play a key role in times of crisis in that they enable a country and its stakeholders to respond quickly and resolve business financial issues on a systemic scale.

The 'Principles' were created in 2001 in response to the emerging market crisis in the late 1990s. From its inception until its first revision in 2005, the World Bank started engaging with a variety of international organisations, countries, and several other actors (such as cross-border operators) to evaluate how the 'Principles' aiming to improve their effectiveness are being used in

34 EBRD (n 13) 35.

practice. Further revisions took place in 2011, 2015, and 2021. The 2005 revision grouped the principles under relevant headings to provide a streamlined approach. The 2011 revision incorporated the updates made to the UNCITRAL Legislative Guide on Insolvency Law to reflect the best international practices in the regulation of the insolvency of enterprise groups. In 2015, changes were made to the 'Principles', highlighting the relationship between the cost and flow of credit (including secured credit) and the laws and institutions that recognise and enforce credit agreements. Also, and in line with the UNCITRAL Legislative Guide on Insolvency, the 'Principles' enlarged the scope of duties and responsibilities of directors in a distress scenario.

Finally, in 2021, the World Bank prepared their last revision with a specific focus on helping policymakers build and improve the insolvency and bankruptcy systems that support the micro-, small, and medium enterprises that were particularly hard-hit by the Covid-19 crisis. This is because – as we have stated in the previous section – micro- and SMEs represent over 60% of private sector employment globally and need efficient, cost-effective insolvency principles in order to either successfully restructure or exit the market. The main provisions of the 2021 reform are focused on strengthening preventive restructuring frameworks. Special emphasis is placed on early intervention mechanisms to avoid insolvency, and debtor-in-possession arrangement is encouraged to allow debtors to retain control of their assets during restructuring. Finally, procedures are simplified for out-of-court or hybrid restructuring to reduce the burden on courts and stakeholders.

6 The EBRD Core Principles of an Effective Insolvency System

The EBRD's Legal Transition Programme (LTP) has conducted a number of assessments of the state of transition in the EBRD region in selected areas of commercial law, including insolvency, seeking to assess the legislation of the EBRD countries of operations. Assessments of commercial legal frameworks play an important role in monitoring the status of legal transition and legal risk for investments, identifying priorities for the Bank's policy engagement and contributing to further commercial law reforms and development. To this end, the role of a well-designed insolvency framework is widely recognised when facilitating the extension of credit and private sector development.[35]

The LTP led assessment of insolvency laws in 2003–2004 and repeated the assessment in 2006, 2009, and 2020. Since the 2009 assessment, there has been a significant level of insolvency law reform globally. This shows the practical importance of such insolvency law assessments as well as the new

35 See, for example, the foreword to the 2021 World Bank, 'Principles for Effective Insolvency and Creditor/Debtor Regimes' *The Word Bank Group* (2021) <https://openknowledge.worldbank.org/server/api/core/bitstreams/3824fe8e-edb3-5f9b-aa28-f5afc759e562/content> accessed 1 January 2025.

emerging role of comparative law as a policy instrument to modify national legislations. Corporate insolvency reforms have been driven in great measure by the global financial crisis (2007–2010), and subsequent economic downturn, and a renewed emphasis on the role and importance of insolvency systems in maintaining financial stability.

As we said in the previous sections, the general goal of most insolvency systems is the efficient liquidation of non-viable businesses and the rescue of viable businesses in temporary financial difficulties. This confirms the relevance and feasibility of running an assessment of the expediency and facilitation of reorganisation options in the region of the EBRD, which is keen to promote further development of insolvency legislation to encourage reorganisation in its countries of operations. Specifically, in recent years, there has been an increasing focus on the importance of statutory restructuring tools, consensual out-of-court restructuring solutions, and early 'pre-insolvency' action to support business continuity.

For these reasons, and because needs and dynamics change over time, the periodicity of insolvency law assessments (ILAs) is fundamental.

In 2020, the EBRD started a new ILA. This is also a well-timed assessment for EBRD countries of operations, which are either EU member states or EU accession countries. Indeed, the Restructuring Directive requires member states to ensure that debtors in financial difficulty have access to an effective preventive restructuring framework that enables them to restructure their debts or business, restore their viability, and avoid insolvency. The directive, therefore, calls for member states to review their insolvency framework for reorganisation.

To this end, the ILA is a comparative tool highlighting major weaknesses that should be addressed by national legislators in order to improve the efficiency of the insolvency framework. This occurs as regards the expedience and facilitation of its reorganisation and gauges the effectiveness of a country's insolvency law, benchmarked against international best practice. Take for instance the Restructuring Directive in the European Union[36] and the Principles of the World Bank Group, which serve as a benchmark to measure the legislative performance of national insolvency law frameworks. Finally, to reflect developments in terms of best practice, in 2020, the EBRD also updated its Core Principles of an Effective Insolvency System, first published 15 years ago. The Core Principles deal not only with financial institutions but, rather, also focus on corporate rescue and cross-border insolvency in relation to companies and SMEs. Particularly important, *inter alia*, is principle no. 15 on cross-border insolvency, which encourages countries to adopt the UNCITRAL Model Law

36 Directive (EU) 2019/1023 of the European Parliament and the Council of 20 June 2019 on preventive restructuring frameworks, on discharge of debt and disqualifications, and on measures to increase the efficiency of procedures concerning restructuring, insolvency and discharge of debt, and amending Directive (EU) 2017/1132 (Directive on Restructuring and Insolvency).

on Cross-Border Insolvency, thus confirming how insolvency procedures can become effective if a mutual recognition of judgements is in place.

7 The New Global Governance of the International Financial Architecture

More regulation does not necessarily imply more transparent or more efficient markets.

We argue that a Westphalian approach to regulation based exclusively on state law can be superseded by a self-regulatory approach where soft law becomes 'harder'. This can generate spontaneous mechanisms of compliance and a voluntary model of self-regulation inspired by market practices and knowledge of financial operators; this has already occurred in other areas of the law (for instance, the Takeover Code in the UK, the international financial regulation of the special-purpose acquisition company, mobile payments and electronic transfer of funds, decentralised finance with smart contracts and virtual currencies, etc.).

In the 'Code of Capital', Pistor claims that financial operators, instead of using self-regulatory approaches, are working towards the codification of the future by enacting a digital code. Even this affirmation might be misleading, because no current legal provision is capable of keeping up with the fast pace of technological improvements. Hence, the law cannot be conceived as the 'input' of a codification process that tends to qualify facts in legal terms. By contrast, we must start from the facts, from the non-legal meanings and the outside-the-law space, in order to identify constants with a common meaning for different markets and financial operators.

In light of this, the law can keep track of the future by initiating uncodified facts into a codification process that does not follow the traditional path of state regulation. For these reasons, the 'uncodified codification' of the law directly contrasts with Pistor's views on codification and comparative law: Accordingly, a universal digital code might or might not exist, depending on the constant meanings that international financial operators and standard-setting will tend to follow or recognise in their quasi-legal frameworks or soft law that is subsequently translated into hard law frameworks.

The failure of direct codification through macro-legislations that tend to echo Pistor's 'universal' code can further sustain the argument that uncertainty rather than financial risk governs the markets.[37] For these reasons, uncertainty-aversion paradigms are obsolete, and where uncertainty has been rejected, profits have dropped too. Hence, the uncodified uncertainty in the Covid-19 crisis is a primary example of how no codification process can ignore the importance of outside-the-law instances in the act of law-making.

37 Daniele D'Alvia, *The Speculator of Financial Markets: How Financial Innovation and Supervision Made the Modern World* (Palgrave Macmillan 2023).

Additionally, this trend has given rise to democratic, discriminatory, and participatory concerns, as well as to the establishment of an ambiguous legal status for private organisations or non-state actors, or better standard-setting, such as the IMF, the World Bank Group, the UNCITRAL, the Financial Stability Board, and so on. Apart from these political issues generated by hybrid regulation and stemming from the privatisation of financial risk, the hybrid feature of the system makes the involvement of private actors a fundamental instance of regulatory responses as opposed to governments or governmental agencies that are part of the public sphere. In the absence of a supreme architect of the financial system or a central planner, the necessary decentralisation of the financial environment allows for new heterarchical relationships to be formed.

It is fair to say that the endemic failure of markets implies that there is a need for regulation or supervision. However, as this chapter has sought to demonstrate, the paternalistic role of the state has been irreversibly modified towards a new global governance paradigm in financial markets. If internal capital controls are reduced or eliminated, then domestic firms gain more room for taking financial risks. This theoretically is not an issue, as long as there is perfect competition and perfect information in the market. However, markets always register a lack of perfect information. Furthermore, the lack of theoretical grounds for the justification that self-regulated markets can really achieve market equilibrium has always enabled the idea of top-down government intervention. To this end, Adam Smith's theory that markets can be efficiently self-governed by an 'invisible hand' has always been contrasted with the Westphalian system, a model based on a paternalistic view of the state in which regulation is imposed from the top as an expression of classic state sovereignty. This view is capable of influencing the expansion of domestic markets through legal impositions and internal capital controls.

One of the most relevant features of financial markets today is that they are not exclusively based on state regulation but, rather, on private actors' decisions and inter-agency forums that give rise to hybrid forms of regulation. In other words, today the current dynamics of markets refers to a conception of global governance where it is not possible to rely exclusively on states' intervention to govern complex financial markets. The final outcome of the regulation process is the result of at least a mixture of sources, deriving especially from self-regulatory responses elaborated by private industry. The role of government is overturned from its classic conception as an entity that acts externally and outside of markets, although the global financial crisis (2007–2010) has provided evidence for the opposite conclusion, that is, a counter-trend, with the re-emergence and reaffirmation of a new Westphalian system that aims to reframe and disempower the traditional role of independent agencies in financial regulation. Although other scholars identify a new role for government as an entity that is external to the market,[38] there are also

38 RC Hockett and ST Omarova, 'Private Means to "Public" Ends: Government as Market Actors' (2014) Cornell Law Faculty Publications n. 1016 54, 55.

hints that government exercises a fundamental role that is internal to markets. For this reason, it can be equally misleading to illustrate the global governance of financial markets as a public–private divide, as it is a potential misconception to theorise an insolvency law framework within the public–private divide with respect to failing financial institutions or collapsing private businesses. Today macro-objectives follow micro-objectives and *vice versa*. Furthermore, beyond regulation's purposes that are getting closer, sometimes governments act in a 'market actor role' using private means to public ends, and in so doing, they behave as private actors in markets.[39]

These new paradigms of global governance of financial markets have necessarily contributed to the emergence of the idea that what we term 'macro-legislations' are progressively abandoned. A *macro-legislation* is an attempt to deal with almost every sector of the financial market (for instance, the Dodd Frank Act in the United States). As opposed to macro-legislations, today we experience the existence of 'micro-legislations' at the national level. These deal with an emerging new crisis (such as Covid-19) in a temporary manner (the rise of national emergency measures) and modify entire national legal frameworks in compliance with established best practices and standards agreed by private standard-setting at the international level (IMF, World Bank, UNCITRAL, etc.), often determined by global legal indicators that serve the role of measuring the performance of national legal frameworks.

Indeed, today, in contemporary financial markets, the idea of top-down state regulation is not followed strictly, and the principle of exclusive state sovereignty has been diluted, thus paving the way to more dynamic sources of power, which are reflected – at least at the international level – more in the frameworks of international financial organisations than in treaty-based regimes (such as the Basel Capital Accord of 1998, the Basel Core Principles for Effective Banking Supervision 1997, the Basle Concordat 1983, the Code of Good Practices on Transparency in Monetary and Financial Policies Rules sponsored by the IMF, etc.). These acts are not international treaties and,

39 Hockett and Omarova (n 38), 56. The authors first mention the existence of private laws that exercise a foundational role of the markets, such as laws establishing proprietary interests in market exchange, or contract law in the case of future performance in market exchange. Furthermore, they identify for expository purposes for four different forms of the 'market actor role' of governments, namely, 'market-making', 'market-moving', 'market-levering', and 'market-preserving'. Governments in 'market-making' roles bear risks that private actors are 'unable or unwilling to bear', such as the risk that some products will not be sold on the market, and they agree to act as a 'buyer of last resort' through a private means, that is, underwriting. Governments in 'market-moving' roles affect prices on certain markets instead of allowing private actors to do this, for instance, when central banks open market operations, such as the purchasing or selling of treasury securities, or 'short-selling commodities whose quantitative easing-inflated prices disproportionately harm the poor'. Governments in 'market-levering' form can improve existing private markets' outcomes, such as in the case of public pensions, whose investments can influence the practices of other firms, and finally, when they act in 'market-preserving' roles, possible collapses of the market are prevented in order to avoid negative externalities; in other words, it is the role of the government to act as a collective agent.

therefore, cannot be defined as a classic source of public international law. However, they constitute part of the international financial architecture in which soft law plays an eminent role as a form of self-regulation. Essentially, in contemporary financial markets, either the code of practices or guidelines on corporate standards, or even a communication by the European Commission, is preferred and can play an essential role that is sometimes preferable to a static civil code. Nonetheless, there are still a few instances of treaty-based regulations, such as the General Agreement on Trade in Services or the Agreement between the United States of America, Mexico, and Canada (USMCA). Finally, the regional agreements in Europe also play a vital role in the development of European financial regulation, such as the proposal for a capital markets union by the European Commission, as well as the free movement of capital enshrined in the TFEU. In all these instances, the main aim is the liberalisation of financial instruments rather than the imposition of regulations – or even the supervision of financial markets. Evidently, the role of public international law has changed, distancing itself from the classic conception of sources of international law where the treaty played a preeminent role.

8 Global Legal Indicators in Corporate Restructuring

Global legal indicators play a remarkable role in building the new financial architecture beyond structural crisis. As we have seen, global legal indicators follow a rational managerial approach by measuring the performance of national legal frameworks in accordance with (legal) constants that are established and enshrined in quasi-legal contexts, rather than hard-law provisions. The Core Principles, the UNCITRAL Model Law on Cross-Border Insolvency, and the Principles for Effective Insolvency and Creditor/Debtor Regimes (which we have illustrated in this chapter) are just some of the new instances that, at the international level, are established as legal parameters at a steady pace or – which is the same thing – act as benchmarks against which national legislations are assessed. Not only does this shift in practice reflect a vision of managing risks under the laws of probabilities and through managerial rationality, but it also specifically promotes a re-evaluation of uncertainty as one of the driven forces of money creation processes. Under such processes, new financing can be secured for preventing restructuring or as a means of investing in the private sectors of developing and emerging countries.

There is a wide recognition of the role of well-designed insolvency frameworks, inasmuch as they facilitate the extension of credit and private sector development. Countries might choose to incorporate several of these procedures into their legal framework, thus providing stakeholders with a variety of tools to address financial distress. Addressing the financial difficulties of a business at an early stage is critical for a successful turnaround and has been a recurrent trend since 2009. Often, these procedures restrict the direct involvement of the court and allocate a greater role to private negotiations between the debtor and its creditors. Nonetheless, reorganisation or restructuring frameworks can take many different forms and are adaptable to each country's financial and real sectors' specific needs. As each country will develop its own restructuring tools and procedures suitable to address their needs and complement their current framework, it is sometimes difficult to classify them in specific typologies, and sometimes the dividing line between the processes might not be so clear.

We have seen how insolvency law is subject to changing dynamics that can be drawn from the new elements introduced in the latest European reforms. Therein, we have witnessed a move towards new procedures that combine court intervention with private negotiations of the parties (the so-called 'hybrid mechanisms') – and this move represents an evolution towards pre-packaged reorganisation and expedited restructurings in general. This new trend was strongly endorsed by the European Commission in March 2014 with its recommendation on a new approach to business failure and insolvency and the Commission's proposal in November 2016 for a directive on preventive restructuring frameworks. Like the Principles for Effective Insolvency and Creditor Rights prepared by the World Bank Group, the Restructuring Directive takes into consideration several best practices in preventive restructuring, aiming to expedite the rescue of companies, and it has taken inspiration from UK schemes of arrangement and, to an even greater extent, bankruptcy proceedings under Chapter 11 of the US Bankruptcy Code. The proposals are ambitious and far-reaching. Since then, a number of countries in Western Europe (including Italy, Germany, and Spain) have introduced new composition procedures for early restructuring of corporate debtors that are not yet technically insolvent, a trend which has been followed in the EBRD region in countries such as Croatia and Slovenia. Another mechanism that has become popular as a means of expediting the restructuring process is the 'pre-pack', that is, a reorganisation plan which is pre-agreed with a majority of creditors prior to submission to the court. Albania and Serbia have incorporated the 'pre-pack' into their insolvency legislation.

Despite the many forms and possible restructuring tools that a country can incorporate, this chapter has hopefully outlined the new legislative process that is likely to take place in the years to come, namely, a decentralised legal system with a global governance that is informed by cooperation mechanisms and coordination, and with the interaction of multiple private organisations at the international level. This new apex contributes to the uncodified codification process that we have explored throughout this work. Whereas benchmarks are established at the international level, the executive decisions of implementation through legislation or statute law are taken at the national level, so that the original apex that was once personified by the national state with its sovereign power becomes the new periphery or 'execution centre'. It is a new encounter of the global-local that is so distant from the times when the law was seen as a rebellious tool (as the French and American Revolutions demonstrate), and it encompasses the law as both an 'output' and an administrative instrument.

Conclusions

In ending our journey through the transnational constellation of private orderings, constants outside the law, and indicators, this coda provides some concluding remarks, drawing together the whole of the book. We do not intend to deliver a synopsis of what we have found on our journey into the new economic world order; rather, it is our purpose to share some thoughts on what we have discovered along the way, that is, the Factory of Global Legal Indicators. This is, in our opinion, an innovative contribution to the field of comparative law. The 'Factory' represents the fruitful outcome of our reappraising comparative legal methodologies in a world completely different from that which saw the birth of our discipline in late nineteenth- and early twentieth-century Europe.

This does not mean that comparative law has lost its pristine character – quite the contrary. It was (and remains) a cultural competence capable of both ordering world knowledge and figuring out the new world (even its new economic order) in its complexity.[1] In reflecting the ambitions of comparative law, a 'method of knowledge acquisition',[2] its 'defining act' still lies in its 'ability to grasp the world intellectually'.[3] In our new world, comparative law has also retained its being a transformative device able to disseminate the fabrication and dissemination of the law across the globe. The practice of ranking legal systems, therefore, remains alive and well even in a time of globalisation.

The expression 'Factory of Global Legal Indicators' grasps this new trend in our discipline. As we have been repeating throughout the book, ours is a time of transnational private orderings, privately made law, and legal-institutional changes, with an unceasing urgency to harmonise the law and favour the smooth flows of goods, capital, and services across frontiers and legal systems. More specifically, the trend is based on the constantly evolving economic conditions and competitive requirements imposed by globalisation, which are

1 For more on this, see Matteo Nicolini, '"Writing the Earth and Representing the World": The Cartographical Ambitions of Comparative Law' (2024) 19 J Comp L 79.

2 Jaakko Husa, *Introduction to Comparative Law* (2nd edn, Hart 2023) 64.

3 Alastair Bonnett, *What Is Geography?* (SAGE 2008) 32.

directly measured in terms of indexes and indicators – that is, two tools that are frequently used today to promote legal change from the 'outside'. Far from being only the preserve of domestic legislators, indeed, our book has disclosed that the law has become the 'output' of private lawmakers, and its ultimate legal source is often rooted in non-legal instances.

The major predicament of this book relates to the 'soft power' of indicators, which makes them particularly apt to accommodate the political use of comparative law with the goals – or which is the same thing, the 'constants' and 'interests' – of external investors, that is, the maximisation of financial returns. Once this is identified as the constant meaning outside the law, it is necessary to supply it with the right legal coding, that is, with the legal 'output' that best suits transnational actors' interests and that states might be willing to incorporate. This is precisely what indicators are supposed to do.

The book thus paves the way to a new understanding of how indicators work; not only are they patterns of governance, but they also act as drivers for legal change. Their output-oriented approach – which is the major consequence of the quantitative turn in comparative law – completely reshuffles the relationship between economics and the law. Owing to its being a cultural competence, comparative law upholds that indicators are part of the broader Factory, producing the law from the outside. Full as they are of transformative potential, they help states identify and recognise legally relevant meanings outside the law.

One of the major objections to the use of indicators lies in this: As the Western legal tradition is the backbone of global law, the law as an 'output' seems to preserve its traditional Eurocentric flavour. The process of quantification in law, the scientific state of mind, and the legal toolkit generalising investors' interests still have their roots in the West. No wonder, therefore, that the (global) standards and benchmarks suggested to developing countries are said to reproduce, through indicators, the legal toolkit of the Global North.[4] In order to reduce such biases, Chapters 2 and 3 have proposed not to embrace economic democracy and activate what de Souza terms as the process of their 'transformation' and 'co-production'.[5]

We assume that the Fabric still possesses some antibodies that might shield it from the Eurocentric objection.

The first of them lies in being publicly made law no longer at the centre of the system. As said, this is now decentralised, thus reflecting, first and foremost, the interests of the actors of the Fabric rather than the interests of the Global North.[6] Decisions are now taken at the 'periphery' (the constellation of private orderings which is transnational law) rather than at the apex, that is, the state level. Today, the apex of the system is located in the

4 SP de Souza, *Designing Indicators for a Plural Legal World* (CUP 2022) 122.
5 See de Souza (n 4) 12 as discussed in Ch 2.9. See also Ch 3.7.
6 See Ch 1.5.

peripheries, and the world has irremediably changed. A second set of antibodies may be found in the cornerstone of our theorisation, that is, the 'soft power' of indicators as a form of law-making and cooperative practice, thus grasping the idea that indicators govern the fabrication of the law from the outside. Cooperative intercourse takes place among transnational actors and extends over national jurisdictions, turning transnational investors' privately made law into domestic publicly made legislation. To this extent, the system is more 'democratic' inasmuch as financial actors use indicators to code their constants – and this expresses the very idea of indicators as a Factory producing the law from the 'outside'. Yet indicators must necessarily nest within each other in a common direction, thus reconciling the extremely concrete – and often conflicting – interests of the members of the transnational community. There is something utilitarian in this process: Each legal solution in the toolkit is the outcome of the cooperative effort among transnational actors.

At the same time, law-making 'from the outside' accounts for another type of cooperative intercourse. The system is less state-centric, but the holders of global capital still need national legislation to legally code their own financial interests. In this sense, the system is probably more 'democratic' because it needs cooperation to avoid risks for both investors and states. This means that the soft power is based not on the 'superiority' of legislative solutions but on their being functional to supplying an objective basis to socio-legal change when it comes to pursuing the constants outside the law.

This predicament discloses a further feature of our cooperative intercourse: Transnational investors might be particularly skilled at handling comparative legal methodologies in the field of indicators. They carry out massive comparative law surveys, and once they have found the legal solution that is better at maximising their profits, they create 'global norms of law', to be subsequently disseminated across domestic jurisdictions.[7] The transformative potential of our intercourse is thus useful for manufacturing 'better' legislation through a comparative process – and therefore for providing lawmakers with the practical knowledge to frame new laws.

To this extent, the book has ventured to explore the shift from the 'old' world to the Factory of Global Legal Indicators. The separation of moral principles from legal arguments signposted this old world, that is, the world of Kelsen, where codifications (and, more broadly, coding assets through the law) mattered. It was also the world of traditional comparative law, where its ancillary function provided lawmakers with the practical knowledge to manufacture 'better' legislation. This is hardly surprising in an era of legal positivism, where 'better' legislation was used to match the politico-legal project through which a given community reimagines itself, and public law becomes the new instrument through which the newborn national or sovereign state

7 M Arslan, 'Differentiating and Connecting Indicators: The Quality and Performance of Law in the World Bank's Doing Business Project' (2020) 16 Int J L in Context 17.

revendicates legal interests. To this end, the law of Parliament not only was a public means to private ends but also favoured the very activity of codification. In so doing, it was also able to qualify private behaviours and conducts to which public law attached legal effects even when private parties did not voluntarily want to settle their private interests in the specific choice that public law had made.

In other words, public law was superior to private law, that is, the law of contractual relations that was perused to settle private economic interests. Such a belief was also confirmed by constitutional documents; in affirming the constitutional value of private property and private autonomy in contractual law, they claimed the remarkable role of public law in determining how private interests should be distributed and settled. Private interests could be afforded recognition and protection as long as they were not against public morality, public order, and public security, that is, the new attributes of sovereignty of the nation state with its domestic law-making machine. Take for example the implied terms of a contract, the legal obligations and responsibilities deriving from entering into a contractual agreement even at the pre-contractual or negotiation phase, the right to compensation in case of expropriation of private land, the public–private contracting between private individuals and state administrative agencies, the implied terms of an employment contract, and the legal effects deriving from the valid registration of a transfer of shares in a private liability company or the property rights in land.

These self-evident examples uphold the features of traditional comparative law – that is, state-centrism, positivism, and formalism – and reinforce the role of public law as the demiurge of private non-fully-codifiable interests. In so doing, the state also provided private parties with private autonomy to allow them to settle their own private interests, but as we said, this could never contravene the efficacy of public interests that had the advantage to be classified and determined at the sole discretion of the new nation state. With a bit of irony, Napoleon's 'ghost' and his fatal defeat at Waterloo still haunt the structure of the nation state, where private interests were 'controlled' through public intervention.

At least at first sight, this legal approach was welcomed by individuals and private parties, who undoubtedly felt freer and in control, because it directly constituted a form of protection of private interests and, at the same time, it constituted the maximisation of private autonomy. It can be said that communities or individuals tend to trust more the good choices of a 'paternalistic' state, especially when such choices are inspired by welfare considerations to protect the rights of 'weak' private parties. Despite good intentions, unintended consequences would have progressively emerged. The shift was remarkable and historical, and a new era soon ensued. With its renovated economic order, private actors became empowered within a superior legal order that would have been qualified as supranational and ineffable. In this new legal order, the role of publicly made law was significantly reduced.

The shift was (and remains) apparent in terms of financial markets: From the state as a sovereign 'in control' of financial markets, we now have the latter destined to be 'in control' of the former. Since then, traditional democratic structures of representation have also shifted towards technocracy, which is seen as the appropriate answer to solve, or at least to deal with, complex issues. Likewise, national risks perceived as important at the national level were translated into 'shared risks' and 'international concerns'.

In so doing, international and cross-border issues necessarily started to require common and shared responses. This directly contributed to increasing and promoting cooperation among nation states to find common solutions to common/shared risks. Think of shared concerns of national security in relation to terrorism; the unification of diverse cultures and languages in continental Europe; the creation of shared policies to establish the free movement of goods, persons, establishment, and capital in the EU; the implementation of a shared trade policy through the World Bank's recommendations; the establishment of common monetary visions in monetary law and economics via the IMF at the time of Bretton Woods – and now through Central Bank Digital Currencies. The era of globalisation has begun. This is also the moment when the local territory of the nation state has become 'glocal'. Indeed, the term 'glocalization' was coined by Roland Robertson, a sociologist and theorist known for his work on globalisation. He introduced the concept in the 1990s to describe the intersection of the global and the local, emphasising how global ideas, products, or practices are adapted to fit local contexts. Robertson popularised the term in his seminal works on globalisation, particularly in his book *Globalization: Social Theory and Global Culture* (1992).[8] It was the new reality in sociological terms of a fluid existentialism in Baumann's conception of the term. Nonetheless, the 'exportation' of national risks into the international arena would have had necessarily significant consequences that sometimes were also able to generate a disempowerment of the local sphere and the national state in particular.

In terms of the Fabric, the book has amply illustrated how the shift took place. The shift was from Pistor's world – that is, one where private and public interests are rendered legal and vindicated by virtue of coding – to the new architecture of contemporary financial markets (or, better, financial systems). These are expressly based on sustainability; as said, decisions are taken at the 'periphery' because a central planner or supreme architect of the financial system is lacking. Sustainability is a (legal) constant that is measured by specific indicators whose role is to grade the societal impact of an investment. For instance, key performance indicators (KPIs) for ESG are now a compelling reality for corporates, and investors and analysts integrate them into a classic spreadsheet analysis. ESG parameters direct investors' decisions too.

Specifically, *sustainability* is a non-legal term that has become legal by virtue of quasi-legal frameworks, such as policy statements, guidelines, and generally soft law instruments that are non-binding and non-enforceable. Nonetheless,

8 Roland Robertson, *Globalization: Social Theory and Global Culture* (SAGE 1992).

this non-enforceability can still create a modification of the legal environment, due to the spontaneous compliance and auto-imposed self-regulation practices of market operators. Numerical assessment adds the finishing touches to the transnational system, because it nudges the less legally attractive countries as regards financial investments. The recipe has always been the same: Recipient countries might attain legal fitness provided that they evolve through various stages of development that lead to the same stage of superiority envisaged by those countries that, in the rankings, have already adopted the legal change proposed through indicators. In case of compliance with these solutions, development aids would soon ensue.

Covid-19 has had a massive impact on our lives, but not necessarily for the worse. In recovering from the coronavirus and in securing an environmentally sustainable and profitable future, companies will need to adapt or suffer the consequences, whether for the sake of their social and human rights practices or just for reputation. For example, Deliveroo is one of several businesses that have been hit with a raft of accusations of shady working practices, poor treatment of workers, and exploitation of individuals whose technical skills, networks, ingenuity, and plain old hard work helped them build big capital in the first place. Energy companies may shout about investing in renewables, but until we experience a global shift away from their reliance on fossil fuels, accusations would appear to be justified.

The new financial architecture is based on sustainability, which becomes a (legal) constant rich in meanings and relevant for financial law, insolvency law, sovereign debt relief practices, corporate governance, constitutional governance, and environmental law in an outside-the-law search for non-legal meanings. The codification era ended, and the instauration or initiation of the future of (legal) constants and outside-the-law meanings has just started.

As said in the Introduction, we are therefore experiencing a new process of knowledge production, which operates at both levels, that is, the practical and the epistemological. Establishing benchmarks for legal assessment is extremely useful for scientific advancements of comparative law; at the same time, it is servient to the 'better' legislation required to harvest profits. This has given consistency to our efforts to identify the contingencies, variables, and operational rules – in sum, the constants – that make up the Factory.

Yet our research unavoidably has a relativist tone. If, as said, the paradigm shift accounts for the remarkable changes prompted by globalisation, some recent events seem to be still explicable in terms of 'normal' (and cumulative) phases of science. The pandemic, the war in Ukraine, the insurgence of populist movements, and the recent US presidential elections seem to be paving the way to a new wave of nationalism, which might have an impact on how the Factory manufactures its own constants and legal solutions. We have seen what the risks are, at least in constitutional terms. If the Factory adopts a 'nominal' approach to 'constitutional (economic) democracy', the critical voices as regards the World of Indicators will indeed intensify in a time of insurgent nationalism and populism. In a fractured, complex, and often non-democratic world, we cannot deny that a given country may want to stick to its own particular idea of what the Fabric, indicators, and the rule of law are (and are not). This is certainly the case of autocracies that, in probabilistic terms, are not excluded from the Fabric. If it were the case, they might also impose their own standards and ideals of the rule of law upon the functioning of the Fabric. Do we really think that it is possible to put constraints on the political discretion of non-democratic regimes? Do we really think that, if it were the case, they would not retaliate, curbing IPRs or overtaxing and overburdening the actors of the Fabric with tax reforms or spending plans? And we add, with all the consequences that this might mean in terms of predictability. The rise of populism and the extreme volatility and unpredictability of the new world order in the aftermath of the 2024 US presidential elections should prompt us to consider that being postmodernists certainly means constructing a reality; that reality, however, still requires a pragmatic state–investor intercourse. What would happen if states' failure to comply with indicators were due to the underperformance (or, which is even worse, the rejection) of the rule of law as a legal constant? In this event, underperformance would cause a non-reception of it and a flaw in the Fabric. With a legal and deterministic approach, states may object that indicators propose a legal solution that is unable to reach their own desired goals (i.e. the economic flourishing of the state).

Economic democracy and nationalism represent a setback for the Factory: Even though the law is still manufactured from the outside, the Factory has to take into account that the politico-economic dominance of transnational financial actors must be reconciled to the interests of state political communities. It is no longer the time for uniform commercial laws to avoid hindrances to trade. Legal nationalism uses comparative law to improve domestic interests and the related economic agenda, even in terms of attracting investments (and using legal solutions) coming from the outside.

From this, however, it does not follow that the future of the Factory is at risk. As the book has demonstrated, we shall continue to interpret the paradigm shift as a remarkable sign of this time of globalisation. We understand that indicators and their soft power are here to stay and govern the processes of legal manufacturing from the outside even in times of resurgent nationalism, and therefore they are still able to explain the state–investor intercourse in terms of cumulative phases of science. As comparative lawyers, we have to revise our existing methodology to allow our discipline to grasp the signs of this changing and fleeting world.

Index

MIX

Papier | Fördert gute Waldnutzung

FSC® C083411

Kolibri 360 GmbH
Ferdinand-Jühlke-Straße 7
99095 Erfurt, Deutschland
produktsicherheit@kolibri360.de